WE SELL OUR TIME NO MORE

TO comrede
Heedi

love from
comrede scutt
xo

We Sell Our Time No More

Workers' Struggles Against Lean Production in the British Car Industry

Paul Stewart, Mike Richardson, Andy Danford, Ken Murphy, Tony Richardson and Vicki Wass

with John Cooper, Tony Lewis, Gary Lindsay, Mick Whitley, John Fetherston, Steve Craig, Pat Doyle and Terry Myles (members of the Auto Workers' Research Network)

PLUTO PRESS
www.plutobooks.com

First published 2009 by Pluto Press
345 Archway Road, London N6 5AA and
175 Fifth Avenue, New York, NY 10010

Distributed in the United States of America exclusively by
Palgrave Macmillan, a division of St. Martin's Press LLC,
175 Fifth Avenue, New York, NY 10010

www.plutobooks.com

British Library Cataloguing in Publication Data
A catalogue record for this book is available from the British Library

ISBN   978 0 7453 2868 3   Hardback
ISBN   978 0 7453 2867 6   Paperback

Library of Congress Cataloging in Publication Data applied for

This book is printed on paper suitable for recycling and made from fully
managed and sustained forest sources. Logging, pulping and
manufacturing processes are expected to conform to the environmental
standards of the country of origin. The paper may contain up to
70% post consumer waste.

10 9 8 7 6 5 4 3 2 1

Designed and produced for Pluto Press by
Curran Publishing Services, Norwich
Printed and bound in the European Union by
CPI Antony Rowe, Chippenham and Eastbourne

CONTENTS

'A Reporter in the back of the room leaned forward and, quoting Smith, hollered: "how can the elimination of 30,000 jobs IMPROVE job security?" Hey, this hack was on the beam. Even the Rivethead hadn't caught how hopelessly inane this statement had been. Remaining completely stone-faced, Roger Smith glanced at the reporter and reasoned: "For those who are left, their jobs will become that much more secure." Ouch .... For those who are left. That sounded awful damn grim for a solution that was intended to come off as some form of reassurance. It was entirely possible that Roger Smith had missed his calling in life. He could have been an ambassador to Ethiopia: "A food shortage, you say? Noo problem. Simply exterminate the vast proportion of your population, stack 'em out of view where they won't upset anyone's appetite and, PRESTO!, vittles aplenty for THOSE WHO ARE LEFT."'

(pp. 114–15)

'The messages [on the electronic message boards] ranged from corny propaganda (... QUALITY IS THE BACKBONE OF GOOD WORKMANSHIP!) ... to motivational pep squawk (A WINNER NEVER QUITS AND A QUITTER NEVER WINS) to brain-jarring ruminations (SAFETY IS SAFE).'

(p. 160)

'We kept waiting for another phrase to come along ....The message blazed on brightly like some eternal credo meant to hog-tie our bewildered psyches. The message? Hold on to your hardhats, sages. The message being thrust upon us in enormous block lettering read: SQUEEZING RIVETS IS FUN! Trust me, even the fuckin' exclamation point was their own.'

(p. 160)

from Ben Hamper, *Rivethead: Tales from the assembly line* (1992)

PREFACE

As we write, the world is experiencing the first major crisis of the new capitalism. The precipitous collapse of the Soviet economy in the 1980s, immortalised by the image of the fall of the Berlin Wall, has been taken to presage the rise of the new capitalism. This new form of capitalist development has been characterised by the international pre-eminence of financial strategies of accumulation which have depended upon a range of social, political and economic relationships, which are sometimes summed up by the term globalisation.

While lean production can be separated in a number of respects from these latest developments, it is also indelibly tied to the trajectory of the current crisis. This is because it allows capital to attempt to displace cost and risk onto labour, just as it seeks to displace cost and risk onto suppliers. Of course, no one would argue that lean production created the current crisis, but it is nevertheless one element in the neoliberal paradigm of business organisation, even if its origins lie outside neoliberalism. At minimum it is a tool adopted and adapted by organisations as they strive to control both their external and internal environments. We would not go further and argue that it can be used to define the current political economy of neoliberalism. Then again, we cannot deny that workers in late neoliberalism have seen ever-increasing areas of their work and private lives delineated by the rhetoric of the lean society. But what is lean production?

Originating in the Toyota production system, lean has been used by pro-business commentators as justification for both material and organisation changes, and ideological assault upon organised labour. It includes the ideological notion that there is one best way to work and to produce goods and services, and that those who employ it, or work under it, will work 'smarter not harder'. Setting aside hotly disputed questions regarding its claims to a revolutionary distinctiveness which can solve the problems of a decline in the profitability of capitalism, its adherents have identified a number of what they take to be its critical organisational features, deriving from the Toyota production system. According to lean's advocates, where companies adopt these, at least the groundwork for success will have been laid. These features comprise:

- continuous improvement – or *kaizen*, to use the Japanese term – to product design and production
- pro-company forms of worker involvement (teamworking and team leaders)
- elimination of waste (waste-*muda*), aided by *kaizen* but also involving the just-in-time delivery of external and internal stock (*kanban* – management of stock flow).

The elimination of waste is to be achieved in a variety of ways, as our book highlights, but for the present waste can be defined as those activities that do not add value to the product. This invariably means, in large measure, workers' time. Workers' time is the space people utilise at work for respite and regeneration, and it is, we insist, indelibly tied to workers' health, well-being, and to the quality of their lives at work and in the wider community.

Lean production is the means by which capital today seeks with ever-increasing intensity to drive work. It is, we argue, the reason for the deterioration in the employment experience for many millions of workers. The elements of lean just described can be interpreted as a means to manage workers and the workplace by stressing them to their limits in order to find, and hence eliminate, obstacles to success. While of course this is not the reason for the current crisis, and financialisation certainly reaches into the heart of auto companies' profit strategies today, our argument is that as a result of the weakness of labour organisation, which lean feeds upon and encourages, lean allows firms to continue to drive down and shift the costs of production onto their immediate workforce and the workforces of their suppliers.

There is constant pressure to drive down costs and remake an automotive industry which depends upon job insecurity. Rather than establishing a new regime of industrial democracy in a thriving manufacturing sector, lean production demands labour subordination. This is another high cost to labour. The unquestioned historical success of the sector cannot distract us from the evidence pointing to the negative impact upon many workers in the world of automotive manufacture, and more widely, as lean sweeps across an ever-widening number of sectors from health care to the operations of government.

Lean production, then, is a managerial agenda that gives capital the leverage to restructure not just for good times, but also for bad – specifically in the face of declining profitability. As such, it can be seen as creating a range of organisational and ideological resources for subordinating opposition to the rule of capital. This is what we mean when we describe it as a new regime of subordination which strives, by necessity, to exclude organised and independent labour. The latter was supposedly a characteristic of Fordism; the objective of lean is to remake the workplace in the light of a management-driven social, organisational and economic agenda. It is, in short, supposed to be a key means for avoiding what capital and its ideologues took to be the weakness at the heart of Fordism: the perceived insubordination of labour. It is a necessary part of lean that this be eliminated.

Still, this has not proven to a straightforward agenda for capital. Despite the growth of the automotive sector over the last 20 years, continuing insecurity, elements of which are central to lean production, has certainly not made workers more subordinate. Indeed, the lean workplace is a tough environment which has led to a significant degree of dissatisfaction. To incorporate labour would be one important plank in a strategy of labour subordination. It is, in fact, as we shall argue, central to the new era of 'class struggle from above'. While not without some degree of success, this has not always proven to be such a straightforward achievement. This is because at the heart of the lean lies the irreconcilable contradiction between the rhetoric of success, security and a range of enriching employment experiences, and the reality for many millions of workers, of exclusion, insecurity and deteriorating employment experience. It is for this reason that we begin with a snapshot of the fate of many workers whose work and lives have been devastated by the ravages of lean production.

ACKNOWLEDGEMENTS

We would like to thank a number of people especially who have given us huge support of one kind or another over the years, because without them this book would not have seen the light of day. In particular great thanks to Veronica Collins, Miguel Martinez Lucio, John Jacks, Barbara and Eric Smith, David Robertson, Wayne Lewchuk, Charlotte Yates, Tony Woodley, Sheila Cohen, Kim Moody, Jose Rahmalho, Marco Santana, Chris Bond and Tom White. Also we want to extend our gratitude to the many autoworkers who gave freely of their time and interest in our project. We dedicate this book to them and to the memory of the many thousands who have suffered, at times great hardship, working in the automotive industry. Thanks too to Anne Beech at Pluto Press whose interest and support for the Auto Workers' Research Network book has never faltered, and to Susan Curran of Curran Publishing Services for her grand work in preparing the final manuscript.

All photos in the book are by Paul Stewart.

ABBREVIATIONS AND ACRONYMS

AEEU	Amalagamated Engineering and Electrical Union
AEW	Amalgamated Engineering Workers Union
APO	Agreement Plant Oxford
BERR	Department for Business Enterprise and Regulatory Reform
BL	British Leyland
CIP	Continuous Improvement Programme
DATA	Draftsmen's and Allied Technicians Association
EWC	European Works Council
Gerpisa	Permanent Group for the Study of the Automobile Industry and its Employees
GM	General Motors
GME	General Motors Europe
HRM	human resource management
IMVP	International Motor Vehicle Program
JAW	Japan Auto Workers
JIT	just-in-time
MDW	measured day work
MSF	Manufacturing, Science, Finance (trade union)
MTM	Management Time and Method
NEB	National Enterprise Board
NMTs	new management techniques
NUGMW	National Union of General and Municipal Workers
NUVB	National Union of Vehicle Builders
PBR	payment by results
PO	Project Olympia Framework Document
QNPS	Quality Network Production System (Vauxhall)
SPC	statistical process control
TGWU	Transport and General Workers' Union
TIE	Transnational Information Network
UAS	Universal Analysis System
UAW	United Auto Workers
UCATT	Union of Construction, Allied Trades and Technicians
VBA	Vehicle Building and Automotive group (TGWU)
VW	Volkswagen
WTW	Working Together to Win

1 UNDERSTANDING THE LEAN AUTOMOBILE INDUSTRY

INTRODUCTION

The perilous state of the US automobile industry has prompted workers to stampede for the exit at cash-strapped Ford, where 38,000 people have chosen to accept voluntary redundancy terms to leave the struggling company.

(*Guardian*, 30/11/06)

This news came on top of General Motors' (GM's) extraordinary redundancy programme earlier in 2006, which saw 34,400 workers pushed out of the company in North America alone. And in November 2006 Volkswagen (VW) declared that it would take the axe to employment at its Brussels plant, reducing the labour force from 5,400 to 3,000 (*Le Monde*, 2006). As we write, whatever the short-term promises for the Brussels plant, its long-term future may be in doubt, with plans for the production of the VW's new Audi A1 focused on Germany. Yet, given this jolt to security and in light of the memory of Renault's closure of its Vilvoorde plant in Belgium, many workers took redundancy to get away from the sector (and indeed many more left than VW anticipated). This has to be seen as an aspect of the lean production factor in labour market insecurity. It forms part of the backcloth to the uncertainty and depression many people in different countries articulate when they talk about the long-term viability of their communities. All this was carried out within the framework of Belgium's 'Social Plan', which included a 'golden handshake' (€140–150,000) for those workers who decided to leave.

Globally, closures in the sector have been a hugely demoralising, quotidian experience. The drip, drip effect of neoliberal rationalisation has left many workers feeling despondent. In the case of VW's Brussels plant, only a comparatively small number of demonstrators turned out to support the VW workers, while the impact of closure will be felt by around 17,000 workers (5,400 direct and 12,000 indirect). While this was disappointing, why would more turn out when 80,000 demonstrators and a significant Europe-wide campaign could not retain volume automotive production at Renault's Vilvoorde plant in Brussels in 1987?

These closures and layoffs come on top of a succession of 'necessary closures' worldwide, and notably in North America and Europe, over the last ten years. They are often described as 'readjustments' to 'get things back on track'. There are other familiar terms used to coax people into accepting more pain, platitudes such as 'increased profitability', 'productivity' and the search for 'capacity adjustment' (a favourite in the automotive industry). These are important because they form the rhetoric of understatement of the central causes of redundancy and closure.

In Britain too, the transition to lean production, among other management strategies, is a move that is supposedly necessary to get things back on track – just one more bit of pain and then everything will be fine – and has led to the devastation of the British and US-owned automotive sector, to the level where only one US-owned plant, GM-Vauxhall's subsidiary at Ellesmere Port, remains open, and only at considerable cost to workers and their families. And yet still there is a good bit of professed managerial wishful thinking – although some, especially those who work there, or have recently taken voluntary severance, might think us overly generous in our choice of words. When Vauxhall-GM called for job sacrifices, it pointed out in its letter to all employees that even these might not suffice – 'This is not a guarantee' – then offered the hope that hard work might see the plant's workforce through. It concluded with the crumb of comfort that 'The best thing that each of us can do now is to focus our current tasks [by] coming to work, building high quality vehicles, and therefore keeping the Ellesmere Port reputation strong and positive. Only by working together can we secure a future for our plant'.[1] Very good, but no guarantees. Was this where the promise of lean production had led in a sector, and with the kind of management strategies, where it was sold on the promise of better and more viable work? What then can we say of the wider context of layoffs and closures?

LEAN PRODUCTION: THE CONTEXT AND THE PROMISES

The 1980s was a watershed for the labour movement internationally, with the fall of the Berlin Wall and the crisis in worker responses to the new offensive by capital. While of course both were related, their trajectories had very different origins and dynamics. Even though capital's offensive may have drawn succour from the collapse of bureaucratic socialism, the social and economic foundation of its new-found vigour was quite separate. It grew out of what we generally understand to be the crisis in its own pattern of accumulation, described as Fordism. If Fordism, with its apparent inability to adapt to the rising tide of neoliberalism and individualism, was believed to have run its course and was unable to deliver, what alternative future might promise more? Greater promise was to be delivered by neoliberalism. Often we use the term neoliberalism to describe the assault by capital on state regulation and labour standards at all levels of the economy and society, and all geographical spaces. This is important to bear in mind because for some researchers and labour activists, failed attempts to find progressive ways of ameliorating the impact of neoliberalism early on led to pessimism. This underlying fatalism proved to be a feature of many of even the sharpest challenges to neoliberalism, whatever their early optimism promised.

One of the aims of this book is to highlight the fact that lean production was, and continues to be, a vital factor in the contemporary assault upon labour standards at work. Labour standards cover a range of features of the way in which the workplace is governed, which in turn depend on the history of workplace struggles between capital and labour. This has a particular impact upon worker health and safety, including workplace stress, work intensification and management attitudes to workers. This can all be summed up as workers' experience of the quality of their life at work. By various means, as we shall see, one of the workplace characteristics of lean production is that it seeks to increase stress and work intensification while reducing workers' collective ability to respond, via corporate management ideologies and practices. This of course affects workers' experience of the quality of their personal and social lives away from employment, a theme we shall explore elsewhere (see Stewart and Murphy 2009).

It is important that we set out our attitude to lean at the beginning, because for some in the labour movement and a number of prominent critical researchers, what came to be known as lean production might have offered positive benefits for labour in an era when any kind of anticapitalist agenda seemed beyond hope.[2] Lean production was a good way to sell neoliberalism to not just the defeated but also the fainthearted, especially the social democratic left in the United Kingdom and elsewhere. In fairness it offered some attractions even to those who might instinctively challenge neo-liberalism. However, a qualified acceptance would have to await the arrival of the High-Performance Workplace and its left advocates, notably Appelbaum and Batt (1994) and Ashton and Sung (2002), who argued that lean would work for all where it was linked to a 'progressive' human resource management (HRM) agenda under-written by strong trade union action. This would be 'win–win' as even the managerialists had never imagined. (For a sustained empirical critique of this widespread view, see Danford et al. 2005).

Meanwhile, for the defeated or the credulous, or both, lean production would seem to have promised something grander than mere survival. The leading ideologues, and especially the Interna-tional Motor Vehicle Program (IMVP) current, talked up the scope for win–win solutions built on honest engagement between employ-ees and management. [3] Successful firms would surely be good for all in the organisation. It would be unfair to group all those who saw something progressive in the lean agenda under the same propa-ganda banner as the authors of *The Machine that Changed the World* (Womack, Jones and Roos 1990). Several prominent researchers who were part of the IMVP team responded to the work of the Gerpisa[4] network highlighting the range of variants taken by 'lean production' (that there was not one 'one best way') by recog-nising that it respected national and local contexts; that it was, in other words, adaptable.[5] Yet lean production was – and remains – an attack on labour, even while it appeared to some, in its early 'Japanisation' form, to allow for a promising planning agenda in the sea of neoliberal destruction of factory plants, companies and communities. We know now that it is lean production itself that is often at the heart of this neoliberal agenda, even if it is not the only approach to labour subordination available to capital today.

Our aim in this book is to highlight the character and consequences of this new offensive from the standpoint of labour in general, so we must be careful in spelling out what we mean by 'success' and 'failure'. It is undoubtedly the case that the restructuring of production, the rebalancing of the capital–labour relationship to the advantage of capital, has allowed capital to reverse many of the postwar social and economic gains made by the labour movement internationally, and specifically, in the context of this book, in the automotive industry. This has come at an enormous cost to workers, their families and communities (as ongoing research on Merseyside by members of the Auto Workers' Research Network demonstrates). Wherever we look we see destruction of social and economic resources on a vast scale

(Moody 1997). For this reason we focus on workers, not only because the voice of labour is often absent in assessments of social and economic success and failure, but also because one of the vanities of advocates of lean production was that it would resolve the problems arising from Fordism's perceived inability to establish economically sustainable production. This was seen to be a result of Fordism's inability properly to measure human and material resources for production, leading periodically to overproduction. Moreover, the advocates of lean argued that lean would increase worker involvement and participation, which in turn would allow for worker understanding of the needs of the corporation, leading to synergy and business success. Goods (and services too) would improve because they would be created in response to consumer needs, and more flexible work would enhance workers' employment experiences. Under Fordism, by contrast, concern with the mass production of goods and services became increasingly divorced from consumer needs. All players in the nexus of work, production and consumption would win out in the new lean world.

In a quite distinct way it would also promise to workers the benefits that capitalism had up to that point been unable to realise. While in the past, forms of capitalist management had tinkered with notions of worker involvement and participation, the adoption of lean production would be unlike anything seen before. For the first time, all workers in the enterprise truly would be heard, their ideas would be taken seriously, and they would benefit from the changes which would in essence reflect, while at the same time creating, a new industrial citizenship. This new industrial citizenship would allow all the old class-driven differences and prejudices of the past to be set aside in a new era of capitalist transformation. So the propaganda insisted, even while the reality was clearly different.

A closer viewing of the lean production workplace tells us that the managers converted to the verities of *The Machine that Changed the World* were really seeking to undermine independent labour organisation and its capacity to fight management, with what Miliband (1989) termed 'class struggle from above' (see Chapter 2 and the Conclusion). In other words, managerially driven commitments to change see lean strategies from a political standpoint, one from which corporate power needs to be reasserted. Unions are fine provided they do not rock the boat, and changes come from above. This is quintessentially a form of company paternalism. For example, there can be worker involvement and worker autonomy – but it is up to management to define their meaning.

We offer a note of caution here. We do not deny the effectiveness of lean production in terms of driving labour harder and in pushing through rationalisation agendas. Furthermore, at the institutional and ideological levels, it is difficult for workers to sidestep continuous improvement groups, for example. However, we need to take into account the impact of lean on union organisation. It can lead, for example, to fewer stewards after reduction of labour and/or the involvement of workers (some of whom are stewards) in managing teamworking. Moreover, companies often introduce rationalisation measures despite worker or broader workplace opposition. More than this, we recognise that many of the lean institutions of involvement enable some workers to participate in planning production: only *some*, because it all depends on where they are in the production process, as our data in the following chapters reveal. For the vast majority of workers, the new lean sector is one of intensive, physically and emotionally demanding employment.

Although the auto industry is a tough one to work in, it is hugely profitable for capital. While job security is a thing of the past, the automotive sector as a whole, while employing less than half the number of workers it did in 1960, still accounts for 194,000 jobs and contributes in excess of £9 billion to the UK economy (more than 6 per cent of the total for UK manufacturing).[6] The point we make, as has been shown elsewhere, is that the cost to labour as a whole has been very high. Even where their livelihood has not been taken away, many workers remaining in lean organisations have experienced deteriorating employment conditions, including increased work intensification and stress, high levels of physically and mentally demanding work practices, and more intrusive management. We must also take into account the psychological impact of job insecurity, a critical feature of lean production. A number of critiques of the character and process of lean production stand out. Some of the exemplary labour movement accounts in the Anglo-Saxon tradition are CAW (1993), Fucini and Fucini (1990), Graham (1995), Rinehart, Huxley and Robertson (1997), Moody (1997), Lewchuk and Robertson (1996), Stewart and Garrahan (1995), Danford (1999), Cohen (1998) and Smith (2000).

While we do not see lean production as having in some sense solved the age-old problem of how to manage labour, we do recognise that in combining a number of new and existing management techniques in the right way and at the right time, and especially in the right context, it has significantly altered the political and industrial relationship of labour to capital, and has achieved this is in a particular way. For the foreseeable future this will not change. Let us be clear what we mean by this. We not suggest that lean production is a new stage of capitalism in the revolutionary sense that it has superseded its social and class antagonisms, especially those inherent in Fordism and in the workplace. We do not deny that high profit rates have been restored to many enterprises and sectors. Rather we contend that the key questions of class subordination and insubordination have not been resolved, unless we agree with the fantastical ideology of the leaners themselves (see again their bible, *The Machine that Changed the World*: Womack et al. 1990). It is a new means by which capital seeks to subordinate labour, yet it has not resolved in a sustained way the global problems of profitability that characterised the crisis of Fordism, even if lean strategies have formed the basis of many individual capitalists' continued or revitalised success.

In countless workplaces across the sector, lean production has successfully undermined union bargaining agendas, both formal and informal, and thus affected their capacity to fight, and the perception of what trade unions are and how they can be successful. We know this, and it could now be held to be something of a truism, because of all the final assembly plants in the United Kingdom in which workers and unions accepted lean production as a way of survival (or felt they had no choice in the matter), only two survive today.[7] Pessimism is an understandable response to this state of affairs, but as our research shows, it is also true that from an international perspective, in many workplaces union organisation has remained strong and vital. Nevertheless, we cannot deny the considerable costs inflicted in terms of employment and the long-term capacity to resist.

Unions often resist the deleterious impact of lean on workers' health, and management almost invariably claims that this is a threat to the existence of the plant. In other words, defence of a union and worker-focused conception of health and safety is seen as undermining competitiveness. The difficulty with the lean view, however, is that even where workers do buy into the management view that all this fuss about quality of working life undermines a plant's capacity to keep competitive, survival is not guaranteed. The employment figures cited above hide the fact that while from a contemporary standpoint, the jobs total looks rosy, it must be remembered that in contrast to the halcyon days of the 1960s, only a small minority enjoy relatively well-paid (by sector standards) jobs in final assembly plants. While insecurity reigns here as much as elsewhere, jobs, and job controls, in final assembly are especially interesting for management for two reasons. First, here labour remains comparatively well organised, and second, this is where the major value-added activities are carried out. This is the last place where the battle for the sector, as they see it, has to be won.

Our view is that while there is clearly no straightforward answer to the destructive impact of lean production, taking its promises of survival at face value and accepting it as a recipe for success has often proved to be hugely burdensome for workers and unions, both at plant level and nationally. We shall illustrate this later, especially with respect to the fate of GM-Luton and the Rover–BMW debacle. We recognise that management threats of closure and layoffs leave workers with few obvious tactics in the fight against lean production. Consequently, although lean production certainly does not resolve the capital–labour antagonism, the threat of disaster restricts labour-centred strategic choices in the route to survival. An absence of obvious resistance should not be confused with an absence of will to struggle at plant level. People need to be provided with alternatives. On occasion, the politics of production leads to an absence of worker-centred alternatives. It may be that in the automotive sector in the United Kingdom no major fight against lean production has straightforwardly succeeded, but opposition, or critical union-labour engagement, seemed to pay the strongest dividends for a considerable period, and certainly longer than anyone thought possible in the late 1990s.

LEAN PRODUCTION FOR WHOM?

Car maker Renault is facing possible prosecution for the suicides of three workers at its technical centre in Paris .... Three employees at the company's state-of-the-art Technocentre killed themselves between October 2006 and February 2007. In linking the three suicides, the inspectorate has added weight to union claims that Renault, as employer, should be held responsible and the deaths treated as workplace accidents. Unions have claimed that harassment at work played a part in the deaths of the engineers, who worked on the conception and design of new vehicles. Renault is also under pressure from France's state health insurance agency, which performed a U-turn and declared that the first of the three suicides should be considered an accident at work .... Separately, an assembly line worker at Peugeot was found hanged at a plant in

Mulhouse in eastern France. This was the sixth suicide at the company since the start of the year, a trend that unions have again linked to work pressures. Police are said to have found a computer disc belonging to one of the victims, containing details of his working conditions.

(Todd, 2007)

Our argument is that the constant pressure to drive down costs has remade the automotive industry into one that thrives upon job insecurity. Rather than establishing a new regime of industrial democracy in a thriving manufacturing sector, the high cost to labour is an inherent, necessary part of the successful political economy of lean production. As we have highlighted, thriving is certainly one way to describe the sector in the United Kingdom, but the evidence for the necessarily destructive other side to this is now indisputable. Our project adds to the ever-widening critique of lean as it sweeps across other sectors from hospitals to the civil service.

As we argued above, lean production is a driving force for what many see as an evolution in the organisation of work and labour in the contemporary political economy. While we accept that the basic tenets of capitalism have not changed in the way that advocates of lean claim, neither do we see it as merely Fordism deepened, or remade, or somehow stripped bare to reveal the inner dynamics of capitalism. If we reject the latter oversimplified view of the historical tensions and contradictions of capitalist work and employment, we certainly do not deny the continuities with Fordism. In this we agree with Tony Smith (2000). Smith's contribution helps to make sense of the way in which lean production can be understood as a form of internal capitalist restructuring, while also allowing capital the means to overcome the crisis of Fordism more broadly at the level of the international capitalist economy. But of course, having the means is not the same as achieving the ends, as trade unions frequently demonstrate.

For us, lean production is a managerial agenda for restructuring in the face of declining profitability. As such it can be seen as creating a range of organisational and ideological resources for subordinating opposition to the rule of capital. This is what we mean when we describe it as a new regime of subordination, including labour while at the same time excluding it. As has been argued elsewhere,[8] lean production necessarily seeks to reconfigure the employment relationship to the advantage of capital by means of innovative value acquisition techniques which lock workers into production (*kaizen*, zero defects, bufferless running schedules and *kanban* production).[9] Two interrelated developments occur in this regime; the level of exploitation is raised, while labour standards, including the quality of working life (and health and safety), compensation benefits and working time/holiday time, come under sustained attack. While the crisis of Fordism can be understood in a variety of ways, it is important to recognise that the origins of the crisis lay in the inability of capital to subordinate labour both in work and sufficiently outside the employment relationship, in the context of the social wage. This is the not so secret 'secret' at the heart of lean. Moreover, and significantly, this is why many of the managerial techniques and ways of thinking so central to lean, originally developed for industrial enterprises, have been adopted (in the United Kingdom and elsewhere) by public sector organisations seeking to develop internal markets, teamworking and just-in-time delivery systems. This is one way to understand the politics of private finance initiatives in Britain.[10]

Lean offers the possibility, as one Canadian colleague put it, to 'checkmate' workers and their organisations for a period (even where these are strong), and lock them 'without strategic struggle' into the circuit of capitalist production. This occurred to a degree in Japan, in the leading export sectors such as electronics and automotives (Stewart et al. 2004, Kawanishi 1992, Hazami 1997, Fujita 1997, Gordon 1998, Kumazawa 1996, Linger 2001, McCormack 2002, Moore 1997). Thus, while far from overcoming the inherent antagonism between capital and labour, lean nevertheless introduces a range of workplace and organisational institutions, such as teamworking and continuous improvement agendas, that either threaten labour autonomy (by reconfiguring or redefining it) or seek to suppress its emergence (see especially Moody 1997). This is why one of the obvious outcomes to the introduction of lean is a deterioration in labour standards. Indeed, even where it is contested, the objective for capital is the same. Then again, this is only part of the story, for it is never straightforwardly a one-way street. As is demonstrated by our research and other work elsewhere, including research by Tony Elger and Chris Smith (2005) on Tamworth in the West Midlands, unless in the context of a greenfield site, lean can rarely be introduced without a fight. Even with greenfield developments there are inevitable local state and cultural variations and forms of regulation that impact on the playing-out of a lean agenda.

Where trade unions can engage robustly, they can be and have been relatively successful in affecting the how and why of lean in any situation. The managerial response to the crisis of Fordism is experienced by labour as an attack first and foremost on the gains concerning worker protection, union autonomy and independence, that were achieved during the rise of Fordism in the postwar era. While we would not deny the ambivalent character of many of these gains, they are perceived by management today as crucial obstacles in their agenda to impose change. It is essentially many of these that are undermined when lean prevails.

We shall return to this later. At present, and in the context of the threat of closure hanging over all automotive plants, it is worth remembering that failure, while never denied by the ideologues, was supposed to affect others: it was the payback for the feckless who refused, or were unable to take up the challenge of, lean production. The new political economy of lean would protect those who embraced its inner truth, which was claimed to be that lean offers more than just survival – it offers world-class success. It was to be seen as a set of production techniques allied to organisational variables that would offer dramatic changes beyond anything traditional Fordist mass production could hope to muster. Yet all the plants closed or threatened by closure (and notably the one GM plant in our project, Vauxhall-Ellesmere Port) were and are lean plants.

The Machine that Changed the World never spelled out what would happen when everyone became lean, when all producers embraced the wisdom of low stocks and buffers, *kaizen* (continuous improvement), the need to get rid of *muda* (waste), teamwork and the other bits of the lean toolkit. But then, success was only part of the story, as we know. In capitalism failure is a necessary part of the narrative whose full dimensions are always reflected in the devastation it wreaks upon workers' personal and working lives.[11]

Failure was not supposed to be an option, according to the lean mantras: 'one best way' and 'working smarter, not harder'. This was not what was being sold in the early days when the ideologues were proselytising the benefits of lean at academic, government or trade union seminars. (See Stewart and Martinez Lucio 2008 for an account of the role of the business academic imparting the latest wisdom of the lean auto producer to the TGWU conference in Eastbourne in 1992.[12]) Or was it? In response to early critiques of lean's evident failure to deliver better work for everyone, meaningful employee involvement and job guarantees, the answer was invariably that the fault lay with incompetent management and/or – peculiarly – plant hyper-efficiency. It was as if lean had nothing to do with it. This was the response by Dan Jones, one of the leading advocates of lean, to the Japan Auto

Workers' (JAW) report on the negative impact of lean production on the health of workers and society more generally (1992). Countering the views of the JAW, Jones argued that lean was bound to go the way of its predecessor if it could not sustain a high degree of employee involvement and move its inherent propensity to greater efficiency and productivity closer to market. Did this mean that it would now be possible to talk of the movement from inefficiency (Fordism) to over-efficiency (lean production)? It is difficult to imagine this was what was meant, but the truth is that lean can indeed lead to overproduction. If we consider its objectives, it is arguably what it is supposed to do. It is about increasing worker productivity. In the context of falling sales this will inevitably lead to plant closure and the possibility of relocation closer to other markets.

There is not one single example of a UK assembly plant that has closed in the last ten years, that could not have been described as 'efficient', 'productive' and 'lean'. Quite the contrary. Manufacturers are candid about this today, as was shown by PSA's rationale for the closure of its Coventry-Ryton plant in favour of the Czech Republic and its cheaper labour costs. According to PSA, Coventry was certainly lean; the issue was labour costs. Yet workers are told that if they are 'efficient' and 'lean', closure is the opposite of what will happen to their plant. Greater efficiency will prove flexibility and worth. This is surely a piece of wishful thinking, but it is worth reminding ourselves of some the reasons for the initial excitement surrounding the trumpeting of lean as the new wisdom of capitalist enlightenment.

Lean was presented as a production regime that was more productive, less wasteful of resources, material and human, and more involving of employees than Fordism (Womack et al. 1990). These observations are only really true if we take a very limited view of productivity, wastefulness and involvement, for we now know that while lean takes employee involvement seriously, its response to employee feedback depends on what they have to say about the system. Those who buy into lean, including team leaders, will thrive, or feel their commitment rewarded, while the critics will be marginalised. Nor is lean production concerned with the elimination of *all* waste, since this depends on where waste lies in the overall chain of production. In other words, involvement is more involving for some, but more wasteful for many others. We can see the consequences of this for workers in physical and psychological terms.

Indeed it is only by seeing lean as part of the jigsaw of contemporary restructuring that the paradoxes of lean production make sense. These paradoxes include the claim of a universal tendency to job improvements, or upskilling for all, despite evidence to the contrary; greater employee participation when evidence highlights the limited nature of this involvement; increased attention to the quality of working life when all employee-based surveys highlight its compromising character; and lastly, the notion that the concept and practice of lean is inherently against waste, when even a cursory glance at the practices of the lean system, in global terms, illustrate the creation of waste. They do so in two significant senses. First, the 'waste' in the system is always held (and thus paid for) by someone else, whether it is suppliers and their factory inventories, or workers in their physical effort. They may think they have 'free' time (how quaint) if they can perform a routine in somewhat less time than the study engineer reckoned, but it is their employer's time that they waste. And the employer wants this time back.[13] All slack and what we would term 'overwork' is carried by and limited to the physical capabilities of individual workers and smaller companies. The second respect in which lean production is hugely wasteful is in terms of the hyperconsumption upon which it thrives. It not only thrives on hyperconsumption, lean is a vital contributory factor its very existence.[14] We shall return to some of these issues in our Conclusion to this book.

OBJECTIVES OF THE BOOK

This book is the outcome of the work of the Auto Workers' Research Network, which was set up in 1993 to research the impact of lean production on the working lives of those at the sharp end of its introduction in automotive final assembly plants. While the crucial issue of broader cross-industry trade union and shop floor alliances was discussed at our meetings (we return to this in the Conclusion to the book), we also considered the whole matter of industry alternatives. This is especially important in the era of concern about carbon emissions, but we decided to focus our attention at this point on an assessment of the politics of lean in the sector, and to address the assumptions about its claimed benefits for workers involved in final assembly. The objective was to track the introduction of lean production in terms of its effects on workers and their lives at home and work, and our book focuses on the latter. The proponents of lean production in the companies, bolstered by their cheerleaders in the academy, had been extolling the virtues of this revolutionary approach to work and employment since the late 1980s.[15] However, trade union stewards and critics were so concerned about the daily reports of intensive and tough work on the assembly lines that it was decided to put together a long-term research project to consider the effects of lean production on workers' health and the quality of their working lives more generally. The project has had its share of problems. These have largely been related to the impact of lean on people's health; also, and notably, it was difficult to maintain contact with the group when plants closed or someone decided to leave the industry,.

Our work focused on two companies in the passenger vehicle final assembly sector, GM (GM-Vauxhall's Ellesmere and Luton plants) and the various incarnations of what had been the British-owned sector until 1994. At this date Rover was sold to BMW, although it continued to trade under its iconic Rover badge. In May 2000 BMW sold Rover to Phoenix, a British consortium, for the princely sum of £10.00, whereupon it was recast as the even more iconic MG Rover. The deal saw BMW retain the Cowley-Oxford plant where it would build the Mini, while Phoenix (MG Rover) would build the large car – the Rover 75 – at Longbridge. In 2005 Phoenix closed MG Rover-Longbridge with the loss of around 6,000 jobs.

Over the years a number of colleagues have contributed in a variety of ways to the project. The Auto Workers' Research Network included John Cooper, Steve Craig, Steve Donnelley, Pat Doyle, John Fetherston, Tony Lewis, Gary Lindsay, Terry Myles and Mick Whitley.

In Chapter 2 we examine the various phases of management–labour struggles over control of the shopfloor and the labour process from the end of the Second World War, from piece work, or payment by results, to measured day work (MDW) and the onset of lean production.

Chapter 3 traces the different forms of trade union engagement with management's lean production agenda. The union strategies are identified as Embrace and Change (Rover) and Engage and Change (GM-Vauxhall).

Chapter 4 examines the fightback that the Engage and Change agenda prompted at GM-Vauxhall Ellesmere Port and Luton in the winter of 1995–96.

Chapter 5 features a round table discussion held at the 'Sandcastle', the TGWU's Regional 6 office in Liverpool in 2001, between shop stewards from Ellesmere Port on their evolving views on lean production and its challenges to labour. The chapter also contains several biographical accounts of workers' experiences of evolving labour and management politics at Ellesmere since the late 1970s.

In Chapter 6, we turn to the British-owned sector and trace the history of negotiation and the trade union embrace of lean production through to BMW's sale of Rover to Phoenix in 2000.

In Chapter 7 we track the trajectories of the various agreements surrounding struggles over the implementation of lean production strategies at GM-Vauxhall, beginning in 1989 with the so-called V-6 Agreement. In this chapter we also assess comparative data from BMW and Vauxhall-GM carried out in 2001 on the impact of lean production on workers' quality of working life. This includes data on stress, workload, bullying, autonomy and union organising.

Finally in the Conclusion we return to the theme of the global social politics of lean production, challenging the key conceits of its protagonists, and notably the claims that it is good for workers and good for society as a whole. The Conclusion ends by examining what unions can do to address the ever-widening reach of lean production.

2 THE PREHISTORY OF LEAN PRODUCTION: EMPLOYEE RELATIONS IN THE BRITISH AUTOMOBILE INDUSTRY SINCE THE SECOND WORLD WAR

INTRODUCTION

Under the piece rate system we directly sold the fruits of our labour. Under Measured Day work we sold our time. Under lean we sell our time no more. Under lean, management determine our labour input and our time with a vengeance. Or at least, that's their aim.[1]

(Peter Titherington, convener, Ellesmere Port, 1992)

In Chapter 1 we posed the question about lean's revolutionary character. It was argued that while it was appealing to view lean as in some sense revolutionary, especially where management wanted to push the idea that it represented an exciting new wisdom about the win–win outcomes of shopfloor involvement, the reality was less attractive (ILO 2000). As researchers in the Auto Workers' Research Network have demonstrated elsewhere, workers on the receiving end have experienced a somewhat less appealing outcome (Murphy 2008, Wilson 2008). Moreover, far from being revolutionary, lean continues many of the characteristic features of labour control strategies in the postwar period. There are some clear points of technical and organisational innovation, for example the use of new information systems for tracking external customers and stock, and the labour surveillance techniques that are central to *kanban* (stock control), but the purpose of lean is nevertheless entirely central to the strategic orientation of management in a capitalist society.

It is important to make this obvious point, since those taking a technological determinist view have foregrounded lean's innovative and socially neutral character. (Although it is understandable why managerialist writers might want to do so, it is dispiriting that there is also a strong strain of technological determinism among some currents on the left.) While the contributions of the Williams team (Williams et al. 1987, 1992a, b and c, 1993) were important in pointing to the historical continuities in production strategies and methods, including particular technical features such as early methods for sustaining quality control and product diversity in Ford's Highland Park complex at the beginning of the twentieth century, both the managerialist and the business history-led debates over lean in the 1990s lacked an understanding that the distinctiveness of managerial regimes was not to be found in either technical procedures or organisational innovation as such. We do not wish to underestimate these technical features (including both accounting procedures and organisational changes), but we would argue that the distinctiveness and the differences are best understood at the level of managerial control and techniques for employee subordination in the broader employment relationship. This, notably, was intended to allow management control in the absence of a trade union counter-agenda.

New techniques have certainly been important in giving management an opportunity to assert a greater degree of process control, and this naturally forms part of our story. But the core of the argument in this book is that lean is not simply about production control, or process control, in any neutral technological sense. What is manifestly different about lean is the strategic role of lean methods in pursuing 'class struggle from above' (Miliband 1989: 115–66). This refers to managerial strategies aimed at achieving worker compliance in the pursuit of capital accumulation. This depends, in turn, on measures designed to shackle autonomous collective representation and trade union autonomy – which is where organisational features such as teamworking come into play. (We discuss this further in the Conclusion.)

It could be questioned, in the manner of Williams and colleagues (1987, 1992 a, b and c, 1993), to what extent the lean interpretation of elements such as teamworking, continuous improvement (*kaizen*) and quality control constitutes something more than a contemporary take on existing elements of management control (see Dan Coffey's 2006 broadside against the assumptions of the leaners). This will become apparent later when we argue that the managerial and strategic imperatives of lean are ineluctably bound to the key control imperatives of MDW. The latter was abandoned with the introduction of the annualised hours regime.[2] Nonetheless, just-in-time (JIT) techniques signalled a change in the relationship between producer and market, to the extent that a more fragmented market required tighter networks and new approaches to surveillance and control, in relation to the new notion of the post-Fordist customer. (The idea of the post-Fordist customer, as opposed to the old Fordist dichotomy, producer–consumer, is distinguished by being both inside and outside the realm of production. We can readily see this in the notion of the internal customer on the assembly line.)

Overall, in our view the context of class struggle from above provides a better way to begin to understand the nature and significance of lean production. This should be seen as in contrast to the notion that lean resolves the problems of overcapacity and diversified customer needs. Otherwise, the argument would necessarily run that lean did not somehow help to create both new markets (and hence post-Fordist customers) and excess capacity. The latter, of course, is the public reason given for so much downsizing in the sector. When lean has accelerated the problems of sector overcapacity (if it did not actually create them from scratch), it is difficult to see JIT and *kaizen*, including teamworking and new audit control measures, simply as technical and organisational concepts that are designed to enhance production to the benefit of capital and labour in equal measure. (See the Conclusion.) This is because we now understand quite a lot about the *actual* social and technical character and consequences of the workings of lean production, as opposed to its professed outcomes (Stewart et al. 2004, 2006).

These sociotechnical and organisational features define the form of class struggle from above that characterises lean production in the two companies central to our account. They are to be defined principally in relation to their impact on workers' experience of lean forms of employment, as later chapters will explore. Elaborating what is unique about this particular form of class struggle from above, a number of us in the Network have argued elsewhere that:

> What has changed from work under Fordism is how managements exert control over labour in efforts to tilt the wage–effort bargain in their favour. In the context of intense international competition, institutions of work and internal labour market regulation such as just-in-time (JIT), team working and *Kaizen,* have challenged established industrial relations regulation. Working conditions and employment standards, including intensity of work, duration of work and the regulations governing work effort, which receded into the

background in the 1950s and 1960s, with the entrenchment of the post-war union-employer bargain, have become significant in the contests between unions and managements in the 1980s and 1990s.

(Lewchuk, Stewart and Yates 2001)

In other words, in contrast to the 'one best way' mantra of the lean school, we locate lean as a specific labour regime 'enmeshed in social relations of contestation in the workplace' (ibid.). Because of the variability that this inevitably creates, the scope for managerial authority (regimes of control) will depend in large measure on union strength (see Chapters 3 and 4). Our view is that change is path-dependent (by company) and continuous with, though nevertheless distinctive from, pre-existing regimes of control. It is possible to discern determinate historical and socioeconomic trends, processes and trajectories in employment relations in the automobile industry in Britain.

REGIMES OF CONTROL: FROM PIECEWORK TO MEASURED DAY WORK

It is beyond the scope of this chapter to provide an account of the full range and content of institutional processes, management–labour agreements, and more broadly the history of employment relations in the sector. However we do need to outline the critical processes and practices that were characteristic of the British experience in the period from the Second World War to the late 1980s, including the formation of wartime and postwar institutions and shopfloor relationships, and how they began to unravel in the 1960s. There are adequate company-by-company accounts of this period available elsewhere (Whisler 1999, Lyddon 1996 and Williams et al. 1994 all have somewhat different takes on the demise of the British-owned sector), so our intention here is to provide a broad-brush narrative, focusing on what we take to be the critical moments in the conflictual relationship between capital and labour. We shall use particular instances drawn from specific companies, predominantly British-owned, to highlight the general trends in the rise and insecure containment (albeit in a quite different register from today's lean period) of trade union and shopfloor power.

Friedman's (1977) argument allows us to characterise the pre-lean period as a shift from a form of bargained autonomy ('Responsible

Autonomy' strategies, 1997: 221) characteristic of assembly-line work under a piece-rate regime, to a regime of 'direct control'. This involved the implementation of MDW across the British sector. It became entrenched earlier in the American-owned firms: it was introduced at Vauxhall in 1956. In characteristically British fashion, some aspects of the way it was introduced and operated in the British-owned sector depended on the strength of local, often informal, trade union organisation. In general terms, we can divide this period into two phases: from shopfloor autonomy and power, to increasing managerial control, and it should be seen as critical in coming to terms with the peculiarities of lean production in the British context.

This trajectory was by no means unambiguous. Even with the introduction of MDW in the British-owned sector, worker resistance was neither eliminated nor ever really shackled. Even today under lean production regimes, and nearly 40 years after the Donovan Commission Report (see below) on the perceived 'problem' of disorder in British shopfloor industrial relations, it is not uncommon to witness stoppages for myriad reasons associated with worker antipathy to the consequences of the new production culture. (See Chapter 4, and Stewart 1997.) In 2005 there was a prominent dispute at Vauxhall-Ellesmere Port in support of sacked temporary staff. More recently in March 2008, staff in the body-stamping shop at Ellesmere Port took wildcat strike action when the company reneged on an agreement on staffing levels. This was especially combustible because the agreement was at the heart of the deal in 2006 on workforce reduction.

CONTEMPORARY CONTRASTS AND CONTINUITIES

Looking at the current nature and role of trade unions in the automobile industry in Britain would give us few clues about the relatively recent past, which was defined by significant union strength at both national and workplace level. There is no longer any automotive assembly plant without a union presence (the recognition by Honda of Amicus in 2002 ensured sector coverage), but the ability of unions to negotiate, let alone set the agenda for change, has never been more precarious. Union power has not disappeared, but it is bounded by the contemporary institutional and political contexts of neoliberalism and anti-union laws. In addition, if union decline is too strong a term (since density remains high in the assembly sector), the current phase could perhaps be described as one in which a particular form of trade union participation has been incorporated, but in a context where employers have not had it all their own way. Yet if trade unions are less combative, management is just as restrained by a proliferation of economic insecurities. Some of these existed in previous eras, but today in the context of a new phase of production and management strategies, a number of them have been amplified extensively. For example, statistical process control, outsourcing and the management of recalcitrant labour go to the heart of management's ability to plan strategically.

This is a far cry from the period of robust shopfloor power in the sector in the late 1950s and 1960s, when union stewards could interrupt production on issues of wage determination, at plant and especially at shopfloor level. These disputes were frequently tied directly to issues of labour control (or in other words, of shopfloor union power). It is important to remember that there are constraints and possibilities for industrial and employee relations in every era, and the current era of lean production is far from delivering on its promise to employers of workplace harmony. Significant difficulties continue to be posed by employment relations and production realities for labour and its union organisations, from Britain to Brazil, and from Canada to Japan and Italy.[3]

If the period from the mid-1960s can be characterised as one of labour–management conflict centred on control of the effort–reward bargain, it can also be interpreted more broadly as the beginning of the consolidation of management's assault on postwar labour standards. By this is meant the microgovernance of the employment relationship at company (or more usually plant) level, determining how hard and for how long workers produce automobiles, for what reward and under what conditions. This chapter concentrates on these issues in the period from the end of the Second World War until the late 1970s: the prehistory, so to speak, of lean production. It covers the change from piecework (payment by results (PBR), or a piece rate) to MDW, and presages the change from MDW to lean production in the late 1980s. We can identify three phases in the battle for control of labour, including labour standards in the industry. These focus on labour's response to each of these three management paradigms.

Lean can usefully be understood as the continuation of management commitment to the elimination of the irritating labour conflicts that beset the politics of MDW. It can be distinguished from both MDW and PBR in one vital way, all other differences notwithstanding: it involved the elimination, or taming, of trade union autonomy in determining the outcome of the inevitable tensions surrounding the effort–reward bargain. If PBR reproduced steward power at the micro (local) level, and MDW, far from eliminating it, changed the content and dynamic of shopfloor conflict (Tolliday 1988), lean was designed to deal with steward power once and for all. In this respect the period from the late 1950s through to the end of the 1960s was crucial, for it was then that the balance began to tip in management's favour. By this we do not imply a linear assault on labour, with power shifting to management along a one-way street. It would be tempting to describe the subsequent battle around lean, both at Vauxhall and in the British-owned sector (including the remnants at Cowley, now owned by BMW) as having been the decisive one for management in the war against organised labour at shopfloor level. This would ignore the constant insecurity for management that arises from the continual insubordination of labour, as reflected by myriad ongoing skirmishes in assembly plants today (what Ackroyd and Thompson 1999, writing about labour insubordination more broadly, describe as the sociological intractability of labour).[4]

BARGAINING IN THE CONTEXT OF CONFLICT AND THE IMPORTANCE OF THE LOCAL AGREEMENTS

There are two principal characteristics that, taken together, have determined the nature of employment and industrial relations in the automobile industry in the United Kingdom since the Second World War. Management–labour relations in the sector were characterised by pervasive informality and localism. These two features came to fruition during the period from the 1950s through to the late 1970s. Unfortunately for Britain's political economy, they were by no means peculiar to the automobile industry. The informality in the negotiation process occurred not just at plant level but also inside the plants of every manufacturer. Since shop stewards depended upon area support (for instance, the paint or body shop) within a particular plant, improving remuneration in any specific area strengthened the trade union on the shopfloor, an obvious precondition for sustained mobilisation. This led to considerable conflict over wage levels, both within and between plants and across companies, where national agreements were either ignored or seen to be ineffectual in their implementation (see the comments on Donovan below).

Whisler argues that:

> In management's view, piecework payment tied wages to effort ratios and paternalism maintained control over workers. The evolution of shop-floor relations, however, indicated that labour's

influence over production was increasing. Piecework provided
workers with a measure of control over their effort levels by definition. Management further enhanced this position by relying
upon labour to maintain production in pursuit of higher wages.

(Whisler 1999: 193)

However, as Whisler goes on to argue, 'management paternalism'
had a very distinctive sting: victimisation of stewards. There is a
well-recognised social and political mechanism at work here. We
would argue that 'management paternalism' depended upon the
incorporation of workers and their representatives, via concessions
which were in turn traded for the relative subordination of stewards
after the battles over control of the line. The conflict was endemic,
and 'subordination' came at a crucial political and strategic cost to
labour. Ceding elements of shopfloor power to stewards implicated
them in the process of labour control, specifically with regard to job
responsibilities, work schedules, job loading and staffing levels.
Nevertheless, subordination was relative in the period of the piece-
rate regime, earnings rose, shop steward influence and job control
practices were extended, and mutuality became the linchpin of trade
union and worker power (IWCMG 1978: 14).

The peculiarities of the 'British system'[5] formed the background
and context, not to say content, of industrial relations at shop floor
and company level.[6] The contours of the British-owned sector
defined the terrain on which labour had to engage with capital. The
fact that the unions were able to achieve a significant measure of
shopfloor control in a different, though no less vociferous, manner
than was the case at Vauxhall and Ford, is for us a strength, despite
a dialectic which arguably hampered unions, because of their role as
intermediaries of labour subordination. We are committed to a positive assessment of this, even though the compromising of union
strength may have been seen by many commentators, then and now,
as part of the unnecessarily high cost to be paid by the British-owned
sector in order to achieve industrial peace – which in any event, as
we know, it did not.

There is always a cost to labour in capitalist societies when
control of workers in production is assumed by their trade unions.
In the Conclusion we consider some of the vital themes unions need
to address in order to confront lean in a broader context.

If organised (and unorganised) shopfloor labour was bound by
the system, it nevertheless made the best of the situation, as Pilkington (1996) and Whisler (1999: 185) point out. From our standpoint,

the prominent and abiding aspect of both the British-owned sector and the regimes at Vauxhall and Ford, despite Whisler's argument (1999: 227)[7], is that 'workers have always developed ingenious ways of "controlling" almost any payment system managers think up' (IWCMG, p. 13). The implications of constant struggle over remuneration were to form a central plank in the deliberations of the Donovan Commission, which famously noted, during the latter stages of this period:

> We attach more importance to the industry's wage structure as a cause of strikes. It is plain that employees' actual earnings are not determined by the negotiations conducted at industry level .... Two major manufacturers (Ford and Vauxhall) are not in any case in the Engineering Employers' Federation, which is one of the parties to such negotiations. In the other remaining companies earnings are a long way in advance of the rates so settled at industry level, and *a crucial part is therefore played by workplace negotiations.*
>
> (Donovan 1968: 104, emphasis added)

Locale, as a vital site of industry negotiations, reflected actual social and economic power. Furthermore, it served to highlight the other feature of the employment relationship in the sector in our period: informality. As Donovan noted, this informal domain, where actual decision making occurred, was inherently unstable, deriving from a highly competitive pattern of remuneration. Yet this competitive facet of the employment relationship reinforced steward power within, but also largely between, plants and different companies (Turner, Clack and Roberts 1967). How was it possible for stewards to attain such a high degree of knowledge of the microconditions of other plants within not just their own companies, but other firms as well? This became possible as a result of the growth of what were known as 'Combine Committees' or 'parallel unionism' (ibid: 216–23). These materialised in the postwar era as organised labour was strengthened by the wartime accommodation between trade union officialdom and the government. Combine Committees were effectively an unrecognised system of union organisation running parallel to the recognised one as defined by the Donovan Commission. Despite being frowned upon by trade union centres, the emergence of the Combine Committees which grouped shop stewards from different plants allowed stewards to get to grips with the minutiae of the industry, making them probably better informed, and usually more articulate about processes, than plant management. Price (1986) argues that a measure of the success of the Combine Committees can be judged by the antipathy of national union officials, and that despite this, although a sector Combine Committee was stymied, they flourished for a considerable period within companies. Combine Committees continued to thrive until the late 1970s at Ford, Vauxhall and British Leyland (BL) (and subsequently Rover). Arguably, the steward network set up and centred on Vauxhall and Rover in the early 1990s to respond to lean vividly played a similar role, even though it would later peter out.

So in the postwar period it was axiomatic that whoever 'called' local agreements determined local power (Turner et al. 1967, Friedman 1977, Church 1994, Whisler, 1999). Since the character and quality of local union power could be said to be central to industrial relations in the British automobile industry, it was local (plant) level agreements that contributed to the unique texture of the industry. While industry-wide agreements existed, they were only ever as good as the local industrial relations environments in which they were introduced.[8] A well-organised plant could, and did, secure significant advances on national agreements (Higgs 1969: 124).

This was the view of the Donovan Commission, which famously saw the absence of national-level control over workplace institutions as the prime cause for the inchoate nature of industrial relations in the auto industry and elsewhere. The consequent fragmentation of bargaining allowed, in the view of the Commission, undue scope for local determination of, *inter alia*, pay and conditions, and was the principal reason for the high level of disputes over pay-related issues.[9] (See Murden 2005 on contemporary questions of payment equity.) The multiplicity of unions, while important, could not be seen as the key factor in the strike rate in the sector: 'Union structure is … a factor which may play some part in the industry's propensity to strike, but we do not believe that it can be one of the major factors' (Donovan 1968).[10] Donovan highlighted the significance of informality in the critical role of local management–shop steward negotiations in resolving disputes. Informality was crucial for managers who needed to resolve local difficulties speedily, and crucial for stewards who needed to hold the line against management in defence of the 'gang' or work group in their shopfloor area (Donnelly and Thoms 1989). Donovan again:

> There is no doubt in our view, that the unions [union officialdom] have not had sufficient influence on the workplace situation. There are a number of reasons for this, one of which is the

readiness of management to deal directly with shop stewards to
the exclusion of full-time officials.

(Donovan 1968)

The growing importance of informal local bargaining based upon
the power of local stewards was the key to the success of trade
unions, even if the ability to generalise this local power along
national lines proved elusive, the importance of the Combine
Committee notwithstanding. Stewards, however, had to prove themselves by providing leadership and addressing the concerns of their
members. This was not easy, and certainly not peculiar to the automotive industry. For example, in 1951, at the Rolls-Royce aero-
engine plant in Hillington, Glasgow, shop stewards complained that
their members frequently took unauthorised action to bring about a
resolution of their grievances, which stewards seemed powerless to
prevent. Internal, departmental identities undermined stewards'
efforts to pursue factory-wide negotiations (McKinlay and Melling
1999: 234; for similar examples in the automobile industry see
Lyddon 1996: 203–4). In the auto industry, unions in the Coventry
area 'appear not have developed a company or even plant wide view
of industrial relations' (Donnelly and Thoms 1989: 107).

The reasons for this relative failure lie somewhat beyond our
remit, but it should be noted that the historical pattern of negotiation tended to reinforce company peculiarities in the way in which
workers sought, as Tom White (a recently retired convener at BMW,
formerly Rover) put it, to 'make deals on their own terms'. Thus
localism in union–management orientation inevitably recreated, at
the same time as it reinforced, local steward propensity to settle
things at source. Inevitably this allowed for competitive wage
bargaining in which, whatever the other disadvantages, labour could
be a relatively powerful player. So if it was the wage and remuneration system that encouraged this practice, what examples can we
find to shed some light on the workings of this process?

WAGES, UNIONS AND CONFLICTS IN THE BRITISH SYSTEM

From the Piece Rate Era to Measured Day Work

While the history of the automotive industry represents a particular story of shifting power within the capital–labour relationship,
it is also a narrative of various attempts by capital to move out of

a crisis of control, which is in turn tied to a profitability crisis. Here, a profitability crisis is seen to lie behind plant-based crises in the cycle of management control. The rise of lean is, in short, a continuation in the story of cycles of uncertain domination at company level (see Ramsay on 'Cycles of Control', 1977, and IWCMG 1978: 13).

> The reason any employer seeks a change in the payment system is in the hope that it will reduce trade union bargaining power and workers control over the pace of work. The issue is not one of payment system but one of power.
>
> (IWCMG 1978: 12)

> Payment systems are used as part of management strategies to maintain and extend their control over work.
>
> (IWCMG 1978: 12)

We can speak of 'fragmented domination' since as numerous commentators have highlighted, management to a considerable degree, notably in the British-owned sector but also in Chrysler (IWCMG 1978: 13–14), agreed numerous concessions in order to make paper agreements on the introduction of MDW. The industrial relations environment at plant level is important in accounting for this, yet it is crucial to note that despite the competition between a number of unions within the plants on the question of wage differentials,[11] according to Friedman, the various companies found that disputes increasingly focused on 'parity between factories of a single firm and between [other] firms' replacing 'disputes over differentials *within factories* as the major source of wage grievances in the motor industry' (1977: 221, emphasis added).

Given that the defining characteristics of labour relations were forged out of local negotiations and disputes over remuneration, it is important to remember that remuneration is indelibly linked to the issue of labour utilisation, or as is commonly understood at the plant level, labour mobility. Because workers tended to be tied to specific job tasks, where payment was by piece rate (PBR), as it was in the majority of car plants during the 1960s, Vauxhall being a notable exception, labour mobility would inevitably have a considerable impact upon workers' wages. There are innumerable instances we could draw on to highlight the interrelationship between wages and union practice; whatever the variants, it is important to point out that we are now making the link to issues of 'job control'. As the IWCMG group argued, pieceworking was double edged: while management would accept the 'automatic regulator linking wages costs to output' (1978: 14), the quid pro quo was that shopfloor localism, including the 'gang system', provided the basis for mutuality sustained though 'shop stewards' influence' (ibid.), including the maintenance of job controls.

We have taken as an exemplar of this invariant relationship across the sector in Britain, the case of the Cowley plant at Oxford, now BMW, and formerly part of BL, the consolidated remnants of the indigenous automobile industry. The history of the Cowley plant (or complex of plants, as it actually was) is an intriguing one. For our purposes we focus on the introduction of MDW there in 1971 (although, it did not achieve complete coverage in BL until 1975, with nationalisation). We have already highlighted broadly the centrality of the piece-rate system as the defining social and political face of industrial relations both at BL and across the industry. Alan Thornett (1987, 1998), in his memoirs of trade union and political struggle at Cowley, sums up the historical significance of the piece-rate system for labour, and why its successor, MDW, was so central to management from the 1970s to the late 1980s. Despite the revolutionary fervour of many of the advocates of lean production beginning in the late 1980s, it often continued elements of management control that had been central to MDW, by different means.[12]

Thornett argues that piecework, when it was first introduced in the 1920s, in an era of weak trade union organisation in the automobile industry, had been an effective tool of management control. This was the case until the 1950s, when unions achieved 'control', or at least a significant degree of regulation, of the piecework system:

> [Management] rightly ... saw piecework as one of the pillars of the shop steward movement in the car industry and they knew that to attack it was to attack the shop stewards.
>
> Our stance [the union, the TGWU, at plant level] was the outright defence of the piecework system despite the fact that the piecework system was originally brought in by [the owner] when his plants were non-union as the most effective way to maximise profitability.
>
> Under piecework workers were 'rated' for each individual operation they performed. When the track stopped, wages stopped. Workers effectively supervised themselves, seeking more work in order to make more money. They would push themselves to the limit of physical endurance. ...

It was an effective system for the employers provided they had complete control of the situation.

(Thornett 1987: 107)

However, in the postwar period, beginning at the end of the 1950s and early 1960s, with the developing strength of the trade unions, the piecework system became more highly regulated by shop stewards at plant level. This was because, as Thornett continues, 'Most importantly the shop stewards won control of the price fixing procedures. Prices could be renegotiated when changes took place and all this was used to push wages up rapidly' (1987: 108).

Hyman and Elger in recalling this period advise 'caution against over-romantic conceptions of the efficacy of workers' job controls .... Frequently they operated within limits acceptable to employers' (1981: 116). Bowden, Foreman-Peck and Richardson make the point that piece-rate systems 'cushioned the company [BMC, Cowley] against production losses, for the basic principle of "no work, no pay" meant that workers, rather than the company, bore the cost of "idle time" or "shut outs"' (2001: 64).

Nonetheless, Thornett's description is really an account of the balance of power in the plant at the level of the assembly track itself; the tug-of-war over piecework defined the period historically, since it told us that management control over production norms was being eroded. Many firms chose to ignore this development: they were preoccupied with output while demand for cars was buoyant in the 1950s and early 1960s (Hyman and Elger 1981: 134). Managers of specific work areas were usually desperate to forge local deals with the stewards, who were recognised by management as the negotiators on behalf of workers in particular areas. In the 1970s, however, as the market situation deteriorated, a pattern of increasing management frustration with shop steward autonomy emerged (Willman and Winch 1985: 65–84). Thornett comments that 'Once management had lost control of the piecework system, they no longer wanted it, and sought to replace it by an alternative system' (1987: 108).

Because shop stewards were the labour intermediaries and inter-locutors, their power in the context of microbargaining was enhanced when the alternative system, MDW, was introduced, despite the fact that MDW was taken up precisely because it was seen as giving management the scope for recovering lost power on the shop floor. In making this point and in our argument more generally, we hope we are not falling into what Tolliday and Zeitlin

(1992) have rightly derided as the 'erroneous' view of a parabola of shopfloor power, rising in the 1950s and 1960s only to be brought down to earth again with the 1980s recession. They must surely be right in arguing that while management could not be said to have had unbridled workplace authority in the 1950s (1992: 103), the kind of effective leverage exerted by labour was episodic and often bound by the micro-obsessions, the specificities, of each area in the shop. In this they are describing a situation in which steward behaviour was hemmed in by the actual politics of a set of local circumstances, and in this respect they are correct to emphasise the extent to which shopfloor politics could never be other than driven by 'opportunism' (1992: 106) which 'meant that stewards could not think or act strategically' (ibid.).

We should also bear in mind Lyddon's argument that in certain companies, 'the decade 1964–73 was the high point of workers' bargaining power, measured by management toleration of their shop stewards and a reasonable degree of control over the wage–effort bargain' (1996: 206). However, the intention here is not to underplay the strategic weakness in workers' various responses to capital in this period. We merely seek to note that, ironically, the possibility of a much more dynamic, strategic, answer to management would have to await the latter's new assault upon labour standards and union organisation. This was lean production, and it signalled the possibility that 'opportunism' could at last be overcome by more strategic and political responses.

Coming back to the question of MDW, Tolliday has revealed the inability of management in the British-owned sector to deal with what it perceived to be the root cause of production difficulties at the time: the piece-rate system (1988: 72). However, management and unions underestimated the force of traditional forms of payment and bargaining, while the company ended up instituting a different set of dynamics which would be just as bothersome.

Remember I'm talking management *intentions* here. MWD represents a concretisation of Taylorism where every job is timed as opposed to piece work, where the job is driven by the employee. Measured Day Work enabled the company to standardise the shop floor, each job was timed individually and the times agreed upon. This helps in planning as well as in the actual production process, for all the obvious reasons, not least of all manning since it is easy to determine the levels of manpower required when you know how many pieces can be produced by a worker. Because of the switch from piecework in general, mainly Ford and British Leyland, there was little idle time. Every minute of every hour was in theory productive and so workers lost out in the switch financially as well. I would say that lost power on the shop floor was in part taken back by the level of control that Measured Day Work gave companies since if you were timed to make say 60 pieces an hour and only produced 30!!! Big trouble. But we fought back. We did.

Ken Murphy, Vauxhall Ellesmere Port, 2005

MDW[13] was intended to centralise decision making, first at the factory level and then at the level of the firm. This was why at Cowley, and at BL's other sites, although with varying degrees of conflict, the unions opposed the introduction of MDW. MDW was a means by which management could set wage rates at plant and later, company level.

The act of taking the piecework bargaining element away from stewards and shop floor trade union organisations would automatically render the irksome negotiating elements unnecessary – and having removed the basis for shop steward power and authority, would leave the company in control of all levels of production, track speed, wages and conditions.

(Turnball Institute of Management, cited in BLMC 1975)

Of course, the centralising drive behind MDW also goes some way towards accounting for the fact that the union centres (outside the plants and regionally) were lukewarm in opposition. Negotiations and decisions on remuneration would be taken away completely from the plants and out of the hands of the shop stewards. However, at Cowley, after a six-week strike in 1970, resistance to the introduction of MDW was broken – but at a cost to management. A so-called 'mutuality' agreement was struck. This agreement reintroduced an element of *in situ* control by the stewards. Basically 'mutuality' meant that any change to the line speed had to be negotiated with the shop steward in that particular area, and this, as Thornett points out, was 'based on mutually agreed "fair effort". Management had been forced into it after successfully abolishing

piecework and forcing in MDW ... after a six-week strike in 1971'
(1998: 19).

The 'mutuality' agreement was management's concession to get
MDW through. As Whisler makes clear, 'Management expanded its
settlement range to avoid the high costs of idle plant and machinery.
In other words, management was willing to pay the incrementally
higher price that labour demanded for continuity of production'
(1999: 212).

While it was undoubtedly true that the 'mutuality' deal returned
a significant element of steward negotiating power, the introduction
of MDW signalled the beginning of the end for shopfloor autonomy
as it had developed in the postwar period. A measure of the threat
posed by MDW to steward power and discretion can be gleaned
from Thornett's ironic comment in support of the strike against it,
that 'Management had offered more pay for less work as a sweet-
ener to get the new system in. It was the first time we had led a strike
demanding less pay for more work' (1998: 19).

The deployment of MDW in BL by 1975, according to the Executive of the British Leyland Motor Corporation Combine Committee, was achieved because 'Concessions had to be made to the men
[sic] on the floor – Carrots despite their price were dangled before
our members as an inducement for acceptance of the system'
(BLMC 1975). Nonetheless, it was the opinion of the Combine
Committee that in the years following the implementation of MDW,
the 'control' management expected from it did not materialise:

> The company has little or no idea of the real labour costs, and
> certainly far less control than they had prior to the introduc-
> tion of MDW and its maintenance. Maintenance of the system
> of MDW [involved] industrial engineers, industrial relations
> department and a growth of foremen and middle management
> ... all or most of them seen in terms of a higher efficiency as
> engines of delay and impediment.
>
> (BLMC 1975)

Tolliday has identified a lack of mutual understanding of shopfloor
politics in the inability to grasp the implications of change:

> As MDW was introduced on a plant by plant basis stewards
> continued to find plenty of bargaining opportunities but, since
> earnings levels were now fixed, shifted their focus from an
> almost exclusive attention to pay and the maximisation of

earnings to the minimisation of effort, better job conditions, and security of earnings. The intensity of effort and the pacing role of piecework fell away. Stewards ceased to correct production problems as they occurred or chase up materials .... 'effort drift' replaced 'wage drift'.

(Tolliday 1988: 72)

By this time the company was in the throes of a financial crisis which threatened its very existence. The government intervened, since it was not willing to see BL go under. The subsequent period was marked by a corporatist engagement between the unions and the Labour government, and the establishment of the National Enterprise Board (NEB) – a vehicle for holding controlling stakes in manufacturing firms 'as a way of injecting public money into private companies, and exercising some control over the use of the funds, while encouraging competition' (Barratt Brown & Coates 1996: 61). This government control was exercised to encourage company restructuring and rationalisation, which BL workers experienced after the NEB took over the company helm in 1975.

This is crucial for making sense of the historical import of MDW. The automotive industry was only one of a number of sectors where the Labour government and official unions struggled to contain shopfloor power. While often exaggerated, on sporadic occasions this local strength significantly undermined national trade union and Labour government industrial and economic strategy. The introduction of MDW at BL (from 1970), followed by the formation in December 1974 of British Leyland under state control, may have cleared the way for the company to bring about the centralisation of bargaining on remuneration and other conditions 'but it was to prove a long-drawn-out and conflict-prone operation' (Willman and Winch 1985: 65). This was both cause and effect of the diminution of shop steward power, a long-sought goal of trade unions outside both plant and firm, and of the government (for relatively different reasons), as codified in the Donovan Commission from as early as 1965–68.

This diminution of shop steward power was reflected in the unions' acceptance of the Ryder Plan, which included the approval of the executive 'right to manage' without union interference, and endorsement of a worker participation scheme. Leading Communist Party conveners Derek Robinson, Peter Nicholas and Tom Steward gave credence to the scheme by enthusiastically taking up places on the BL Cars Council. Together with other council members, and union national secretaries Jack Jones (TGWU) and Hugh Scanlon (AUEW), they supported a strategy of company survival at all costs, even though this meant accepting redundancies and plant closures, and opposing strikes (McIlroy 1999: 240). Senior stewards became 'dangerously detached from their membership' (Hyman and Elger 1981: 139). Their actions, however unwittingly, paved the way for the appointment of Michael Edwardes as chair of BL (1977–82). He was to preside over reducing the workforce by half, significantly intensifying the pace of production, cutting real wages and sacking leading shop stewards, including Derek Robinson (Whisler 1999: 372).

Edwardes, by jettisoning recent commitments to worker participation, as defined by the Ryder Plan, was able to break union solidarity on the basis that it had no alternative strategy. As Edwardes himself put it, his aim was to 'put management back in the saddle' (Edwardes 1983). According to him, the Ryder Report reinforced bureaucratic decision making. It would have to go. It was 'a bureaucratic paper chase dissipating management resources and effort. Some management decisions were delayed by months while the joint consultative machinery tried unsuccessfully to grind out a consensus' (Edwardes 1983: 37).

Edwardes' hardline approach was signalled by his determination to tear up existing agreements and sweep away the remnants of mutuality. His aim was essentially to destroy traditional job controls and rationalise production. Plant closures followed, first the Speke Triumph TR7 factory and then plants at Canley, Abingdon, Castle Bromwich, Liverpool and Park Royal in London. Edwardes' final triumph came in November 1981, when the TGWU agreed to take international levels of competition as 'the bench mark for all future negotiations on pay, conditions and manning'. Automotive workers across the globe were increasingly subjected to 'chasing each other's effort under the watchful eye of bankers and managers intent only on the preservation of their profits and the capitalist system' (Rudder 1983: 45).

REGIMES OF CONTROL: MEASURED DAY WORK AND THE RISE OF LEAN PRODUCTION

The advent of lean production in the 1990s transformed the landscape of employment relations in the global automobile industry, arguably nowhere more so than in Britain, considering its significant role in production in postwar Europe and more widely. Our argument is that it is important to properly identify its origins and the factors that determined its trajectory. These are divided evenly between changes in the wider political economy, including a crisis in accumulation, and the never-ending problem of insubordinate labour. While the proponents of lean have a powerful narrative, we have demonstrated how it could not have appeared fully formed as a strategy created by the conceit of either the IMVP or Andersen Consulting. Management variants of lean would be built upon existing organisational and labour practices in the sector, in the context of conflictual social and political relationships.

The critical features that various organisational and technical components of lean would seek to confront and subdue were labour (shopfloor) controls of production, including labour utility/ flexibility; mutuality (trade union independence); and in broad terms, worker orientations in opposition to company imperatives. It was here that the big ideological battles would be fought. While management never won this fight in any straightforward fashion, nevertheless organisational features promoting teamworking and *kaizen* groups would eventually become, as we shall see, important means by which management would attempt to fragment and control labour in pursuit of their main goal. This was, we argue, an attack on postwar labour standards, not by negotiation, but by imposition. Tony Richardson, a steward at Cowley in the 1970s and 1990s, suggested that the difference between piecework and lean production was that 'With piece working, management asked you whether the timing was right for certain tasks – they had to negotiate – whereas with lean production management told you what the timings were' (interview 5/7/02).

In the 1950s and 1960s, informal localised bargaining came to characterise union–management negotiations in the automobile industry. The importance of shop stewards directly representing their members in these industries, as indeed elsewhere in manufacturing, increased to the extent that this development became the subject of a major inquiry, the Donovan Commission (1968). By the time the Donovan Report was published, however, the intensification of international competition had already compelled automotive producers to put in place plans to reassert management authority; piecework was to be eliminated and replaced by MDW. The ending of piecework was strenuously opposed, and took over a decade to achieve. Only management concessions such as the shift to mutuality in conjunction with an increasingly hostile economic climate cleared the way for employers to establish MDW.

This major reform was buttressed by state intervention, particularly in the automobile industry. By taking control of BL, the state
set in train an extensive restructuring and rationalisation
programme in the context of increasing international competition
and a history of low capital investment. That this was undertaken
under a Labour administration served to heighten the expectation of
union leaders and most – but not all – leading shop stewards that it
would be the salvation for the company and indeed the British automotive industry. Instead, as we saw, it opened the door for
Edwardes, on his appointment as chair of BL, to carry out a further
rationalisation of the company and reassert managerial authority.

The days of the British-owned volume producer were numbered.
Broadly, the aim of centralisation and the reassertion of management and official trade union control (over workers and members
respectively) had been brought to fruition. In retrospect we can see
that this period represented a vitally significant element in the
prehistory of what later came to be known as lean production.
Earlier descriptions, such as Japanisation, proved less serviceable for
management, as we have argued elsewhere (Stewart 1996, Danford
et al. 2005).

While lean production eventually established an especially
accomplished pattern of management control both in the United
Kingdom and internationally, we can now begin to see that its
current weaknesses in the British case can be traced to the less than
conclusive, and sometimes rebutted, assault in the late 1980s and
early 1990s on shop steward organisations in the sector. However,
as we shall see, even where significant change has led to extensive
rationalisation, labour remains relatively powerful in significant
instances. For management it was not meant to be like this. To a
profound extent workers and their unions in the international auto
industry have been able to respond to the myriad initiatives and
organisational forms: first lean production, and more recently the
so-called High-Performance Work Organisation (Lewchuk et al.
2001, Danford 2005). Unions have responded to new patterns of
global competition on the basis of path-dependent (company-
specific) employment relations featuring a strongly organised labour
current or trade union centre.

Lean was distinguished from its predecessors, PBR and MDW,
because these were concerned with the problem of labour control in
the context of an employment relationship forged upon an acceptance of the inherent power of organised labour; lean production, by
contrast, perceived labour itself as the problem. Or rather, the prob-

lem was the management of labour, although it is true, of course, that the 'problem of labour' had been presented by the early advocates of lean as having arisen because of management failings, and in particular the failure to control and subdue labour, if the ideologues were to be entirely candid. As our long-term research on the sector demonstrates, both in the United Kingdom and elsewhere, their rhetorical idea of empowerment was a necessary means for selling the fiction. This must remain the judgement, for the issues were never about saving jobs and protecting livelihoods, avoiding injury or 'working smarter not harder'. Still less was there much concern for empowering what would be a much smarter work force.

Chapter 6 follows the story of implementation of lean production in what remained of the British-owned sector, charting the introduction of lean under the auspices of state-of-the-art so-called Japanese management techniques ('*Rover Tomorrow*' in 1992) through to the sale to British Aerospace in 1988 and BMW in 1994, and finally to the brink of collapse in 2000. In many respects it could be a parable for everything that was deceptive about the proselytising lean mantra, 'one best way'. The leaner the company became, the more organised labour 'Embraced and Changed', the more shopfloor workers sensed a growing disempowerment. High levels of stress, injury, and personal disaffection with a production regime driven by job and plant rationalisation at both Rover (subsequently BMW) and Vauxhall are reported in later chapters. No sensible person today would lightly utter the three nostrums of the ideologues of lean production – job security, 'better' work and employee empowerment.

Before looking at this story of decline in some detail, Chapter 3 examines the responses by labour to the introduction of lean production in the British-owned sector and GM-Vauxhall – these responses we term 'Embrace and Change' and 'Engage and Change' respectively.

3 FROM 'EMBRACE AND CHANGE' TO 'ENGAGE AND CHANGE': TRADE UNION RENEWAL AND NEW MANAGEMENT STRATEGIES[1]

INTRODUCTION

This chapter is concerned with the relationship between the introduction of new management techniques (NMTs), trade union responses and employee attitudes in the automotive industry in the United Kingdom. Influential commentators have been pessimistic about the survival of independent trade unions and traditional industrial relations in the industry, predicting marginalisation and erosion, either as a result of increasing anachronism as unions fail to adapt to the circumstances of the new management agenda, or as a result of complete accommodation to this agenda (Coriat 1993, Marsden et al. 1985, Womack et al. 1990). This view has been challenged in recent years by reports of trade union recovery (Fisher 1995, Martinez Lucio and Weston 1992, TGWU 1995). Certainly, unions have demonstrated an ability to accommodate to the introduction of NMTs, but this falls well short of an unqualified acceptance, and unions have succeeded in retaining an independent influence over the implementation and outcomes of NMTs. It is against this background of evidence of innovative adaptation and constrained dissent that this study provides a re-evaluation of the pessimistic prognosis for the fate of industrial relations in automotive assembly operations in the United Kingdom.

The fieldwork upon which the study is founded was carried out at Vauxhall Motors (GM) (Vauxhall) and Rover (UK) (Rover) during 1992 and 1993. Structural and organisational change was formally 'imposed' at Rover via a company-wide management agenda. The Transport and General Workers' Union (TGWU), the senior union in the sector, responded with a national policy prospectus initiated under the defining nostrum 'Embrace and Change', which left unions at the plant level with little alternative but to accommodate it. By contrast at Vauxhall, under locally adapted interpretations of this policy, redefined by the Stewards' Committee as 'Engage and Change', NMTs were implemented through a process of local bargaining which resulted in joint control over outcomes in many areas. The shop stewards in both companies described a process of struggling to preserve, and wherever possible build on, traditional industrial relations institutions. The parameters of this struggle were determined by the companies' agenda (and as such were company-specific), and to a lesser extent, by the unions' response at the national level. Paradoxically, however, these parameters were extended by the opportunities presented by NMTs themselves. New labour processes were mediated by unions through the company's organisational strategies such as *kaizen*, teamworking and quality control processes, the very institutions which were intended to replace the unions, and the effect was to strengthen the influence of the union at the plant level.

The research highlighted that perceptions on the shopfloor were consistent with those of the senior stewards, namely that implementation of NMTs was achieved largely through imposition at Rover, with a degree of subsequent informal negotiation, while the prevailing view at Vauxhall was of a formally negotiated settlement. The research also afforded the opportunity to collect information about the impact of NMTs on the shopfloor in terms of experience of work, industrial relations in the plant and attitudes towards NMTs. These data provide the basis for inter-company comparisons of the outcomes of NMTs, which were then analysed in relation to perceived differences in bargaining in each company.

INDUSTRIAL RELATIONS WITHOUT INDUSTRIAL RELATIONS?

A central tenet of the lean production school, the dominant management paradigm in the sector, is that Anglo-Saxon (in other words, non-Japanese) forms of industrial relations in the automobile industry are antithetical to change (Coriat 1993, Womack, Jones and Roos 1990). The prescriptive character of the lean production school argues that non-Japanese trade unions are necessarily subordinate to the company, that there can be no distinctive trade union agenda under the auspices of traditional Anglo-Saxon forms of bargaining, and that trade union members have a passive role to play in positive changes to the industrial relations climate. In other words, trade unions in companies embarking upon lean production strategies have a conditional role in the organisational change process. Where trade unions accommodate this conditional and subordinate role, organisational change can proceed as planned, management failures notwithstanding (Lowe, Delbridge and Oliver 1996, Oliver 1991, Oliver et al. 1993, 1994, Womack et al. 1990). The possibility that trade unions might develop their own agenda is inconceivable within the strictures of the lean production school, and considered to be against the interests of 'a new industrial citizenship' (Jones 1992). It is significant that this treatment of industrial relations in the process of organisational innovation and change is made without empirical reference either to plant- or firm-specific trade union practice or to employee attitudes.

The lean production account of change in the automotive sector is not alone in considering that traditional forms of trade union practice are becoming outmoded. Marsden and colleagues (1985), in their trenchant account of the major trends and developments in industrial and employee relations in the UK automotive industry in the 1970s and early 1980s, shared the view that traditional trade unionism cannot accommodate change, and concluded that unions can only survive through adaptation to management's agenda. They predicted that managerial authority, based largely upon new labour relations initiatives (mostly drawn from experiences abroad) and new investment strategies and overseas competition, would be re-established across the sector by the late 1980s, leaving traditional forms of union organisation and strategy looking increasingly anachronistic. Moreover, they claimed, the inability of unions to adapt to the circumstances of the new management paradigm must, of necessity, lead to the fragmentation and possibly long-term erosion of traditional trade unionism in the sector.[2] Studies by Willman and Winch (1985) and Jurgens, Malsch and Dohse (1993) in many ways confirmed this view against trade union renewal along traditional lines.[3] Together these studies continue to influence perceptions of the nature of the social and political character of employment relations in final assembly operations in the United Kingdom.

While we do not wish to gainsay many of the arguments of Marsden and colleagues about developments in the 1970s and early 1980s, a number of significant changes occurred in the 1990s which called into question some of their pessimism from a union standpoint (Marsden et al. 1985: 183–7).[4] There was increasing evidence from researchers that traditional industrial relations is central to the development of new work patterns, *in both implementation and outcomes* (Babson 1995, Fucini and Fucini 1990, Gerpisa 1996, Rine-hart et al. 1994, Robertson 1992a, 1992b). Much of this literature derived from North America, but an increasing body of research in the United Kingdom pointed to union recovery in sectors other than the automotive sector (Fairbrother 1996, Fairbrother and Waddington 1990, Fosh 1993, Heery and Kelly 1995, Kelly 1996, Smith 1995), and to the significant impact of plant-level trade union intervention in determining the outcomes of new patterns of work and employment (Beaumont 1985, Fisher 1995, Martinez Lucio and Weston 1992, Stewart and Garrahan 1995, Turnbull and Wass 1997).

The programme for renewal of the TGWU, the dominant union in the automotive sector and traditionally considered to be an adversari-alist, was informed by the experience of union strategies in other coun-tries including the United States, Germany and Japan, such that an interesting and persuasive set of traditions from these countries now overlays the established practice of the TGWU. This reorientation of the union's policy and practice needs to be borne in mind when discussing the development of the micropolitics of shopfloor industrial relations, and it is against this background of innovative thinking by the TGWU at plant level, as a response to NMTs, that our study provides a re-evaluation of Marsden and colleagues' predictions about the fate of industrial relations in the automotive industry.

DATA AND METHOD

Two sets of data form the basis of this study. The first comprises the unions' response to NMT initiatives as interpreted by the senior shop stewards in each plant, and the second comprises an evaluation from the shopfloor of the impact of NMTs on work and the unions' role in the implementation of NMTs. In contrast to the more tradi-tional benchmarking approach to the evaluation of the impact of NMTs, these data consist of subjective accounts of the effects of NMTs from the people most closely involved with their implemen-tation: employees and their union representatives. The study was undertaken during 1992 and 1993, two years into the process of implementation, and the data were collected from matched samples of ordinary employees and employee shop stewards from two Rover plants (Rover A and B) and two Vauxhall plants (Vauxhall A and B).

In the first instance, individual and group interviews were conducted with 32 senior union representatives from the TGWU, the Manufacturing, Science, Finance Union (MSF) and what is now the Amalgamated Engineering and Electrical Union (AEEU) at each of the four plants (including one from the Union of Construction, Allied Trades and Technicians (UCATT) at one of the Rover sites). The TGWU, numerically the dominant union, was the leading strategist in the joint union response to NMTs. These data were collected by means of individual face-to-face and telephone interviews and focus group discussions, and utilised a semi-structured schedule with common themes which were supplemented by detailed references to local and company peculiarities. The focus of the qualitative information was the stewards' descriptions and explanations of the unions' response to NMTs.

The focus of the quantitative data was workers' perceptions of the impact of the unions' response. These data were collected by means of a questionnaire survey, and include information about employees' perceptions of the effects of change associated with NMTs and their attitudes towards these changes. The role of the union in negotiating the implementation of NMTs was emphasised in the questionnaire, along with the impacts of NMTs which impinged on industrial relations. Administration of the survey was undertaken by a shop steward at each of the plants, who was responsible for explaining the content and purpose of the survey to individual participants. The purpose of individual counselling was to ensure a high response rate (a recent employer survey had achieved a response rate of less than 20 per cent). This methodology did indeed achieve a high response rate −70 per cent of questionnaires were returned − but it restricted the sample size to 200 employees (50 employees from each of the four plants). Employees were selected in equal numbers at each plant, and within each plant the sample was stratified by section (body shop or assembly line) and by whether the employee was a shop steward or an ordinary member.

The sampling method used, disproportionate stratified sampling, and differential response rates across strata generated a sample of respondents in which the employees from the body shop and employees who were stewards were over-represented. In the statistical analyses of responses the data are weighted to reduce the influence of responses from stewards and workers from the body shop in accordance with their representation in each company.

Inter-company comparisons in shopfloor perceptions of the unions' role in the implementation of NMTs, the impact of NMTs on industrial relations, the impact of NMTs on the work process and employees acceptance of NMTs are presented as frequency distributions separately for stewards and ordinary union members. The statistical significance of any difference in responses between each company is evaluated using the χ^2 test of association. Interview data are used to explain and develop these inter-company comparisons. The bivariate analyses and qualitative data together suggested an association between the company-specific nature of union participation in the implementation of NMTs and shopfloor attitudes to NMTs. This hypothesis was formally investigated using multivariate techniques in which the impact of union influence in the implementation of NMTs on employee attitudes towards NMTs was distinguished from the impact of other potential explanatory factors such as personal characteristics, company characteristics, the perceived impact of NMTs on work and the perceived impact of NMTs on trade unionism. The dependent variable, employee attitudes to NMTs, is ordinal,[5] and thus an ordered probit regression is an appropriate estimation technique.[6]

UNION RESPONSES IN EACH COMPANY

The UK operations of Rover and Vauxhall are, in the words of Roy Edney (former convener, Rover A), 'survivors in the game' of global inter-plant competition. Each plant had survived the economic insecurity of the 1970s and 1980s, and in the early 1990s was experiencing capital expansion and technical and managerial innovation. The broad objectives of the latter were the same at Rover and Vauxhall: organisational rationalisation and the transformation of industrial relations, both of which were presented as prerequisites to securing a new programme of capital investment.

The official response of the TGWU to managerial innovation was initiated under the defining nostrum 'Embrace and Change'. The strategy was seen by the Vehicle Building and Automotive group (VBA), the trade group within the TGWU responsible for the automotive sector, as a realistic approach to what were generally perceived to be the anti-trade union effects of NMTs. It was argued within the VBA that NMTs, despite their anti-union objectives, could be ameliorated through a strategy of accommodation. Provided the trade unions agreed to substantial changes in working practices on the tracks, together with a broad acceptance of organisational changes across the company, including the transformation of the pattern of collective bargaining, the unions would survive without having to undergo fundamental change (TGWU 1995). As the convener at Rover B justified, 'Why can't we live with them [the innovations]? We've lived with them in the past.' While shop stewards viewed the proposed technical changes (just-in-time, JIT), statistical process control (SPC), body shop automation, online quality intervention and so on, as being at the heart of NMTs, and as such irreversible, they argued that the social and organisational changes (teamworking and labour flexibility initiatives) which management wanted to introduce were not. Rather, the latter were aimed at preventing union obstruction of the former. It is in the light of this understanding that the TGWU's explicit emphasis at the national level upon its own flexibility and willingness to accommodate change, and its implicit focus on communications and the process of legitimacy with respect to the character of teamworking, begins to make sense (Fisher 1995).

While 'Embrace and Change' is a suitable description of the TGWU's response to the dirigiste and centralised approach to the implementation of NMTs at Rover, at Vauxhall, NMTs were implemented against a background of corporatism and inter-plant autonomy, both of which allowed the union a degree of leverage which was absent at Rover, and thereby offered the opportunity for strategic intervention. The initial strategy of 'Embrace and Change' was interpreted by the plant conveners at Vauxhall as being locked into a management agenda, and was replaced by an alternative understanding described as '*Engage* and Change' (Peter Titherington, former convener, Vauxhall A). At Rover, NMTs were central to the agenda known as *Rover Tomorrow* (1992), and were introduced throughout the company as an all-embracing package. Implementation was driven from the top downwards, and the unions were left with little choice but to accept the broad terms of immediate corporate change. By contrast, at Vauxhall the corporatist approach was maintained in such a way that it was hoped the unions would be brought along with the changes. As Warman, a leading manager at Vauxhall B, argued, 'the unions are partners in change' (1992), and this afforded the union an opportunity to 'engage'.[7]

The distinction between the TGWU's responses to what were, after all, rather similar agendas for change in two companies in the same sector – that is, the difference between a strategy of 'embracing' or one of 'engaging' with the management's agenda for change – is explained below in terms of the stewards' understanding of that agenda and the circumstances in which it was encountered.

ROVER: 'EMBRACE AND CHANGE'

The aims of the twelve-month implementation programme of NMTs known as *Rover Tomorrow* were the consolidation of past changes in working practices, together with the introduction of contemporary management and technological innovations. These can be summed up briefly as technical innovations including JIT, SPC, online quality practices and managerial innovations relating to labour flexibility, including organisational and social changes associated with teamworking and the equalisation of conditions of all employees (that is, the removal of demarcation boundaries). From the management perspective, the realisation of technical innovations was considered to be dependent upon reducing trade union regulation of labour flexibility. This was to be achieved through the subordination of trade union agendas to those of management, and at an institutional level, through the centralisation and flattening of collective bargaining, the latter being achieved by means of biannual single-table bargaining.

Formally, *Rover Tomorrow* was implemented through imposition. Management insisted that the unions accept the deal and this was not opposed by the TGWU's national negotiating position. However, union lay officers were far from unanimous in their support for this strategy, the chief negotiating officer describing the process as 'all one way' (*Rover Tomorrow*: 9). The absence of explicit formal opposition from the union led to the general feeling on the part of the employees that the deal was being 'bulldozed through' (senior steward in the paint shop at Rover B), and inevitably this perception cast a veil of suspicion over the unions when the agreement was signed. This could reasonably be offered as going some way towards accounting for the very small majority in favour of *Rover Tomorrow*.[8]

Employees' perceptions that the agreement had been imposed had significant repercussions for the company too. According to the stewards, Rover continued to experience problems with mobilising staff around NMTs away from the production line, and if the introduction of NMTs was also linked to the 'battle for hearts and minds' in the delivery of the new practices such as teamwork, the company had much ground still to achieve:

> [P]eople weren't over the moon about teams and team leaders, and all that the deal [*Rover Tomorrow*] did was make what they were about formal . . . you know they're coming anyway so you may as well have an input into it.
>
> (AEEU steward, Rover B)

A steward from the paint shop at Rover B observed that 'teams are everywhere, but no one believes in them, the old hearts and minds thing is with us here'.

Despite the formal successes of the company in implementing much of its agenda, stewards had some success in redirecting management objectives, including the management intention to redefine and limit the scope of collective bargaining, and significant concessions were achieved with respect to the retention of informal regulation of many day-to-day labour practices. Stewards at the largest production facility in the company, Rover B, brought off a significant coup in the way in which *Rover Tomorrow* was consolidated with respect to lay member activity. The implications of their success reverberated throughout the company's other assembly plants, where local agreements were negotiated covering control of absence regimes, labour mobility and steward density, including the delineation of areas of representation. In this way, the stewards secured the retention, albeit implicit, of joint regulation in a number of areas, although sticking to such agreements often depended on the leadership skills of the local steward (fieldnotes), since 'they [the company] keep pushing and pushing, always testing us and then trying again to erode the local agreements on job ownership' (steward on Rover 100 track).

Whatever problems *Rover Tomorrow* presented the unions with, their vigilance on what they considered to be vital issues of survival was in many ways assisted by the operation of NMTs in the labour process on the line. A paradoxical feature of the outcome of *Rover Tomorrow* was that three elements contained in the NMT agenda (absence control, labour mobility and union rights) themselves provided sites for union recovery. Stewards in different plants successfully mobilised members in defence of separate plant agreements. It was an ironic outcome because *Rover Tomorrow* sought to flatten the terrain of collective bargaining by denying the peculiarities at each plant. In addition, the general insecurity of front line management in the transition to the team leader system helped the unions in their attempts to redefine and limit the role of the team leader. Despite the intention of *Rover Tomorrow*, the team leader often had less discretion in the regulation of day-to-day activities on the shop floor than the foreman once had.

VAUXHALL: 'ENGAGE AND CHANGE'

The broad objectives of management's agenda for change were the same at Vauxhall: that is, organisational rationalisation and the transformation of industrial relations. The specific detail of Vauxhall's programme of restructuring involved stock reduction, delayering, and reduction in the use of relief workers and indirect labour (Jurgens et al. 1993: 295–6, 305), all in the context of reduced union influence through its replacement by teamworking. In practice, what the company achieved was some measure of all but the last of these: 'Teamwork, which is supposed to be the panacea for the motor industry, is so ineffective because of the way we've controlled it round the negotiating table and *on the shopfloor*' (convener, Vauxhall A 1995).

The union recognised from the outset that the introduction of teamworking was the company's key to the transformation of industrial relations: direct communication between the company and the shopfloor was designed to bypass the stewards. In hindsight, the terrain of the team turned out to be the linchpin of the strategy for union recovery. Indeed, it could be argued that one of the outcomes of the introduction of teamworking was the politicisation of the debate in the plants about changes to the labour process, both in and away from assembly operations (see Stewart 1994).

The union's response to teamworking was to 'engage with' rather than to accept the proposal. The strategy of engagement which followed, described by Peter Titherington, the convener at Vauxhall at the time, as 'a strategy of disagreement', allowed the stewards to gain control over the implementation of the social changes associated with NMTs by placing their own interpretation on the nature of team meetings and teamworking. This was achieved through daily circulars and formal and informal education forums: between 1988 and 1993 the TGWU organised an unprecedented 155 education sessions for stewards.[9] The result was a 'hollowing out', as Titherington described it, of management's substantive strategy because the unions were successful at highlighting the antithesis between teamworking and employees' general interests. By gaining control over the implementation of teamworking, the union was able to influence its field of impact, and in particular to restrict the agenda to work task schedules and to exclude industrial relations concerns.

Thus, the content of many of the social and organisational features of NMTs was limited by the manner in which the unions achieved control of the agenda. That the union was afforded the opportunity to negotiate at Vauxhall can be attributed to the corporate policy approach to the implementation of NMTs, which emphasised distinct variations and local adaptations throughout Europe in what the company described as its European human resources strategy (Quality Network Production System (QNPS) nd). Thus agreements on the introduction of NMTs (Vauxhall A Agreement 1989, Vauxhall B Agreement 1992) were negotiated and adapted to the peculiarities of each plant.[10] The unions mobilised over a twelve-month period prior to implementation, and successfully ensured a quid pro quo from management. In return for securing support for NMTs from their members, they won the right to determine the meaning of the NMTs. They did this in the first instance by successfully opposing management's principle of team leader elections and subsequently intervening at Vauxhall A, when occasion allowed, to 'constructively dispute' (as one steward wryly put it) the claims to participation which were central to the new teamwork strategy of employee involvement in *kaizen* meetings. This was followed by a similar pattern of intervention at Vauxhall B where, according to one senior steward, 'we've won the issue about the limits of democracy in those team meetings' (senior steward, TGWU).

In addition, the unions benefited more generally as a result of management's apparent underestimation of the progressive disjuncture between the rhetoric and experience of new management practices of involvement, including the mantra of 'working smarter not harder' (Stewart and Garrahan 1995: 530). Another critical aspect to communication is linked to leadership at shopfloor level, and management had problems resolving this. Evidently either management underestimated the significance of ensuring that the 'right' people became team leaders, or the stewards, having retained the support of the shopfloor, were successful in articulating employee experiences of NMTs to their advantage. In any event, the appointment process led to 'totally the wrong people' (steward, Vauxhall B) being appointed, such that 'we basically minimised the effects it [teamwork] would have'.

However, what was 'minimised' was less the technical innovations of the new labour processes, and more the organisational and employee relations aspects of the change process: teamwork, *kaizen* and the all-important battle for 'hearts and minds'. In short, the company was successful in implementing change in the technical labour process with reasonable ease (Stewart and Garrahan 1995), but the unions were successful in retaining collective bargaining, and moreover its extension via a novel form of regulation of the social organisation of the labour process. Stewards had de facto negotiating rights over any aspect of the labour process addressed in team meetings.

Clearly, then, the unions survived the critical offensive of NMTs and remained active in the automotive industry. The unions' response, though constrained to a large extent by parameters set by the company, was nevertheless innovative and largely effective. *Rover Tomorrow* was 'imposed' by the company, and officially the unions had little alternative but to accept the broad terms of the agenda. However, victories at plant level over the regulation of day-to-day working practices and influence over teamworking secured for the unions a continuing relevance in the determination of terms and conditions of employment. At Vauxhall the continuing role of the union was accepted at the outset, and NMTs were jointly implemented through local bargaining. In return for delivering employee acceptance of technical change, the union effectively secured control over the organisation of work around the new technology. The next section examines the impact of NMTs on employees' experience of work, and in particular whether and how the outcomes of NMTs, as evaluated by the employees, were affected by the distinct processes by which they were implemented in each company.

THE EXPERIENCE OF NMTs ON THE SHOPFLOOR: AN INTER-COMPANY COMPARISON

The perception of the unions' role in the implementation of NMTs, and the perception of the effects of NMTs and attitudes towards NMTs on the shopfloor (the definition of variables is provided at the end of the chapter) are reported separately by company and by the employees' role within the union in Tables 3.1 to 3.4. The significance of differences in responses at the inter-company level was tested statistically using the χ^2 test.

Table 3.1 reports responses to the questions concerned with the implementation of NMTs, namely the extent and nature of bargaining over the implementation of NMTs, the financial compensation to employees, and the role of training in respect of the additional job requirements associated with NMTs. Employees' (both stewards and ordinary members) perception of the union's involvement in the process of implementation was one that reflected the stewards' descriptions of the distinctive union strategies adopted in each company. At Rover, where management insisted on the wholesale adoption of *Rover Tomorrow* and where the negotiating process was described as being 'all one way' (see page 45), this was reflected by the fact that around half (45.9 per cent) of all employees considered NMTs to have been imposed without reference to the union. This view was significantly greater among non-steward employees. This is in sharp contrast to shopfloor perceptions of union influence at Vauxhall, where the unions were considered to be 'partners in the process of change' (Warman, manager, Vauxhall B). At Vauxhall 81.4 per cent

Table 3.1 Perception of implementation of NMTs[1]
(percentage of respondents in each company reporting each category)

Shopfloor perceptions of:[2]		Shop stewards		Ordinary members	
		Rover	Vauxhall	Rover	Vauxhall
Bargaining over NMT	Formal negotiation	34.8	81.4	20.6	70.0
(stewards and members*)	Influence	30.4	13.6	15.7	30.0
	Imposition	34.8	5.0	63.7	0.0
Comparison of financial reward[3]	Greater	0.0	10.8	0.0	8.2
	Same	9.8	8.0	0.0	16.4
	Less	90.2	81.2	100.0	75.4
Provision of training in NMT[4]	Training provided	42.1	54.9	9.2	50.9
(members only*)	No training	57.9	45.1	90.8	49.1
Quality of training where provided[4]	Satisfactory	34.9	66.5	n/a	61.5
(stewards only**)	Unsatisfactory	65.1	33.5		38.5

Notes

* Indicates significant at 5 per cent level, ** indicates significant at 10 per cent level.
1 Data weighted by employees' section of plant.
2 Definitions of explanatory variables are reported at the end of the chapter.
3 Lawal test used because of small expected values.
4 Yates' continuity correction applied to 2 × 2 contingency table.

of stewards and 70 per cent of ordinary members considered NMTs to have been implemented through formal negotiation.

The workforces in each company were equally dissatisfied with their financial reward for the considerable productivity gains achieved under NMTs. A steward at Vauxhall B gave some indication of the magnitude of the growth in labour productivity: 'if you take what we was doing here with the Cavalier in 1989 and what we do now [1993], what we do now is nearly twice the number with the same number of men'. This dissatisfaction was unresolved, and resulted in industrial action at Vauxhall during the summer of 1995 (see Stewart 1997, and as adapted below, Chapter 4).

Reskilling and upskilling are purported to be central to lean production, and consequently the education and training necessary to underpin these new skills (Womack et al. 1990: 100–3). In practice, the provision of training in NMTs was less than universal. At Vauxhall over half the employees surveyed reported having received training, and nearly two-thirds of these rated it as satisfactory. It is significant that training was jointly managed at Vauxhall, where the union was 'on to the propaganda potential' and was consequently 'well sorted on that score' (steward, Vauxhall B). By contrast, at Rover, training was concentrated among the stewards, with less than 10 per cent of non-steward employees participating. Of the stewards who received training, a third rated the training as satisfactory. According to a senior steward at Rover A, training largely consisted of 'how to get SPC [statistical process control] and do "just-in-time", where to stand and how to move and such like … it has nothing new to it from a production point of view, it's not like craft training'.

Teamworking is heralded by managers and proponents of the lean production model as the preferred democratic alternative to traditional industrial relations (Jones 1992) and it is in this respect that teams have been viewed as the key threat to unions. The results reported in Table 3.2 indicate that the impact of NMTs did indeed undermine the role of the union. However, the greater union involvement in the introduction of NMTs observed at Vauxhall (Table 3.1), the principle of joint ownership over NMTs and the unions' effective control over team meetings appear to have limited the potentially negative impact on the union and on industrial relations. Employees' perceptions of industrial relations outcomes were significantly less negative at Vauxhall than at Rover, particularly among ordinary union members. Around 40 per cent of employees surveyed at Vauxhall reported a negative impact on the industrial relations climate, and around a quarter reported a reduction in the

Table 3.2 Perception of change in industrial relations[1]
(percentage of respondents in each company reporting each category)

Shopfloor perceptions of:[2]		Shop stewards		Ordinary members	
		Rover	Vauxhall	Rover	Vauxhall
Impact on current industrial	Positive	10.9	13.3	2.4	44.4
(members only*) relations climate	Neutral	22.7	32.0	28.6	16.6
	Negative	66.4	54.7	69.0	40.0
Change in role of trade union	Increased	12.5	35.9	4.5	19.6
(stewards and members*)	Unchanged	30.4	35.2	2.3	54.1
	Decreased	57.1	28.9	93.2	26.3
Change in recruitment to union[3]	Easier	1.8	1.6	0.0	16.4
(members only*)	unchanged	52.7	60.4	20.0	47.7
	More difficult	45.5	37.9	80.0	36.0

Notes

* Indicates significant at 5 per cent level, ** indicates significant at 10 per cent level.
1 Data weighted by employees' section of plant.
2 Definitions of explanatory variables are reported at the end of the chapter.
3 Lawal test used because of small expected values.

role of the union. At Rover 69 per cent of non-steward employees reported a negative impact on the industrial relations climate and 93 per cent reported a reduction in the role of the union.

Table 3.3 examines employees' experience of the impact of NMTs on various physical aspects of the labour process. The results are not indicative of fundamental change to the labour process in either company. Only around half of employees considered the work process to have changed substantially, and there was little evidence of any significant reduction in job demarcation between production and craft jobs, any increase in job mobility or any increase in the technical or skills requirements of the job. Rather, NMTs appeared to be associated with an increase in the pace of work, not its content.[11] In general employees indicated that their work was considerably more intensive in its physical and mental demands and less interesting than before.[12] A convener at Rover A described just how the company had won the 'hearts and minds' of the workforce: 'we work smarter and harder, constantly jacking up the pace of things. They'll have us doing bleedin' *kaizen* in our sleep! But it hardly makes for an interesting life.'

In fact, there was little difference in employees' perception of the physical work-related outcomes of NMTs between the two companies (or according to the union position of the employee). Taking NMTs as a whole, employees at Vauxhall and Rover reported a similar impact on the overall change in the labour process.

The remainder of Table 3.3 considers the various elements of NMTs separately. When respondents were asked to compare the different aspects of their current work to their job two years earlier, only two aspects of change were significantly different (at the 5 per cent level) at the inter-company level. In both cases significantly more employees at Vauxhall reported a greater impact. Job mobility was compared before and after NMTs, and significantly more non-steward employees at Vauxhall reported an increase in mobility over time. Significantly more employees (both stewards and non-stewards) at Vauxhall reported an increase in the physical requirements and work intensification in their jobs. However, in terms of the majority of changes in job characteristics, demarcation between jobs, the skill, technical and mental requirements of the job and job interest, the perceived impact of change was the same in each company.

In summary, there were significant differences in employees' perception of change in each company. Importantly, the major differences did not pertain to the impact of NMTs on the physical

Table 3.3 Perception of change in labour process[1]
(percentage of respondents in each company reporting each category)

Shopfloor perceptions of:[2]		Shop stewards		Ordinary members	
		Rover	Vauxhall	Rover	Vauxhall
Overall effect of NMTs on work[3]	Substantial	50.0	60.6	45.7	58.6
	Marginal	51.1	30.3	37.0	41.4
	Not at all	8.9	6.1	17.4	0.0
Change in mobility[4]	Mobility before NMT	32.1	31.1	24.5	40.9
	Mobility after NMT (members only*)	36.2	38.7	23.5	55.5
Change in demarcation between skilled and production[3]	No change	18.1	49.9	20.0	34.1
	Small reduction	68.6	41.0	74.3	65.9
	Large reduction	13.3	9.2	5.7	0.0
Change in demarcation between production and skilled[3]	No change	30.9	22.9	36.4	41.4
	Small reduction	61.8	57.7	57.6	55.1
	Large reduction	7.3	19.4	6.1	3.5
Work intensification[1] (stewards and members**)	Work harder	52.7	77.3	43.1	62.0
	Same effort	47.3	22.7	56.9	38.0
Change in skill requirement[3]	Greater	11.6	13.1	29.4	25.5
	Same	67.4	77.1	70.6	68.9
	Less	20.9	9.8	0.0	5.6
Change in technical requirement[3]	Greater	14.0	19.3	0.0	33.0
	Same	86.0	71.1	100.0	67.0
	lLess	0.0	9.6	0.0	0.0

Shopfloor perceptions of:[2]		Shop stewards		Ordinary members	
		Rover	Vauxhall	Rover	Vauxhall
Change in physical requirement[3]	Greater	26.8	68.6	27.5	43.1
(stewards*) (members**)	Same	68.7	31.4	72.5	47.6
	Less	4.5	0.0	0.0	9.3
Change in mental requirement[3]	Greater	59.6	71.6	58.8	57.6
	Same	40.4	25.5	41.2	34.1
	Less	0.0	3.0	0.0	8.3
Change in job interest	Greater	23.3	5.0	11.8	10.9
	Same	53.5	54.5	29.4	63.9
	Less	23.3	40.5	58.8	25.3

Notes

* Indicates significant at 5 per cent level, ** indicates significant at 10 per cent level.

1 Data weighted by employees' section of plant.

2 Definitions of explanatory variables are reported at the end of the chapter.

3 Lawal test used because of small expected values.

4 Yates' continuity correction applied to 2 x 2 contingency table.

experience of work, but rather to employees' perceptions of the process of change, and specifically the union's involvement in the implementation of NMTs and the impact of NMTs on the continuing role of the trade union in the plant. Workers at Vauxhall were significantly more likely to report union influence in bargaining over the implementation of NMTs, more likely to report an intensification of work and less likely to report a deterioration in industrial relations than their colleagues at Rover.

The next section examines respondents' attitudes towards NMTs, specifically the degree to which they supported and were prepared to cooperate with the process and outcome of change, and seeks to link more positive attitudes to change with union involvement in the implementation of change.

THE ACCEPTANCE OF NMTs ON THE SHOPFLOOR: AN INTER-COMPANY COMPARISON

In Table 3.4, employees' attitudes to NMTs and the physical impact on their work (which was reported in Table 3.3) are presented. In contrast to the results reported in Table 3.3, attitudes towards NMTs among non-steward employees showed considerable variation at the inter-company level. Excluding the stewards, employees at Vauxhall displayed significantly more ambivalence about NMTs and less hostility to their impact than employees at Rover. Over three-quarters of employees at Vauxhall reported a positive or an ambivalent attitude to NMTs, compared with less than half at Rover. Acceptance of NMTs appeared to be closely associated with the perception that they were necessary for the company's survival, with 62 per cent of employees at Vauxhall considering NMTs to be necessary for the company's survival and only 20 per cent of employees at Rover considering this to be so.

It is clear from the survey data and the interviews that the most distinguishing differences at the inter-company level are employee attitudes to NMTs and the perceived extent of union involvement in their implementation. However, it is not possible to establish a causal relationship between these inter-company results on the basis of the bivariate results reported above. For example, the degree of union participation is only one of a number of potential causal factors explaining the variation in employees' attitudes to NMTs. Other factors include differences in the nature and extent of reform, as measured by different levels of impact on physical work, differential

Table 3.4 Attitudes to NMT and change in labour process[1]
(percentage of respondents in each company reporting each category)

Shopfloor attitudes and perceptions[2]		Shop stewards		Ordinary members	
		Rover	Vauxhall	Rover	Vauxhall
Personal attitude to NMT (members only*)	Positive	8.9	6.4	17.6	11.0
	Neutral	47.3	55.8	31.4	66.6
	Negative	43.8	37.9	51.0	22.4
Perceived necessity of NMT for survival	Necessary	24.1	37.1	19.6	62.0
of company (members only*)	Qualified necessity	32.1	34.3	12.7	14.2
	Not necessary	43.7	28.6	67.6	23.8

Notes

* Indicates significant at 5 per cent level.
1 Data weighted by employees' section of plant.
2 Definitions of explanatory variables are reported at the end of the chapter.

industrial relations outcomes, and unobserved inter-company differences (such as relative market position, management style, historical legacies of past innovations and conditions in the external labour market).

The *independent* effects of each of these factors on the levels of acceptance of NMTs reported by the workforce in each company were examined using an Ordered Probit Regression in which the effects of personal characteristics, company characteristics and employee perceptions about the impact of NMTs, the necessity of NMTs, the impact on trade unionism and the level of trade union influence over their introduction were estimated. The results are reported in Table 3.5. Eight separate regressions were estimated using different combinations of explanatory variables, starting with company and individual characteristics and including, successively, employees' perceptions of the impact of NMTs on their work, the perceived need of NMTs for the survival of the company, trade union influence over the implementation of NMTs and the perceived impact on trade unionism in the plant.

Positive coefficient estimates are associated with more positive attitudes to NMTs, and conversely negative coefficient estimates are associated with more negative attitudes. The relative size and significance of the coefficients (the latter indicated by the t-statistic) reflect the relative importance of each variable on employees' attitudes to NMTs. In each specification, the log likelihood ratio is significant. In the first specification, the company variable indicates that attitudes among the workforce at Rover were more negative than at Vauxhall. However, the company variable becomes insignificant as other explanatory variables are included, indicating that inter-company differences observed in Tables 3.1 to 3.4 are the result of inter-company differences in employee characteristics and perceptions. With the exception of the company variable, the impact of all the other explanatory variables, where they are found to influence attitudes, is robust to changes in specification.

In terms of employees' personal characteristics, length of service with the company had a significant negative impact on their attitude towards NMTs: longer-serving employees appeared to be more resistant to the impact of change. Whether or not the employee served as a shop steward did not determine acceptance of NMTs. Regression (iii) includes employees' perceptions of the overall impact of NMTs on their work, and indicates that where the perceived impact was substantial, the employee was more likely to report a positive attitude to NMTs. However, the impact of a perceived increase in work effort, introduced in regression (iv), is negative (although this is significant only at the 10 per cent level). In regression (v) trade union influence included, and is seen to have a very strong and positive effect on an individual's acceptance of change. Consistently, this variable has the greatest impact on employees' attitudes. Regression (vi) indicates that the impact of trade union involvement was independent of the perceived necessity of NMTs, although this latter was an important determinant of employees' acceptance of change. The final two specifications suggest that attitudes were independent of industrial relations outcomes.

CONCLUDING REMARKS

The unions at both companies were initially sceptical of the NMTs. For different, and largely economic reasons, they felt under considerable pressure to accept the change process. It could be said that during the pre-implementation period the unions were acting out the final drama of the UK auto industry in an era defined, to paraphrase Wood (1988), as cooperation in the context of conflict. In the new drama that has been unfolding since 1989, two different phases in shopfloor industrial relations can be delineated, which might be termed 'cooperation in the context of compliance' (at Rover) and 'cooperation in the context of bargained dissent' (at Vauxhall). Willman's (1988) prescient view which underlined communication, as opposed to work restructuring, as the basis of employee consent has in many respects been vindicated. However, our findings also highlighted the contested nature of the communications process, and in particular the institution through which it was channelled: the team. It hardly needs to be said that the final irony was that union renewal and the distinctive employee–management relations developed on terrain largely of the companies' own making. Recovery was driven, at least in part, by the political nature of the agenda around NMTs. Unlike previous management attempts to change the workplace, trade unions were directly engaged in issues concerned with organisational power, including involvement strategies such as *kaizen* and teamwork, quality control processes, labour flexibility initiatives, and even negotiation over key personnel policies of suppliers (see Vauxhall 1989, 1992).

The significance to employees of union involvement in the process of change was revealed in comparisons of both shop stewards' and ordinary members' perceptions of and attitudes to NMTs

Table 3.5 Ordered probit shop floor attitudes towards NMTs[1]

Explanatory variables[2]	(i)	(ii)	(iii)	(iv)	(v)	(vi)	(vii)	(viii)
Personal characteristics								
Job tenure in plant (years)		-0.045*	-0.037*	-0.039*	-0.036*	-0.036*	-0.034*	-0.037*
		(-0.487)	(-3.374)	(-3.519)	(-3.094)	(-3.006)	(-2.322)	(-2.729)
Shop steward		0.078	0.081	0.141	0.063	0.149	0.201	0.101
		(0.041)	(0.042)	(0.074)	(0.033)	(0.079)	(0.109)	(0.056)
Company characteristics								
Rover	-0.745*	-0.181	-0.211	-0.295	-0.022	0.258	0.214	0.210
	(-5.041)	(-0.940)	(-1.059)	(-1.473)	(-0.101)	(1.006)	(0.671)	(0.782)
Overall impact on work								
Substantial			0.426*	0.609*	0.835*	1.146*	1.243*	1.081*
			(2.947)	(3.106)	(4.268)	(4.777)	(4.466)	(4.095)
None			-0.075	-0.069	0.428	0.699	0.825	0.679
			(-0.180)	(-0.166)	(0.598)	(0.851)	(1.070)	(0.832)
Work intensification				-0.368**	-0.599**	-0.404*	-0.425**	-0.403**
				(-1.867)	(-1.651)	(-2.039)	(-1.831)	(-1.841)
Perceived necessity of NMTs for survival of company								
Necessary						0.702*	0.521**	0.735*
						(3.315)	(1.940)	(3.313)
Not necessary						-0.501*	-0.561*	-0.523*
						(-2.356)	(-2.364)	(-2.371)
Bargaining over NMTs								
Trade union influence through formal negotiation					1.222*	1.139*	1.188*	1.407*
					(4.795)	(5.465)	(3.877)	(5.554)

Explanatory variables[2]	(i)	(ii)	(iii)	(iv)	(v)	(vi)	(vii)	(viii)
Impact on industrial relations								
Positive impact on industrial relations climate							0.096 (0.336)	
Negative impact on industrial relations climate							-0.411 (1.314)	
Increase role trade union								0.603 (1.084)
Decrease role of trade union								-0.229 (-0.843)
Constant	0.239* (3.062)	0.726* (5.688)	0.403* (2.489)	0.531* (2.948)	-0.796* (-2.405)	-1.314* (-3.245)	-0.927** (-1.855)	-1.446* (-3.511)*
Mu (1)	1.552 (13.310)	1.605 (13.342)	1.062 (12.018)	1.679 (11.513)	1.781 (11.342)	2.004 (8.987)	2.089 (8.226)	2.126 (7.800)
Log likelihood	14.04	22.01	26.00	27.94	42.13	60.30	63.36	62.95
% correct predictions	52.8	52.8	52.8	48.5	57.8	63.6	61.4	64.2
No.	140	140	140	140	140	140	140	140

Notes

Reference categories: in descending order of Table: union member; Vauxhall; marginal impact overall on work; no work intensification; qualified necessity of NMTs; agreement imposed without union influence; no impact on industrial relations climate; no change in trade union role.

't' statistics in parentheses. * indicates significant at 5 per cent level. ** indicates significant at 10 per cent level.

1   Data weighted by employees' section of plant and employees steward status.

2   Definitions of explanatory variables are reported at the end of the chapter.

at Rover and Vauxhall. Respondents at Vauxhall, who were significantly more likely to report union influence in bargaining over the introduction of NMTs than respondents at Rover, were also significantly more ambivalent about NMTs and less hostile to their impact on terms and conditions of employment. Importantly, from the company's perspective, this relationship was independent of the work-related impact of NMTs (and also the impact on plant-level industrial relations and unmeasured inter-company differences). It appears that traditional bargaining makes a difference in the new management environment, not in terms of outcomes normally associated with union activity (demarcation practices, terms and conditions of employment and so on), but rather in terms of employees' acceptance of the necessity and outcomes of employment reform.

APPENDIX: EXPLANATORY VARIABLES

Variable name	Question/coded response
Company	Do you work for Rover UK or Vauxhall GM?
Shop steward	Are you an officer of the union or an ordinary member?
Job tenure in plant	How long have you worked in this plant?

Shopfloor perceptions of/attitudes towards:

Bargaining over over NMT`	How would you best describe the nature of bargaining the introduction of NMTs? *Formal negotiation* *Consultation with informal negotiations* *Consultation* *Imposition*
Comparison of financial reward	Do you feel that you are satisfactorily rewarded for your agreement and participation in NMTs? *Very satisfied – Very unsatisfied* (five-point scale)
Provision of training in NMT	Have you received training in the company's use of NMTs?
Quality of training where provided	How satisfied are you with the quality of that training? *Very satisfied – Very unsatisfied* (five-point scale)
Impact on current industrial relations climate	How would you describe the impact of NMTs on the industrial relations climate in the plant? *Strongly positive – Strongly negative* (five-point scale)
Change in role of trade union	Has the role of the union changed as a result of NMTs? *Substantial increase – Substantial decrease* (five-point scale)

Change in recruitment to union	How has the recruitment of new union members been affected by NMTs? *Substantially more difficult – Substantially easier* (five-point scale)
Overall effect of NMTs on work	To what extent have NMTs affected your work? *Great effect – No effect* (five-point scale)
Change in mobility	Did you move jobs within the plant before the introduction of NMTs? Do you move jobs within the plant since the introduction of NMTs?
Change in demarcation between skilled and production	To what degree are skilled staff doing jobs previously done by production-line staff? *High degree – No degree* (five-point scale)
Change in demarcation between production and skilled	To what degree are production-line staff doing jobs previously done by skilled staff? *High degree – No degree* (five-point scale)
Intensification of work	Do you work harder since the introduction of NMTs?
Change in skill requirement	How would you describe the changing skill requirements of your work? *More, same or less?*
Change in technical requirement	How would you describe the changing technical requirements of your work? *More, same or less?*
Change in physical requirement	How would you describe the changing physical requirements of your work? *More, same, or less?*
Change in mental requirement	How would you describe the changing mental requirements of your work? *More, same or less?*
Change in job interest	How would you describe the changing level of interest you have in your work? *More, same or less?*
Personal attitude to NMT	Which view best describes your attitude towards the NMTs in your plant? *Strongly positive – Strongly negative* (five-point scale)
Perceived necessity of NMT for survival of company?	Do you consider NMTs necessary to the survival of the company? *Yes, qualified yes, or no?*

Note: reclassification of five-point scales to three-point scales in analysis.
Source: *New Technology Work and Employment* (1998, 13: 2).

4 STRIKING SMARTER AND HARDER: THE NEW INDUSTRIAL RELATIONS OF LEAN PRODUCTION? THE 1995–6 VAUXHALL DISPUTE[1]

[We aim to] form a partnership between all the Vauxhall people, working together to win, by focusing on customer satisfaction through teamwork and continuous innovation and improvement.

(Vauxhall, 1992)

They don't understand that we are taking action because of the situation they have created. They can't see that it's their lean production that has pushed the lads to it. I tell you this though; we are definitely playing it smarter now. Anyhow, people are voting with their feet and clocking off early on Fridays.

(Vauxhall-GM shop steward December 1995 in response to spontaneous action by assembly line workers against lean production)

Between the late summer of 1995 and mid-February 1996, Vauxhall Motors, the UK subsidiary of General Motors (GM), struggled to come to terms with the new industrial relations of lean production. For the first time in many years the company faced well-planned action by employees and trade unions, in particular the Transport and General Workers' Union (TGWU), at its two assembly plants at Ellesmere Port in the north-west of England (the Astra plant) and Luton in the south (the Vectra plant). The carefully contrived public relations image extolling the virtues of lean production lay in ruins. Workers at the two sites, which together employed almost 10,000, took action in support of their claim for a reduction in the working week and an across the board wage rise. Their campaign included a two-hour unofficial strike every Friday.

Vauxhall had a major problem in tackling this de facto assertion of shopfloor power. This power, according to one production manager at Luton, initially embarrassed the plant management because the rhetoric of consensus and participation, which had been built up around lean production, was being exposed. In the context of discussing what he referred to as the new 'person to person approach' embodied in the Quality Network Production System (QNPS), GM's 1988 European quality and human relations initiative, he described in somewhat graphic terms management's initial reluctance 'to use the boot' to achieve its aim of transforming the industrial relations environment. Indeed, far from transforming it in management's sense of improving things to their own advantage, the mix of lean production and old-fashioned shopfloor management was leading to a perceptible deterioration of the industrial relations climate.[2]

A deteriorating industrial relations climate was precisely what many employees felt underlay the cosy assumptions of involvement and consensus espoused by protagonists of lean production in the assembly plants. As one steward at Luton put it,

> 'I am still the manager and you are still the worker' – it's there in the so-called 'walk the talk' Americanism. A lot of people ... have seen management change their position.... People are starting to smell the ... shit because their nose is being rubbed in it by the employer and they do this in the most distasteful way. [And] what happens is that the person learns for themselves that they don't do that any longer. They don't do this, they don't do that because it isn't going to bring the rewards the employers say that it would.
>
> (JJ 14/11/1995)

The same steward went on to say that:

> If you take our current dispute on wages, I would like to bet that when we get the ballot we anticipate.... I wouldn't be too sure whether it was totally about wages or ... containing some elements of the [lean] system itself and I think that cannot be ruled out.
>
> (JJ 14/11/1995)

Whether from paint and body shop or general assembly, shopfloor workers were directly critical in their interpretation of management attitudes and practices since the introduction of teamworking. (Lean production was frequently referred to by a range of terms, as has been highlighted elsewhere (Stewart and Garrahan 1995).[3]) Jenny from trim made the point that we 'Get too much pressure off management', a point emphasised by John (paint shop), when he said that, 'What management want they get – that's democracy' (11/1995). Opposition was not straightforward, since as Peter (trim) pointed out:

> As have many other people I have a family and a mortgage. This is the reason I have not walked out of this shit pit. The team leaders think they are gods with the management and treat you like shit. The only answer you get from them is if you don't like it go elsewhere.
>
> (11/1995)

Indeed, despite the rhetoric of inclusiveness, Peter's experience of attempting to engage with management was, he felt, deeply disillusioning:

> Why can I never get any satisfaction when talking to my supervisor or manager neither of which can give me or my colleagues the time of day? They basically don't care how we feel as long as the track is running.
>
> (11/1995)

Together with the 1995 action by unions at Ford (UK) (which also witnessed unofficial strike action), the Vauxhall dispute represented a watershed in the social and ideological restructuring of workplace relations in the UK automotive sector. Not since the so-called 'We Will Manage' dispute at Ellesmere Port in 1979, recalled by Marsden and colleagues (1985: 32), had workers at Vauxhall been involved in action of such widespread significance. In November 1995, workers voted by over 70 per cent[4] in favour of strike action in pursuit of their claim, and by almost 90 per cent in favour of action short of a strike (Electoral Reform Ballot Services 1995). This was a remarkable result in the political and economic circumstances of the time. Yet many involved in the industrial and employee relations developments at plant level were not too surprised by this result. A worker with more than 20 years' experience felt that 'Supervision do not take enough notice of what the workers say to them', while Jim (paint shop) remained unconvinced by the supposed novelty of Vauxhall's lean production methods, 'I would like to say that I feel like the workers in *Metropolis* [the 1930s film].

Just as brain dead and not being able to utilise my abilities.' This perception was echoed by James when he commented drolly that 'The Company talks about quality – in reality quantity's more important.' Jill, from final trim, situated management rhetoric around lean, including the teamwork concept, within the wider 'business' of capitalist production. For her, claims about participation and improvements to working conditions were not borne out by experience, and just as significantly, she also saw it as a direct attack on union power:

> The teamwork concept gives the impression of taking an active part within the team. But the reality is team members have no real say about the running or organisation within the team. Most team members are aware of this deception but are reluctant to say or do anything about it as there is a great feeling of job insecurity. As for health and safety the emphasis appears to be on production first, safety second. It is not uncommon for management to say 'we have a business to run' totally disregarding safety problems. Union involvement is now getting less and less. Team leaders are informed of any changes before shop stewards thus undermining union positions. The overall opinion is we are working a lot harder and things can only get worse and not better.
>
> (3/11/1995)

MANAGEMENT MISJUDGES THE SHOPFLOOR

> Last night down in the compound there they would have torched the Vectras if we hadn't have stopped them. The company just don't see that the lads and lasses too has had enough of lean.
>
> (Luton shop steward)

The trigger for the Vauxhall dispute was management's response to the August 1995 pay and conditions claim by the unions, which the company argued could jeopardise important elements of GM's long-term investment portfolio in the United Kingdom. However, management seemed blithely indifferent, or at best oblivious, to the impact that its own remuneration would have on workers' sense of fairness. Commenting on Charlie Golden's[5] (Vauxhall's managing director's) pay rise, one track worker from the body shop said:

I think the fact [is] that the wage offer is such an insult and people were expecting more and their expectations had been built up over the years by the company. 'You will share in the spoils'. Oh yea – unless you're after Charlie Golden's 60% pay rise earlier in this year. Charlie Golden, Managing Director, GM England got a 62% increase in his wages. That was Charlie Golden's raise for you! And a lot of people were thinking, 'charging himself 60% raise and there is plenty of money around' and when the wage offer finally hit the table, people were saying 'what the fuck is going on here'. They were saying 'You were telling us over the years that we were the best thing since sliced bread and we are the most important piece in the factory and you come up with the insult of a wage deal – not like you had.' That really pissed us off, you know?

(13/12/1995)

The unions were calling for £20 across the board in year one and a 10 per cent increase in year two; a shorter working week, down from 39 to 37 hours; a track workers' allowance of 3 per cent and sick pay entitlement from day one (in year two) of absence. The main elements of management's initial response in 1995 consisted of a two-year (eventually described as three) pay deal (3 per cent in year one with only a cost of living increase in year two), inferior sickness benefit and the consolidation of the various local bonus schemes. Vauxhall clearly felt this would assuage employee claims in respect of productivity and quality gains made since 1989, particularly in their view at Luton (Vauxhall *Negotiations Update*, 13 October 1995, no. 5). Indeed, the company recognised that these gains were predominantly attributable to increases in employee productivity tied to the introduction of key elements of lean production, mostly as these affected assembly workers. However, against the background of increased productivity in the context of lean production, it would appear that Vauxhall had misjudged the feeling of shopfloor workers. The reality is that the impact of lean production on the labour process had begun to undermine the rhetoric of participation in decision making on vital matters such as job development schemes. This is because change was (and still was at the time of writing of this chapter at Ellesmere Port) increasingly linked to staff cutbacks by way of outsourcing in particular – one of the central objectives of lean production. The real story here was how the unions were able to capitalise on the inherent contradictions of the new technical and social arrangements at the heart of lean production.

The Enchanted Kingdom Newsscroll

A First Taste of Victory?

At the Luton Plant's first mass-meeting in living memory (virtually), the workforce took a decisive and essential step towards fair wages and conditions when they unanimously told the company "shove it!".

It is obvious that the workforce, has finally had enough of Vauxhall's arrogant "We can do what we like and you'll put up with it" attitude. It seems that this time the Company might just have pushed things a little too far, even for the Luton Plant workforce, who Vauxhall see as a bunch of cowards who haven't had the courage to stand up and fight for donkeys' years. It pains your friendly Elf to have to admit that up until now they were right.

Over the last few years *we*, the workforce, have turned the white-elephant Luton Plant into a profitable, efficient factory. We have allowed our numbers to be whittled down as outsourcing stole our jobs. We have worked smarter and *much* harder. We have delivered what was asked of us, and more. When the Company tells the media that we are being offered a fair deal they do not mention the fact that the reward we are claiming is for years and years of back-breaking effort. Years during which the Company has shrunk from paying us what we are worth while hiding behind a legion of contrived excuses.

As our convenors so rightly said: if we don't stop the rot now it will be too late, and we will be condemning ourselves to a bleak future. Our workload will increase – Vauxhall knows that as the old and frail succumb to the increasingly barbaric demands of Vauxhall track-work, they can replace them from the pool of young, fit unemployed that the Tories have so thoughtfully provided in the Luton area.

At the mass meeting we enjoyed our first taste of defiance for a long time – too long. This is our last chance to fight for our survival.

Why We Can Win

Everyone knows there will never be a good time to strike – it will always be too close to Christmas, or to a holiday, or... get the idea? There will never be a good time, so let's just do it *now*.

The management cannot afford a strike any more than we can. The longer we hold out, the more pressure they will get from GM. Do you really think Barber and co. are going to put their nice cushy jobs on the line by letting a strike drag on indefinitely? And don't listen to any bullshit scare-mongering about closing the Plant. After all the money GM have invested in Luton? Close it? Your elf thinks not.

Know your enemy

We made the mistake of trying overtime bans and one day stoppages in the past – they achieve nothing. This time let's do it right - *All out until we get a fair offer!* The Company has much more to lose than we have – and they know it – especially as they struggle to launch the new model. They have enough problems already... This time *we can win!*

Justice for Defeated Management: Top Ten Suggestions

○ *Castration ... if not too late*
○ *Crucifixion*
○ *Sentence to track-work*
○ *Burning at the stake*
○ *A fucking good kicking*
○ *Needles under fingernails*
○ *Hang, draw and quarter*
○ *Impale upon own golfclubs*
○ *Force to commit ritual suicide*
○ *All of the above*

Published by ELF (Employee Liberation Front) & Vauxhall Independent

Samizdat 1, ELF (Employee Liberation Front) and *Vauxhall Independent*, 1992–2000.

```
                                        VAUXHALL MOTORS LTD
    OCTOBER 1992                        KIMPTON ROAD
    INTERNAL MEMO                       LUTON
    ATTN : JOHN BARBER                  BEDS
    Dear John,
            Thank you for your kind letter received last week. I did
    not appreciate the dire problems facing us at the moment, and I'm
    sure I speak for us all. In fact we would go as far as to say that
    if we did, we would have double checked the orders to ensure that
    we did not encounter the shortages that caused such a loss in
    production in recent weeks.
            By the same token, we deeply regret the incident several
    weeks ago when, due to inattention to the weather forecast, we
    carelessly allowed the paint shop to be struck by lightning, and bad
    flooding in the body shop, causing further loss of production. We
    will endeavour to ensure that we do not make such mistakes in future.
            We also believe that by implementing short time in the
    single most productive factory that General Motors has ever had,
    (Cardiff University report) together with replacing successful working
    methods  with 'old fashioned'  Japanese methods  (Bob Eaton, former
    director G.M.Europe) is really good business practice.   Probably.
            We may have to think about giving up our floating vacation,
    but we do realize that by our selfish desire to take holidays when we
    want them, we may jeopardize the completion of vital projects that are
    urgently required, such as the fifty million pound landscape garden
    and redecoration one.
            To finalise, thanks for your tremendous morale boost, it
    could not have come at a better time. We will never forget your
    immortal words that still guide us as much today as they did then...
                "DON'T ARGUE .... JUST DO IT !!"
    LOTS OF LOVE.....


    JOE PRODUCTION WORKER ESQ.
```

Samizdat 2 (ELF 1992–2000).

CONFRONTING LEAN: LAYING THE BASIS FOR UNION ADVANCE

Keep communications and good relations with the shopfloor.
(shop steward, Luton)

In the end, the unions had to settle for a deal on pay and conditions
which was less than was hoped for at shopfloor level. When the

Vauxhall Independent

NEGOTIATIONS STATISTICAL ANALYSIS EDITION

Right: David Cato yesterday, who recieved our first ever distributor of the month award

SMEGMA

Just about as popular (not to mention greedy) as the Tory Government, John Barber and his cronies have really scraped the barrel this time. In a spiteful revenge attack for being thrashed in the ballot, the low-life scum that is Vauxhall management issued an injunction to prevent us taking the action that we justly and lawfully decided on.

Mere words cannot describe the revulsion felt throughout the once dedicated workforce. Men and women who have given so much and worked so hard, only to see the almighty buttocks of General Motors repeatedly dumping on them from a great height. But not for much longer. The press releases, injunction threats and fallacious propaganda have only served to strengthen the resolve of the underlings. So you have been warned, SCUM. The worm has turned, and you're in for some heavy shit.

BRUCE WARMAN, an apology.

An apology is due to all our readers. Over the past few weeks a grave injustice has been done that we hope to correct forthwith. Bruce Warman, charming, witty, considerate, loyal Director of Personnel not, has aired his opinions to just about any quarter of the news media stupid enough to listen to them, in the belief that if *you throw enough shit, some of it will stick.* This philosophy (as used in CIP, Competetive Tendering, JIT, etc) has back-fired on the conceited git in a big way over the past month. In his press release to the Herald newspaper (9.11.95) he was quoted thus; '...3.5%, extra holiday, nearly new car subsidy is generous by any standards.' The article then told of Charles Golden's 60% pay rise, giving him a salary of over £0.35 Million PER YEAR! I for one would seriously consider accepting 60%, or 30% come to that. Warman, who recently changed his name from David Icke when nobody believed that he *was* the Son of God, then suggested to local TV stations that the loyal workers would vote against their Trade Unions and reject industrial action. Again he was made to look a foolish half-wit when the results were announced.

Statistics show that Mr. Warman is actually a fifth-wit, as you can see from this specially prepared graph. The shaded area shows the total amount of votes cast against strike action by all hourly paid workers, that being how many votes *he* got, and the big bit shows that he's not as smart as he thought.

This is how many people think that Bruce Warman speaks out of his arse.

This next graph indicates that Bruce, catch-phrase 'come on down, the price is right', tends to talk more shit than John Barber,- and that takes some doing.

To sum up, the reason Company cannot afford to give us any more than they have offered (see Fig.3) is because they have already given it all to Charles Golden.

BRUCE WARMAN, a sphincter.

In association with ELF, Employee Liberation Front.

Distributor of the Month

As you are probably aware, the Vauxhall Independent is reliant, almost in its entirety, on its supporters to facilitate distribution. To show our appreciation we have set up an award scheme for our most worthy ally.
We are honoured to announce that the first ever winner of the Distributor of the Month Award is David Cato. David's solo effort struck gold when he faxed the last issue direct to John Barber. On recieving the award David said, 'I think you lads and lasses are doing a great job cheering up your fellow workers. I am proud to accept this award, but it was nothing, really.' What can we say? Keep up the good work!

Fax a million Dave

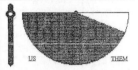

Make your own 'Peter Snow' Swing-o-meter!

When we heard the ballot results we exitedly rang the BBC and asked to borrow the 'Swing-o-meter' used by political pundit Peter Snow. Unfortunately this was not available, but in true Vauxhall Independent style,- here is how to make your own. All you need is a pin, some card and a pair of rounded end scissors.

Cut out the swing-o-meter and pointer, and glue them to the card. Then push the pin through the centres (marked) and 'hey presto' a swing-o-meter just like Peter Snow. You can now have hours of fun humiliating defeated directors (like Bruce Warman).

WIIICH? Report - What are you worth to GM? Fig.3
Hourly paid average.
Charles Golden
1 2 3 4 5 6 7 8 9 10 11 12 13 14 15 16 17 18 19 20 21 22 23 24 25 26 27 28 29 30 32 WAGES FOR ONE YEAR x £10,000
Fact: Charles Golden's wages alone would feed a starving 'third world' country for eight months, or fund a cancer ward for one year.

Merry Christmas and a prosperous New Year to all our supporters, distributors, and editorial staff. No surrender.

Samizdat 3 (ELF 1992–2000).

company's final offer was made, after six months of an often bitter struggle, particularly at Luton, workers still voted to reject the deal although the majority against Vauxhall's offer was considered by the TGWU to be too slim to continue the dispute.[6] The final deal, based upon a three-year cycle, comprised a reduction in the work week from 39 to 38 hours, a 4.5 per cent pay rise in year one plus cost of living top-up in years two and three, a new car plan scheme and the

VAUXHALL INDEPENDENT

Who said Vauxhall are scared?

NOVEMBER 1995 STRIKE EDITION

MORE BULLSHIT!

John Barber has written to *you personally* from the luxury of his air conditioned expense account to tell *you personally* how you should vote in the union ballot. He explains how concerned he is that *you* might expect a reasonable standard of living in return for the hard work and high standards achieved over the last two years, and how that expectation could cause the total collapse of GM Europe. What a load of bollocks. Mr.Smug Bastard informs you that *we* could lose money this year. Well perhaps Vauxhall should not have wasted all of last year's profit buying Avis, setting up 'outside contract firms' eg. T&D Automotive to take our jobs, installment of mega bucks robots to replace workers and sending the rest to America-pretending that the vast profit never even existed.

"The costs of introducing the Vectra have been enormous," we are told, yet he failed to mention that most of the expense was unnecessary.

Motoring experts declared, "Vectra? You could have launched a space shuttle for less!" He also neglects to note the vast improvements in productivity where almost a thousand people have left Vauxhall, none have been replaced and more cars than ever have been built. What planet is he living on?

The replacement scheme for Flexx, the new hospital hours, and the floating vacation are out of touch with reality and have nothing to do with a pay deal. These subjects should be discussed at JNC, not forced upon us under the guise of 'working conditions'.

If industrial action does not take place, Mr.Comfy Mansion in the Hertfordshire countryside will have won. We are not fighting for what we deserve, we are fighting to return our standard of living to where it was ten years ago.

In his penultimate paragraph we are warned, "...(industrial action) casts a shadow over the possibility of more investment-investment which is essential to help provide job security in future." This is another lie. Over the past seven years the bulk of investment in Luton has been spent on making the hourly paid worker work harder for what, in real terms, equates to a far lower standard of living.

THE TIME FOR ACTION IS NOW. WHAT EVER THE COMPANY TELLS YOU IS FOR THEIR OWN GOOD, IT'S TIME TO LOOK AFTER NUMBER ONE. JOHN BARBER IS RICH, SMARMY AND DEVOID OF CONSCIENCE. HE WOULD NOT CARE IF LUTON PLANT CLOSED TOMORROW AS LONG AS HE KEPT HIS JOB AND HIS FAT SALARY. IT MAY BE A LONG STRUGGLE AND IT CERTAINLY WON'T BE EASY. GOOD LUCK, NO SURRENDER, TAKE NO PRISONERS.

In association with ELF, Employee Liberation Front.

BELOW: John Barber, 1995 winner of the Slitty-eyed Fat Bastard of the Year Competition, and Runner up in the Conceited Wanker Awards to Charles Golden (inset).

NOSE A   NOSE B   NOSE C

JOHN BARBER'S 'MATCH THE NOSE GAME.

Below are some of Johnny's biggest fibs. All you have to do is match the nose above to each fib using your skill and judgement, and send your answers to; BARBER'S BULLSHIT COMPETITION, V Block Vauxhall Motors, Luton, or just play for fun! Start picking your noses!

NOSE   QUOTE

"It is possible that we may lose money this year...best offer that can reasonably be expected, improves pay and conditions."

"....accepting this pay offer means that your jobs will be secure in the future."

"The nearly new car roll scheme is worth 2.6% per employee so the company cannot afford to reduce your working hours."

In the event of a tie, the competition will be judged on a tie-break.

I think John Barber is a wanker because (not more than ten words)

For people entering for fun the answers are at the foot of the page.

Hi ho, hi ho, it's out on strike we go..........

EXIT

Answers to Barber's Nose: 1.C; 2.C; 3.C.

9

Samizdat 4 (ELF 1992–2000).

reduction in family hospital allowance time for night shift workers. (Table 4.7 highlights the problems identified by workers on this issue.) This last element left a residue of discontent with some workers, who argued that they had been, in the words of an Ellesmere Port shop steward, 'sold down the river'.

The thing to understand is that we get hospital appointments that you are entitled to four hours if your wife, husband or child goes to hospital, you can go with them, you get paid for it. At the first meeting they had the firm said we had to drop the idea for your wife, husband and your children where you'd be able to go to the hospital with them and everybody looked and said it is out of order! First they say it's about teamworking employees and we are the most important thing in the factory and all this ... and how we should be pulling together and the next minute you cannot even get paid to take your child to the hospital. That is despicable, that is. That's going back a hundred years and their argument was they'd stop the supervisor taking his child to the hospital, but they wouldn't, that's crap. The supervisor can have time off any time he wants.

(11/1995)

However, the cut in the length of the working time could arguably have been seen as a tangible gain, since agitation around time and effort had grown out of a general dissatisfaction with the nature of the labour process under lean production (see Tables 4.3 to 4.5). In this sense, company acceptance of the hourly reduction could have been understood as an important and tangible gain. If time represents even bigger money under lean than under the regime of Measured Day Work, a reduction in work time is an important gain since it begins to undermine some of the logic at the heart of teamworking in a very concrete way for workers. The unions had been campaigning for 15 years for a 37-hour week but this was often the first demand to be dropped in pay negotiations.

The additional feature that eroded employee confidence in management was the company commitment to a three-year deal. Management's assumption was that this would eventually force the unions out of their historical, political and institutional role as key players in the bargaining process, since shopfloor conditions would increasingly be addressed by team briefings under the auspices of the Continuous Improvement Programme (CIP). However, this view was premised on a fundamental misunderstanding of the source of the original discontent, which provided the basis for union (and TGWU especially) strength on the shopfloor.

The dispute was infused with irony. Having poured tens of thousands of dollars into the improvement of employee relations (via team briefings and the CIP strategy) in the United Kingdom, GM and Vauxhall management felt it was inconceivable that a dispute would develop around precisely the core message of involvement, encapsulated in both the Luton plant agreement, 'Working Together to Win' (Vauxhall 1992) and the so-called 'V6' Agreement covering Ellesmere Port (Vauxhall 1989).[7] After all, these agreements promised to promote employee involvement and participation in key aspects of the lean labour process, from *kaizen* to teamworking on the line. Yet this was far from the perception of line workers, as Sandra (a steward in the trim shop whom we quote at length) argued:

> Teamwork? We have argued this amongst ourselves. Team working is not working out in our factory. It is just not friggin' worth it. They have got where they got today on the back on the threat of redundancies – that there might not be a factory here in five years down the road. Also added to this they brought out the carrot – an open chequebook. They went around the shopfloor with an open chequebook and said you come up with a suggestion to take time out of the job and you will get a whack. That is not how teamworking should work. Teamwork should be based on the fact they are doing it willingly for the right reasons for the good of the company. No one is doing it for that, they are all doing it for the money and of course that has run out. Teamwork … is working for the good of the company and not for the good of the individual. You are all meant to be keen and willing to put in these suggestions to make the company more profitable, not to have a fat cheque in your back pocket, it is just not working. You go out on the shopfloor half an hour every day and ask what do you think of teamworking. They will say 'fuck all', although it is there but in real terms it is not there, if you know what I mean. They are having these so-called team meetings before each shift and the latest innovation is a six-minute team meeting, they are now calling it a team briefing. It's not a two-way thing. It's just the team leader talking to the team about what is going to be the bill today. That has always happened anyway and it's just absolute rubbish … it's just not working. The lads are not turning up and no one is bothering and the team leader is talking to himself or his best blue-eyed guy is talking. The concept is just a way of telling people this is how we have arrived where we have arrived. We have got our rate of production through teamwork, but if you would like to, just analyse teamwork and the real meaning of teamwork going through the Japanese philosophy or even the American in the first place. Our company talk bollocks on this.

If you see the blue-eyed boy or girl doing the job instead of the person who really deserves it, then you won't take much notice of it, that person just becomes the old-style supervisor and you will turn off to them the same as you would against the old team leaders. The team leaders are company, they virtually got no training whatsoever and they were told here we are you are a team leader.

(14/12/1995)

Joannie's view (also from trim) reinforces the perception that the jargon of teamwork was being used to dignify already existing managerial practice:

It is just as though it is the flavour of the day. Since teamwork has supposedly come in here we have had CIP, we have had everything. It is a new set of words every time you come in to work through the door.

(13/12/1995)

Later on she reinforced Sandra's view of teamworking:

I think business had just come round to the stage where they have just had enough. Enough is enough, we always expected the day to come when they turned around to say that as far as they were concerned they had enough of the team concept and what this really meant to them was harder work. That is all it ever meant. They can see it through now in a team, we all work together, we work harder, you work harder, and that is it you don't get any benefit, nobody has seen any money from it. They have started to see all the benefits as they have created and they are all going to management, none of them are coming our way, enough is enough we want our share, if we don't get our share we are not having any more of this. Maybe the day will come when they turn around and say you can scrap the team altogether, they won't have it because they know what the concept means. The idea of working together is fine but management's idea of the team concept is not what it means to us. That is where the problems arise.

(13/12/1995)

Only later in the interview did Joannie reveal her belief that shopfloor management was fairly cynical:

Teamwork only works for certain people (team leaders). They've got a monopoly on overtime. Members of a team did the CO_2 course. They were not asked to do overtime on bodies that needed CO_2. The team leader got that overtime. He didn't not do a CO_2 course until overtime on bodies that needed CO_2 finished. Another team leader received a bottle of whisky because his team reached a certain number. He showed us his appreciation by taking the bottle home and told his team it was his and they could have a photo of it. The team I am in has not had a team meeting since September 95. We were told what to do. We have not been asked our opinion.

(13/12/1995)

Moreover, besides this gap between rhetoric and reality, a further problem was that the language of participation and 'smarter work' was pushed increasingly onto a vanishing direct labour force. The reality of lean management began to bite during this period. Work was becoming increasingly onerous on the tracks with speed-ups, destaffing, job loading and reduced job cycle times (see Tables 4.3 to 4.5). When asked about the increasing frustration on the shopfloor, a steward from the body shop replied that the issue now was not only about remuneration, nor could payment be seen in the usual way as a straightforward compensation for increased work pressure.

Q. 'Why has it all come to a head now, do you think?'
David: 'Because people have accepted one-off payments to settle disputes in the past and they're finding that their base money is rubbish, they are working harder; the tracks are not even up to what they are supposed to be. People are struggling now in the paint shop; people are doing an extra 25 an hour.

(14/12/1995)

Although this is a characteristic of work processes in both plants, the introduction of production of the new Cavalier at Luton, the Vectra, with its reduced cycle times, added another turn to the screw of work intensification. In many cases these work processes could only be achieved through a more aggressive management style. In this respect, a critical contradiction for management was that aggression always has to be an option under a lean production regime. Employee experiences of lean production have been mostly negative, with reports of work becoming more physically and mentally demanding, with scant regard for employee expectations of greater training and financial remuneration (Stewart and Garrahan 1995). Moreover, there is increasing evidence of the detrimental effects of lean production on workers' health and safety. (See Tables 4.8 to 4.11 on quality of working life.)

These employee experiences, together with the strategy laid out by the TGWU at plant level (Fisher 1995), suggest that the significance of the dispute cannot be judged solely in terms of the unions' limited success in pursuit of their substantive claim. For sure, the unions achieved less than their memberships had expected after having endured a difficult six-month dispute. The irony for the unions was that this pressure for change had grown as a direct consequence of both their own proactive strategy of direct engagement with the politics and ideology of lean production, and workers' own experiences of the reality of so-called 'smarter work' (see Joannie's comments above). In the assembly plants the TGWU especially had been preparing for lean production since the late 1980s, to such an extent that before the plant agreements were signed in 1989 and 1992 (at Ellesmere Port and Luton), the shape and content of team meetings were subject to joint regulation. (Martinez-Lucio and Weston (1992) provide a compelling account of some of the background to this in what they term the 'workplace response' strategy.)

The TGWU's strategy for mobilisation depended upon control of the communication process at shopfloor level, and their success in this was acknowledged by management. A concerted campaign of education was developed to counter the easy management rhetoric which associated lean production, employee participation and trade union subordination with company success. During the period of initial mobilisation against the politics and ideology of lean production, the union organised several dozen training sessions while the local leaderships drew the participation of the *Labor Notes* current in the United States (see Ken Murphy's comments, pp. 80–4). The effect of this successful ideological offensive by the TGWU was to point up the relationship between Vauxhall's lean production strategy, the danger of subordinate trade unionism and workers' experiences of 'harder work'.

The implementation of the TGWU's campaign in defence of workers' collective and individual rights and interests drew management's sting because it focused on two key aspects of the change process. The first related to changes to the technical labour process in which responsibility for product quality was continually pushed down to the shopfloor with inadequate financial compensation for workers (see Chapter 3). Workers also considered that insufficient consideration was given to their requirements for physical and mental recovery from the stresses of working lean (see Tables 4.10 to 4.13). As a consequence of the 1989 and 1992 agreements at Ellesmere Port and Luton respectively, the unions established controls on labour mobility; criteria and limits for the proportion of track relief staff; some conditions, in theory, covering outsourcing; the redefinition of spheres of influence between unions and management, and at both plants an increase in shop steward density. As regards questions relating to just-in-time (JIT), 'zero waste', low buffers and employee responsibility for aspects of statistical process control (SPC), and other critical technical features of lean, the unions acknowledged from the beginning that little could be done to inhibit these. However, it is in respect of the second aspect of the change process that the unions made some notable advances. Away from direct production, the TGWU was particularly successful in challenging management aims in areas relating to team briefings, continuous improvement/*kaizen* and the company's broader ideological paraphernalia promoting the benefits to employees of lean production. It was a feature of union strength that management at both plants had been woefully unsuccessful in winning the 'hearts and minds' of the workforce. The battle for 'hearts and minds' is crucial for both management and unions, as each side recognised, and it was a fight that led directly to the second feature of the change process – trade union power and autonomy.

Lurking behind the technological (JIT and *kaizen*, for example) and ideological changes flowing from lean production, there had been another management agenda which required the success of three interrelated developments. The first was the substitution of traditional employee and union-regulated gang working with a team leader-managed work process. Second, the success of this depended on the creation of a collaborative system of company–union industrial relations, known within GM in the United States as 'jointism'. In the United Kingdom, we can understand this in terms of a weak trade union, company-driven partnership agenda. Third, and as a consequence of the latter, Vauxhall required the development of an employee involvement programme built upon union marginalisation (Vauxhall Luton 1995). The evidence from this dispute suggests that whatever immediate gains both sides claimed, they tell only a limited part of the story. Management had in its arsenal the ability to play the investment game, known in the United States as 'whipsawing', but the threat of disinvestment is a dangerous threat to make in a context where you are trying to convince the labour force of the honourable nature of your intentions. What is known for sure about the 1995–96 dispute is that the TGWU were remarkably successful in combating a number of social, organisational and industrial relations features of management's offensive. On the crucial matter of the ideological campaign for 'hearts and minds', management trailed the TGWU.

CONCLUSION

From the point of view of industrial and employee relations, management's objective in signing the Ellesmere Port and Luton plant agreements was to break the TGWU's shopfloor prerogatives from above and below. From above, they aimed to do it by involving the union in joint problem-solving exercises on everything from corporate strategy to ergonomics and health and safety. From below, it was done by drawing individual workers, via *kaizen* and team briefings, into a more limited but no less significant process of employee–company 'jointism'. In this fashion, workplace problems would cease to be industrial relations issues around which to mobilise a distinctive trade union agenda, but rather would be seen as matters of common concern 'to us all, management and employee alike – we can all solve this problem together'. Nevertheless, as the dispute demonstrated, and later events revealed, management increasingly found the going tough, as at least three interrelated features of the period continued to be reproduced. First, management were unable to close the gap between the rhetoric and the reality of lean production with respect to the claims made for employee benefits. Second, and indelibly tied to the first point, was the fact that the lean labour process continued to have a negative effect upon workers' physical and emotional lives. Finally, the unions, by virtue of their ideological hegemony, continued to outpace management when it came to delivering on promises to their members. Lean production as class struggle from above without doubt, but in this instance labour was engaging with great ingenuity.

Of course, it is true that in contrast to the trade union experiences at Ford and Rover, plant-based union organisations at Vauxhall weathered the 1980s reasonably well, while eventually all three, GM-Vauxhall's Ellesmere Port aside, were devastated by the political economy of lean by the beginning of the millennium. Yet one of the factors that distinguished the Vauxhall experience in the 1990s was that the TGWU began with a rejectionist position based upon a sharp and essentially correct view of new management practices (see Chapter 3). The point is that whatever compromises were inevitably made on outsourcing and staffing levels, these did not, because of the political understanding of lean production at plant level, undermine the union organisation and its hegemony on the shop floor. In other words, early preparation and oppositionism allowed the unions to stay ahead of the game when management's full anti-union agenda was revealed.

While this argument was made against the backdrop of a resurgent form of labour organisation that had been relatively successful in confronting GM-Vauxhall's lean production agenda, inevitably, as we would anticipate in this period of neoliberalism, the company clawed its way back into contention. As we shall see in Chapter 7, the change in corporate strategy, defined above all by the shift away from a Vauxhall-UK agenda to GM Europe, signalled the beginning of the long-term erosion of the utility of 'Engage and Change' for labour. With the increasing shift to a European framework of planning, R&D and vehicle manufacture, the scope for an arena of union action comprising several plants in one country where struggles could be reasonably well organised was now about to disappear.

Chapter 5 features an abridged version of a round-table discussion which took place at the TGWU's regional 6 office in Liverpool between members of the Auto Workers' Research Network, some of whom are stewards at GM-Vauxhall's Ellesmere Port. In the debate they assess the nature of the fight against lean production and how the union developed a critical agenda at plant and company level. Following this, in Chapter 6, we recount the travails of Rover and the politics of the demise of the British-owned sector from *Rover Tomorrow* in 1992 until the debacle over Longbridge in 2000.

The History of the Fight to Control Lean Production

The automotive industry has undergone many changes over the last 50 years or so, but over the last 20 years I think that the changes have been more deep-rooted and thought-out than in the past.

When I started in Vauxhall Motors in 1978, the model mix was poor, labour relations were poor and more importantly, the quality of management left a lot to be desired. All in all this led to an unmotivated, poorly paid and poorly trained workforce. Over the years a lot of the shortfalls have been addressed, but not all, not all by a long chalk.

In the early years, our means of control of our labour was 'We Sell Our Time'. This was 'Taylorism', or more commonly, time and motion study. This was easy for unions and management to understand and easy to administer. However it did require man-hours and an extra department to undertake the various time and motion studies that took place around the plant. At the introduction of a new car this would be a considerable task, and a lot of studies ended up as agreements between the shop steward, the foreman and the time study engineer. This meant of course that on paper, all jobs and tasks were 100 per cent efficient.

The changes for Vauxhall began in earnest in 1979, and I think that it was no coincidence that the Tory government were also elected in that year. We had just finished a dispute over wages with the company, which we lost, and the company gradually asked employees back to work in a piecemeal fashion. This was how the company had planned to break down the trade union organisation within Vauxhall, and but for a handful of committed shop stewards, it could have been the end of our organisation. The company were particularly ruthless and sacked several shop stewards who, in their opinion, were troublemakers or ringleaders. In reality, these shop stewards were sacked in order to send a message to everyone that management were in charge and they were prepared to make ruthless and snap decisions.

A lot of the shop stewards who were pre-1979 chose not to stand again. Indeed when the company introduced a separation programme in the early 1980s, they left the company altogether. However this meant that the Shop Stewards Committee, as well as the company, had to reinvent itself and promote the union in a different way. In many ways this was a successful path that the shop stewards took. Everything that the union did was T&G this and that: for example, an annual T&G May Day dance, an annual T&G pantomime for members' children, an annual T&G Fun Day for members and their families, all done to promote the union and find a way of letting people see that the union was a family and they were members of that family.

During the 1980s we saw a lot of what was happening in Japan, the new work practices that were being introduced and the pressures that were being put on Japanese workers, pressures that we could see could be transported to the United Kingdom in the blinking of an eye.

Because the warning bell had been tolled we decided to embark upon a serious education programme for our shop stewards. This education programme was developed by us for us, and it would be many a year before the union nationally fully understood exactly what was happening in industry, and especially what was happening in the auto industry.

We invited Mike Parker, a writer and researcher for *Labor Notes* in Detroit, to come and take some educational sessions with our shop stewards; this was done on the back of work that Mike had written a book on 'quality circles'. Mike was also an ex auto worker, so had a good idea of what was happening in the industry generally.

This initial tutorial was perhaps the springboard for a lot of our shop stewards to get to grips in a more positive way with what the company were trying to achieve, and I certainly found this to be a turning point in my own education about the whole area of new management techniques (NMTs).

At the time NMTs were largely regarded as 'teamwork', and the whole concept of teamwork and NMTs was not taken seriously by the trade union movement as a whole. This of course made it difficult for us to educate our stewards and the workforce, mainly because all the necessary material needed for the educational process was nearly all our own, or what we could glean from other people. We had made many friends over the years in the rest of Europe and had some contacts with Japanese unions, and this held us in good stead, with a steady stream of information and ideas, which at the time was invaluable. Forewarned really was forearmed, and it would not be over-stretching if I said that we had more of an idea of what the company were trying to achieve than did most of the senior managers within Vauxhall, and judging by what other colleagues in other plants were saying, the situation was no different anywhere else in Great Britain.

The next step for us was to try to spread our knowledge around the car industry, not just within our own union but around as many of the other unions and shop stewards' bodies as were interested in what we were trying to do.

We did hold several conferences with shop stewards, not just from Great Britain, but from around the globe. One of the aims was to educate our people, but not just in NMTs but also educate people on the need for solidarity, also to show workers in this country that workers around the globe have similar and often worse problems than we do here in Great Britain.

All over Britain at this time, towards the end of the 1980s, new agreements were being drawn up, and inexperienced negotiators ended up signing deals on teamwork and NMTs without understanding the wider implications of their actions. Indeed it was at this time that we heard the phrase 'no-strike deal' being used.

We signed a deal at Vauxhall at this time, known as the 'V6 Agreement' [see Chapters 3 and 6], which was an agreement on teamwork and so on that the company insisted had to be agreed in order for Vauxhall to receive investment for a new engine at Ellesmere Port. The convener at the time, Peter Titherington, was a shrewd negotiator and along with his deputies, strung the negotiations out over many months. This gave us the opportunity to put in the agreement safeguards for our members, safeguards that have kept us in good stead till this day. The company have however striven for more and more changes within the plant, and some of the agreement has been watered down by successive pay deals. The V6 Agreement was negotiated by the conveners, but it was also put to the membership, who voted to accept it and saw it as a way for us to achieve investment in our plant.

The 1990s again saw attacks on our working conditions, and where we previously worked within a strictly Taylorist environment, we were now working within different constraints. For example, new jobs would not be timed (although within the V6 Agreement we reserved the right to use a stopwatch on any job). Instead the times for jobs were worked out before they were introduced, and the operator was then left to try to work within the time. In the event that the operator couldn't, then either an element of work was removed or the job was rejigged. In some instances, where there was a dispute a watch was used, but this was unusual.

Over the years, we have seen many changes, but I think that the biggest impact on us, was when the company started to coin the phrase 'lean production'. This was in the beginning to mid-1990s and was really when people started to feel the full effect of NMTs, because this is where the company always wanted to be, a minimal amount of core workers assembling parts made outside of the main factory, by workers on less pay, with inferior agreements. This in effect gave the company more control of its product, and more control of its workforce. The company are now in this position in many of its plants around the globe, but it's not just GM. All the major manufacturers are using this 'system' to produce not only cars, but a multitude of goods.

There are no morals in the history of where we are and how we got here, but workers and national and local unions cannot rest on past laurels. Change in industry is constant, and firms like GM will spend millions on a concept to bring down the cost of its product. If it doesn't work for them, then they will just start again, and so it goes on. What we as trade unionists have got to understand is that we can't make an agreement and then go to bed, we have got to keep on top of those agreements and make sure that they work for us.

Ken Murphy

ADDENDUM: DATA SUMMARY

In this addendum we include some data collected for the period, from early 1995 to February 1996, covering the build-up to and the dispute at Vauxhall (Ellesmere Port and Luton). Questionnaires, together with other field data, were also collected at Rover's Cowley (Oxford) and Longbridge (Birmingham) plants during the same period. Some of the interview data from GM-Luton is included in this chapter. The questionnaire was distributed at both companies in November 1995. (See Appendix 1, Questionnaire '96, page 214.) Rover workers reported they were less affected by NMTs than Vauxhall workers, while younger workers in their 20s did not appear to notice any lean effects, which may not be so surprising since mostly they had been appointed after the introduction of lean at both companies. Table 4.2 apart, the tables do not report worker experience over a five-year period: that is indicated in the text.

Overall, when we looked at the issues of quality of working life (physical work load, work pace), job control and autonomy, stress and management, and health and safety, workers reported largely negatively.

Specifically, what we can say of this period is that work was perceived to be getting 'harder' and 'faster': around half of respondents thought their work load was too heavy and that it had become more so over the previous five years. Moreover, 70 per cent of respondents thought that the pace of work was too fast, with nearly 83 per cent noticing an increase over a span of five years.

Regarding the significant issue of the impact of 'harder' and 'faster' work on their health, around half the respondents had experienced working in pain for at least half their working time. Just over half the respondents had spent at least half of their working day in an awkward position.

It was reported by 63.5 per cent of respondents that they were either 'very' or 'moderately' tense as a result of their work, and 63.2 per cent reported this had increased over the previous five years. It was reported by 78.8 per cent of respondents that they were exhausted after a shift at least half of the time, while 68.4 per cent reported that this had increased over the last five years. For 62.3 per cent of respondents tiredness restricted family activities.

Finally, on the vital matter of job control, 82.2 per cent of respondents found it difficult or impossible to change things about their job, 75 per cent reported close monitoring at work and over 61 per cent of respondents reported difficulty in taking time off for minor sickness.

Industrial relations

Table 4.1 In general how would describe the industrial relations climate in the plant at present?

Industrial relations climate	Total sample %	Vauxhall %	Rover %
Positive	12.4	18.5	17.9
Neutral	25.9	19.8	32.1
Negative	61.7	61.7	50.0

Note: difference significant at 5 per cent level.

Table 4.2 How does this [industrial relations climate] compare with five years ago?

Change in industrial relations climate over five years	Total sample%	Vauxhall %	Rover %
More positive	10.1	10.0	10.3
Unchanged	44.2	31.8	56.9
More negative	45.7	58.2	32.8

Note: difference significant at 5 per cent level.

Quality of working life (physical work load, work pace, job control and autonomy)

Table 4.3 How would you describe your current physical work load (moving, lifting objects, loading and unloading machines, air tool torque, etc.)?

Physical work load	Total sample %	Body shop %	Assembly %	Vauxhall %	Rover %
Much too heavy	14.0	14.4	13.0	18.9	9.1
Too heavy	32.5	29.3	35.0	34.8	30.3
Not a problem	53.4	56.3	52.1	46.3	60.7

Note:: difference between sections not significant; difference between companies significant at 5 per cent level.

Overall when asked, 'Do you work harder in terms of physical work load compared with five years ago?' 78.4 per cent of the sample reported that their physical work load was harder than five years ago, 73.5 per cent in the body shop compared with 81.9 per cent in assembly (significantly different at 10 per cent) and 73.4 per cent at Vauxhall compared with 83.1 per cent at Rover (significantly different at the 5 per cent level).

Table 4.4 How would you describe your current work speed or work pace?

Speed of work load	Total sample %	Body shop %	Assembly %	Vauxhall %	Rover %
Much too fast	17.6	12.4	19.5	20.3	15.0
Too fast	52.4	49.9	58.4	54.1	50.7
About right	27.7	36.7	19.1	24.2	31.2
Too slow	2.3	1.0	3.0	1.4	3.1

Note: difference between sections significant at 5 per cent level; difference between companies not significant.

When asked, 'Do you work faster in terms of work pace compared with five years ago?' 82.5 per cent of the sample reported that speed of work had increased since five years ago.

Table 4.5 How easy is it for you to change the things that you do not like about your job?

Change job	Total sample %	Body shop %	Assembly %	Vauxhall %	Rover %
Easy	3.7	5.2	2.8	4.0	3.4
Neither easy nor difficult	14.1	17.1	11.8	14.7	13.5
Difficult	58.7	62.4	56.8	55.5	62.0
Impossible	23.5	15.3	28.6	25.8	21.1

Note: difference between sections significant at 5 per cent level; difference between companies not significant.

Table 4.6 How closely is your work performance monitored by management?

Speed of work load	Total sample %	Body shop %	Assembly %	Vauxhall %	Rover %
Closely	75.2	81.9	72.5	83.8	66.5
Not closely	15.7	13.1	19.2	6.7	24.8
Not at all	9.1	5.0	8.3	9.5	8.7

Note: difference between sections significant at 5 per cent level; difference between companies not significant.

Table 4.7 Would it be easy to get time off for personal reasons such as illness in the family for a medical appointments?

Time off	Total sample %	Body shop %	Assembly %	Vauxhall %	Rover %
Easy	38.1	42.6	35.5	29.1	47.2
Difficult	56.3	51.4	60.5	64.0	48.5
Impossible	5.6	6.0	4.0	6.9	4.3

Note: difference between sections significant at 5 per cent level; difference between companies not significant.

Stress and management, health and safety

Table 4.8 In the last month how many days have you worked with physical pain or discomfort which was caused by your job?

Frequency of pain at work	Total sample %	Body shop %	Assembly %	Vauxhall %	Rover %
Every day	17.5	11.8	21.9	15.7	19.3
Most days	20.7	15.8	24.7	24.0	17.3
Half the time	10.4	8.6	11.4	10.3	10.5
A few days	51.4	63.8	42.0	50.0	52.9

Note: differences not significant.

Table 4.9 On average what part of each day is spent in physically awkward positions?

Time spent in awkward working positions	Total sample %	Body shop %	Assembly %	Vauxhall %	Rover %
All the time	15.9	17.2	17.1	14.7	17.1
Three quarters of the time	18.4	15.3	20.1	17.8	19.0
Half the time	18.1	12.6	21.3	18.1	18.1
One quarter of the time	29.1	30.3	26.9	34.5	23.7
Never	18.5	24.6	14.6	14.9	22.1

Note: differences not significant.

Table 4.10 In the last month how tense and wound up have you been at work?

Level of tension	Total sample %	Body shop %	Assembly %	Vauxhall %	Rover %
Very tense	32.3	27.9	33.9	30.5	34.1
Moderately tense	31.2	29.2	33.9	32.5	30.0
A little tense	26.9	27.3	26.3	27.5	26.2
No tension	9.6	15.6	5.9	9.5	9.7

Note: difference between sections significant at 5 per cent level; difference between companies not significant.

When we asked, 'Compared with five years ago, does the job make you tense and wound up?', 63.2 per cent reported an increase in tension since five years ago, 55.8 per cent of workers in the body shop and 67.5 per cent of workers in assembly (significant at the 5 per cent level), and 55.0 per cent of employees at Rover compared with 71.3 per cent of employees at Vauxhall (also significant at the 5 per cent level).

Table 4.11 In the last month, how often have you felt exhausted after 8 hours of work?

Frequency of exhaustion from work	Total sample %	Body shop %	Assembly %	Vauxhall %	Rover %
Every day	29.9	28.4	30.9	29.4	30.2
Most days	36.9	32.4	39.8	37.4	36.8
Half the time	12.0	11.1	14.3	14.4	9.5
A few days	17.2	23.4	13.9	17.0	17.3
Never	4.0	4.7	3.1	1.8	6.2

Note: differences not significant.

In response to the question, 'How does this exhaustion compare with five years ago?', 68.4 per cent reported that the frequency of exhaustion was greater than five years ago, 61.1 per cent in the body shop and 73.4 per cent in assembly (significant at 10 per cent), and 61.4 per cent of employees at Rover compared with 75.4 per cent at Vauxhall (significant at the 5 per cent level).

Table 4.12 In the last month, how often has tiredness due to work restricted your participation in family and social activities?

Frequency family and social life suffers because of effects of work	Total sample %	Body shop %	Assembly %	Vauxhall %	Rover %
Every day	13.3	13.1	11.5	15.4	11.1
Most days	28.1	22.9	32.6	30.3	26.0
Half the time	20.9	17.2	23.0	19.5	22.3
A few days	27.4	34.1	23.0	27.7	27.1
Never	10.3	12.7	9.9	7.1	13.5

Note: difference not significant.

5 ROUND TABLE DISCUSSION ON LEAN PRODUCTION

This chapter is an abridged version of a round table discussion between General Motors(GM)-Vauxhall conveners (current and past), shop stewards and a university researcher, held at the 'Sandcastle', Liverpool TGWU Office in 2002. In the editing process care has been taken to preserve the authenticity and tenor of the full discussion and, with some revisions, to retain the original dialogue. Reordering the sequence of the interchange has enhanced cogency and coherence. Fundamentally, it is the story of Ellesmere Port shop stewards' struggle to understand, engage with and fight against the effects of lean production. Their aim was to reduce the impact of lean on present and future workers employed at Ellesmere Port. The issues debated reveal the contradictions, and problems, associated with fighting lean, together with the struggle to understand it in an effort to capture the objective character of the lean agenda.

This approach enables us to share with the reader the experiences of some of those intimately involved in the world of lean production. It is from their experiences, and those of others, that we can deepen our understanding of lean, to work towards intelligently arming unions and workers with the knowledge to resist the worsening conditions of lean employment relations.

At the end of the chapter several participants in this struggle offer accounts of their experiences of the politics of production during their time at Ellesmere Port.

The round table participants were John Cooper (JC), Tony Lewis (TL), Gary Lindsay (GL), Ken Murphy (KM), Paul Stewart (PS) and Mick Whitley (MW).

INTRODUCTION

PS: I would like to address five core questions. One is the origins of lean; the second is the struggles around lean, with a small 's'; thirdly is where we are now; fourth is how do we get beyond the current situation? Finally, what does the future hold?

JC: How do you want us to focus this then?

PS: We could begin with history of lean production, how it came about. Do you remember the TIE conference here, remember in January 1992?[1] People were talking about lean production, and how we can fight it; we can fight it, which was very much, as I understood, the attitude of Rover stewards. They were very 'oppositional' in words and very determined in that they would stop it, but your attitude was much more along the lines of 'You've got to fight and oppose it, but it's going to come so you have to be able to deal with it, on a day by day basis.' It's not about defeats or accommodation, you argued. You have to engage with it to change it.

So it's about lean production and the ideology of it, the way it was introduced in GM-Vauxhall and all the other issues that came out of discussions. The T&G had conferences, nationally, where there was a debate around lean production, with Dave Robinson [CAW] and then Dan Jones [Cardiff Business School]. I couldn't imagine that being organised now. Could you? I mean that's partly due to the shift in the union as well.

At the demonstration in Luton against closure, 2001: foreground left to right, Phil, Andy Dunn, Pat Doyle, Kenny Moran, Jimmy Flemming

JC: I can remember the lad coming over from America too.

PS: Mike Parker?

JC: Mike Parker. Yeah, I can remember the discussions we had with Mike Parker – I've still got his two books – and with Jane Slaughter.

PS: *Inside the Circle* and *Choosing Sides*?[2]

JC: *Inside the Circle* and *Choosing Sides*. Yeah, that's them, and it was so revolutionary at the time, reading *Inside the Circle*, but in all honesty it's old hat now, isn't it?

We had a system in place, it was in 1985 or 1989, it escapes my memory at the moment, how they determined how long it took to build a vehicle, which was part of the wage deal that year called 'We Sell Our Time'. It was a dramatic and universal change, in how we measured what work people did, and they moved away from the stopwatch to 'Management Time and Method' (MTM), and that progressed and progressed, and they came up with Universal Analysis System (UAS), and the UAS is based on a whole series of movements known as 'gets' and 'reaches'. It could be a 'reach' and you get a value for that, and a 'get', you get a different value for that, and that's how they do it. The person that gives Gary the time never has to see the job, never has to understand what continuous production

At the demonstration in Luton against closure, 2001: foreground left to right, Pat Doyle and Kenny Moran

is, all he knows is the job contains a 100 'gets', 50 reaches and X number of yards walking, which he'll give a given value, and all of a sudden there is a time there.

But it's based on values, that I said you couldn't breathe that fast, in fact you couldn't blink that fast, some of them, the way they break them down. At the bottom you will get a value and that value will be equated into minutes and seconds. That was the start of lean.

PS: We're going right back now. So before, people were talking about changes, like Taylorism and Fordism and post-Fordism, but what you seem to be saying is, what characterises the period right from the 1980s was that rather than being piecemeal, management became more strategic actually, political in a way. There was some-thing strategic about the way that it deals with the change in a way that they hadn't before. So that it incorporates all the lessons from stopwatches and time and motion people, industrial engineers, but perfected – that's not the right word – doing it all more strategically.

GL: They have definitely got their act together, but it is a strategic way as well.

MW: The thing is, people didn't really understand the extent of what lean production was. I mean, in 1984 we invited Mike Parker over – you know, he wrote the book [above]. We could see what was coming and that was a lot to do with our involvement in TIE and speaking to the likes of Mike Parker. We flew him over and he gave us an insight, but even then it wasn't as in-depth as it is now.

Even now there's no end to it. You know where it starts, but where does it end? I mean what's core product one day mightn't be core business the next day.

... That's the problem that you've got, I think people, the likes of us, we never embraced it as other plants did embrace it. You had the likes of Toyota, you had just-in-time companies starting from a greenfield site, brainwashing workers and saying this is the way we do the business. We come from a traditional brownfield site which was changed over to a lean field or greenfield site.

I think every time a company or GM put a plant in, they experiment; it's an experiment with them. ... Make the comparison now with Poland, they've just built a plant there with very minimal investment, but very, very lean, lean principles and all this, that and the other. Then you look at that vis-à-vis the Russelsheim plant where they've thrown millions and millions of dollars into that plant. Now they don't know what the return is going to be on that. It's like here's a model with very minimal investment in it, *vis-à-vis* an old brownfield site, they're gonna change it to a lean field site.

So what's confusing to me is, when you go to different plants, different plants are at different levels of lean production .... You've got some levels in some countries, who oppose the team concept, then you've got other ones who are models there, the ones the company say, 'That's where we've got to get to, from there to there.'

PS: How do you characterise the situation, if in 1992 you were still coming to terms with lean, ten years on? Lean's reaching its new development, whatever that might be.

KM: Have we taken lean to another plane? We haven't, we're just living with it. They took it to another plane, don't forget, when they started with teamwork and all the rest of it, they didn't *really* know what they were doing, they were just kicking around a few ideas that they picked up from other places. They got all sorts of firms in, consultancy firms, paid them all sorts of stupid money.

It wasn't that easy for the company. One reason was because we wouldn't let it happen the way they wanted, but the other one was they weren't ready for it themselves. They never had the talent, they never had the people who were good enough, and they never had the managers, who were dynamic enough, who could cope with those changes. You talk about change for us and how hard it was for us to cope with change. For them it must have been just as hard,

Gary Lindsay at the demonstration in Luton against closure, 2001

because you're talking about people who winged it. Managers, right, who were on a wing and a prayer, for reasons I said to you before, who were made up on the nod and everything. They weren't good enough, they just weren't good enough.

PS: If you had to compare, if you had two or three things to say about what lean production meant to you in 1992, after you'd agreed the V6 was implemented, what would you say?

KM: It's hard because I mean, in them early days, lean production as a phase, to what it is now, it was new then. In 1992, we didn't know the breadth of it.

PS: You didn't in what sense?

MW: Not in 1992, no. We know it's bigger than what we thought, because even right now, when you say continuous production or lean production, call it what you will, you don't know where the end is.

KM: There is no end though, is there?

MW: That's what I'm saying.

MW: People used to say outsourcing and all that, lights-out production – completely automated.

KM: They don't want that though.

MW: No, no, they want low tech and lean.

KM: They want control, that's what it is.

MW: Yes, because robots break down and when you've got continuous flow and a robot breaks down, right, everything stops and you might have to get technical engineers out and all that.

PS: Yes, but they do – they are investing huge amounts in technical change, aren't they?

MW: Yeah, they have done. And it's true it's not like the 1950s or 1960s, obviously. When you go back to those years it was labour-intensive; it wasn't automated to the extent that it is now, of course. When you are in a mass production situation you didn't worry, you had loads of people.

KM: And you could naturally whack the work around between you as well. If there were four of you on a job, three of you would do it and one of you would get a blow, you know, you could put your own respite into the job, and as long as the company got their product at the end of the production line, they were quite happy with that.

Not any more. What they do now is, they revamp a job. In other words, every job has got a time element, and what they do is, they say, where can we save a second? If we can save a second by moving that element from man A to man B, we'll do it, even if it may not make a ha'pence of difference whether it makes that man B's job

Ken Murphy at the demonstration in Luton against closure, January 2001

more complicated and more difficult. He's got the time so he can do it. Then they'll put the element on the other feller, just to save a second.

Now this is where the company came unstuck, because the quality of the job goes down the pan, because they haven't thought it through. I see it all the time, honest to God, to try and save a second on a job, and the thing is, it's not good enough then. It's inbred in them … that they've got to save time.

I see it in audit; they have a team in the hard trim. They call the Area Improvement Team, and all they do is go round trying to shave seconds off jobs. Their job is to take a second off here, a second off there. They don't take it completely out of the job and make you work a second harder. Oh no, they're cuter than that. What they do is, they give that to someone else. Someone's got a second shy on his job, you can have this second, do you understand me? Then they find another second to give to the other feller, to try to make up, at some point in the process. It's like a second off every job and they'll eventually be able to take a man out, half a man out, or put another job element on somebody else.

MW: The safeguards we put in [the V6 Agreement in 1989]: there is no change unless all agreed by all shifts, so it's like a safeguard for us, so no one can play one shift off against the other and say, well, they're doing it. We say, no, we don't do that. We say each shift will look at that job and agree it or disagree it, so if there is a problem on one shift, there will be a problem on the other two shifts, because that's where we used to fall down a little bit, didn't we?

KM: You see, at one time, we talk about the evolution, the way that work's evolved, at one time we had time study, Taylorism, 'We Sell Our Time' in the 1980s, which is like straight time study. From 'We Sell Our Time', we've evolved from that now, to lean. The thing is it didn't suit them to say, well, it takes you a minute to do that job, because that was your little safeguard that, it takes you a minute to do the job so it's going to take me a minute to do the job. And they say, OK, we won't say it takes a minute, we'll just see how long it takes you.

MW: They can time a job now and tell you what the manpower is, before they even build a plant. As John said, it's part of the UAS. It's pretty sophisticated.

KM: Overnight in work, when they did away with the old time study, a whole department went, there was like dozens and dozens of people just lost their jobs overnight.

You talk about outsourcing things: the company started outsourcing, probably before we even realised it, like getting paid wages through the bank and all the rest of it. Again, a whole department just went. We have two people in wages now. We probably had a hundred in there, we've got two now. How long ago was that?

MW: The financial centre now is in Spain, it's in Barcelona. They've got a new system called SAPS. I forget what it means but it's all based on North America and Europe. They've had a few problems with it, you know?

PS: With these changes and the attack we've seen on your power – why have you survived?

MW: Why has Ellesmere Port survived? That's a difficult one, but I'll try to answer it as best I can. I think Ellesmere Port, the investment that went into the new Astra, over £200 million worth of investment went in. We had a car there [Astra] that was selling, and obviously when you look at General Motors when they made the decision to say, which plant are we going to close, I think Ellesmere Port was in the melting pot, as was Luton. And I think one of the factors that Luton was selected to close was because the life cycle of the model they were making was going. Although everything was in situ, obviously within General Motors there was an overcapacity of 350,000 vehicles and they had to take something out, and when they announced that closure, they looked at that Luton plant and I think it was like on the toss of a coin. I think it came down in favour of Ellesmere Port in my view because the Astra was a model that was selling at that particular time and the Vectra was on the way down, and I think there was more scope for developing the Ellesmere Port plant than the Luton plant.

I think they were the ingredients but it was a strategic board decision. I don't think it was a UK decision. Because General Motors have got overcapacity in Europe they wanted to sell the Eisenach plant[3] to Volkswagen. The Volkswagen people didn't buy the plant because it never had room for expansion. But I mean there's a tale in itself. Here's the most efficient plant that has done everything, all the outsourcing, everything. It's the most lean plant with the exception of Poland now – Poland became lean. They would have off loaded that really, so you know that's worth a debate in itself. If I was a worker in Eisenach, I'd say, 'Hang on a minute, we're the most efficient plant in GM but you want to close it down?'

LEAN PRODUCTION

JC: The lean production cycle has evolved now to some extent. You could have a conference on lean production to try and understand it, and the people that would attend are those that live with it every day. Eat, sleep and drink it. We understand it now. We need to know and understand how we combat it, because I think the only way you can combat it is to negotiate, understand it, understand it and minimise the effects that it has on our people, because I don't believe for one minute we can stop the capitalist drive for lean production. If we say no, I think they are clever enough now – and it goes back to what Gary says, they're so sophisticated now and they have global figures. They can use those to decide about how and what to move in terms of product and production. It's nothing to move production of the Astra from Ellesmere Port to Melbourne, it's nothing to move production of the Zafira from Germany to Thailand. It's nothing, they can do it.

GL: So for want of a better expression, we have got to get in bed with them to be ... able to kick them out of it. I don't mean get in bed to go along with it. It's like being in the Labour Party, you've got to be in it to try and change things, rather than being on the outside looking in.

PS: So you have to engage them to change them, you've got to go along but not believe in it?

GL: And then try and fight them from within.

PS: So in that case if you had to sum up lean production, taking account of course of the deterioration in the quality of working life you've described at other times – we can come to that later – over the years what would you say are the three things that characterise it? What would they be?

GL: It's just that, profits, profits, bigger profits and the biggest. That's four! [Laughs]

JC: You mean why lean production …?

PS: Yeah.

GL: For the company, why are they doing it do you mean?

JC: Why lean production? Because there is always gonna be a maximum of a certain model you can sell in the world, and any one company, given the opportunity, wants to maximise the amount of the maximum, if that sounds right. They want to make sure. Fords want to make sure that they've got as big a share of the world auto-motive sales as General Motors have, which gives to Gary's point, which is, the more they sell, the more the return on the dollar they invest, but how can I maximise that? I'm going to build as many cars as possible with as few people as possible. If I've got to move it a hundred times I'll do it if it gives me one more cent on one more dollar.

PS: Even if you've got overcapacity?

JC: If I've got overcapacity, I'll just close it down. Just close it. I'll do away with the capacity or with the knowledge that when the upturn comes I can either increase production there or open a new plant. It's not a problem, because … countries are queuing up outside car manufacturers' headquarters to say, come and build in our country. They are knocking on General Motors' door: 'Will you build another plant in Sao Paulo?'

PAUSE FOR TEA AND COFFEE

PS: Can we continue this theme of lean generally in the plants? Lean production is not just rhetoric, it actually does impact on people in a very practical way.

MW: I think there are a lot of things, a lot of building blocks to lean production. Maybe globalisation in 1992 wasn't so high on the agenda as it is now. What does it mean for us with competition within the actual firm that you work for, whether it be Ford, GM,

Toyota, playing one plant off against the other? If you're making a similar type of model, they judge you on quality performances, man hours per car, things like that ....

They use that rule of thumb to turn round and say, 'Look, you're 28 man hours per car and your sister plant, like for like, is like 20 man hours per car. You're not efficient,' and things like that. So the threat then becomes, 'We're gonna build a replacement model for this model, what are you going to do?' I mean the unions prioritise job security, you know?

PS: So Mick, how would you characterise the elements of lean now?

MW: You're laughing: you're saying you know what they are but how would you articulate them?

PS: Maybe lack of labour standards, which you've mentioned on other occasions, might be one?

MW: Lean production has always been mean: lean and mean. And that's what it exactly is, it's doing more with less. People like to articulate lean production as, 'Oh, it's just the way we do the work now, and all this, that and the other', but they don't look at the human side, the physical side, and all that it brings. You know, repetitive strain injury, stress, because I mean right now because it's such a cut-throat industry, cut-throat competition, now they're saying every car, whether you're working 9 and 3/4 hour shifts or 8 hour shifts, that car's got to be done right first time. And that's the stress.

Because I mean, a person working at 9 o'clock at night or 10 o'clock at night is totally different from a person working at 8 o'clock in the morning. He's a human being and he starts to flag, you know? That's not portrayed in the car; if I want a car I want the same build, the same quality as I got at the beginning of the shift, as I get at the end of the shift.

There's a constant thing all the time, there really is. I don't know how you're going to measure that, stress and things like that, people. You know a lot of people go off sick, absentee levels are rising.

There are all kinds of aspects. And they'll come round and review a car section, and say, 'Can we take any manpower out of that, swap the job round?' And all that, constantly doing it, constantly what they can save, continuous improvement, which is a never-ending demand.

LEAN AND OUTSOURCING

MW: So it's difficult, when you ask, do you oppose it [lean]? I mean the question's got to be asked, how do you oppose it when people are supplying seats, but not only supplying seats to your plant but supplying seats to other plants as well, because they've got that contract with General Motors? If they've got a contract, where does that leave us? Or a component or a commodity that's been outsourced or bought in by another supplier, so you're out – and that business gives them a wrap-around agreement, a handcuff agreement, for seven years to supply that particular part. So they [GM] give them money for R&D and things like that, so that's gone, so therefore where does that leave you?

In an experiment in South America for GM, the actual supplier was making the component, taking it to the line and actually fitting it to the car. You know, I think GM only had inspectors on there, inspecting the work, but it was basically built by suppliers. So that takes you back then, to outsourcing, what's yours and what do you define as core business? Sometimes you think, they will never outsource that, but they do the unthinkable.

GL: Well, you were talking about lighter jobs, and I see the lighter jobs as the prime target for the company for outsourcing. You know like the seats and all that, which are off the line, they seem to be the jobs that the company target to take out. They're easier to take out for someone else to get £5 an hour or something.

Billy Swain (Swagger) and Tony Lewis at the demonstration in Luton against closure, 2001

JC: The lean production in itself is concentrating on core business, isn't it? It's the outsourcing of seats and truck drivers, and anything else they can get away with. I mean we mentioned the CAW before. The Canadians, one of the people we were speaking to, that big guy from Ford; they've just outsourced their door build, and the cockpit assembly. Now you look at the doors and cockpit assembly over in our place and it's about a quarter of general assembly that would be gone. You know we don't lose sight of the fact that over the channel in Antwerp they outsourced all the body shop.

GL: Underbodies.

JC: No, it wasn't Antwerp, was it? They outsourced part of the body shop in Antwerp, gone, completely gone, you know, so their goal for lean production is, one day there will be someone standing on the dock in a shed, and these cars that are built in Thailand or Indonesia or Mexico or Brazil, the English guy or the German guy, the European guy will stand there putting on the Ford badge or the Chrysler badge or the General Motors badge, and that's their goal.

PS: And that's the ultimate value then, the badge?

JC: Of course it is. It doesn't matter who makes it. It's like Nike, that chap Nasser, the famous quote from Jack Nasser, that Ford Motors have got to get out of building cars, we want to be a Nike in the world village of globalisation, where we don't make cars, we sell them. We don't make sports shoes, Nike just sell them, don't they?

JC: The difficulty for us whether it's the 1980s, 1990s or even today, because of the global economy and the concept of a world car, they can put production where the hell they like; it's just a flick of the switch.

To change from paying for it in euros to paying in pesos, whatever it is – and if we say no, we're not having it, the company … can do a number of things. They can say, 'Look, we hear what the trade unions are saying but, we'll implement it anyway.' And they'll implement it over our heads. We can pretend it's not happening and they'll do that anyway.

Or we can say, OK. We understand the realities of life, in this world, in this capitalist world, no matter how much we want to change the capitalist world. We live in a capitalist world. We can't defeat capitalism in isolation, but we can dent it. You know, we can't eat the whole elephant but we can eat a bit at a time. The only way forward – and this is just my view, by the way – you can't, you shouldn't ignore it, and you shouldn't say, no, we're not doing it, because they'll do it anyway. The third option, and it's the only option for me, is, 'OK, what's your proposal? You want to outsource seats? How do we negotiate the outsourcing of seats?' First of all our position is saying, 'They're not going', and in all honesty and being brutal, it's rhetoric. The fact of the matter is, the flavour of the month is lean production, and they are going to outsource as much as they can. How can we as a trade union minimise the effect on the people that are left?

We should negotiate from a position of strength, from a position of equality, with the company who want to make the changes, and nine times out of ten, we'll come out on the right side. We could give you in our own experiences a number of instances where we have said, 'Hold on a minute, we understand. We understand your desire to change. We don't like it, we don't support it, but how can we minimise the effect, in all honesty, on the people we represent?' And we have done that since the 1980s. Part of our V6 Agreement was that philosophy. 'OK, all right, we hear what you are saying. If we say no, you're going to close the plant and switch production to Germany, because that's the nature of the beast, isn't it?' So we negotiate it, but the problem we've got now is, we're being faced with a position where once again, in General Motors that is, they've made a decision in Europe to cut production by something like 300,000 units. And it's the old whipsawing effect: you know, 'What will you give us to keep your plants open?'

So we are not just fighting the company, we're fighting in all honesty our colleagues on the continent. Now I don't pretend to have all the answers. I don't think anyone has all the answers, but all we can do is to learn from our experiences and take it forward that way.

PS: Lean production is more than just outsourcing, OK, but let's just push this issue of outsourcing a bit more. Could we explore just a little the relationship between outsourcing, in terms of the company taking cost out, and the internal features of lean, such as *kaizen*?

JC: Yeah, there was a suggestion about production from someone in Ellesmere Port which saved the company £100,000 per year, so let's look at that one. ... At one time ... that idea stayed in Ellesmere Port, but now because and perhaps with the aid of technology and communications, the fact of life is, if it's a good idea in one place, then it's going to be a good idea in all the other places. So the best values, best practices philosophy comes in, and lean production is a question that's wide and gets wider as we debate it.

PS: So you find cost-cutting measures through the continuous improvement groups at Ellesmere, say, and so they go to all GM plants, and vice versa.

JC: That's it, yes. But there are so many other strands to it: the implications of what that outsourcing means, of what *kaizen* means for outsourcing. And it's not just about outsourcing core business, it's about making the remaining business, for the people who remain building the vehicle, producing more with less, and we're going to get a taste of that next year [when Luton closes[4]]. We're going to get a taste of their desire to build more cars, a lot more cars and with less people. It's not just about outsourcing. Some companies now are looking at insourcing because it's cheaper to insource it. Instead of having quality problems at an outsourced company, a lot of multi-nationals won't tolerate it if there is a bad contractor. Some of them say, 'OK, can we do it better in house? It might cost us a penny more, but can we do it in house?' And some of them are looking at that now, aren't they? ... Fords are looking at it. What can we do? Can we do it better in house or outside?

GL: Yeah, it's gone right round.

JC: Yeah, It's gone full circle, but the fact of the matter is, the one who pays the penalty, whether he works for Ford or Vauxhall, or the first-tier supplier or second-tier supplier, it's going to be us who pay the penalty, it's their goal. Lean production equals greater profit on the dollar.

Demonstration against Luton closure, January 2001

KM: Because like we've took our pain, we've swallowed the pill. It's a lot easier to outsource much of the work, and I mean, what's down the road? Electricians, fitters?

MW: Now I think that sooner or later – and I think sooner – they're gonna look at that. I mean there are little bits now, stacker truck maintenance: that's gone, you know. All the big installation work all gets done by contractors. By stealth they're doing it.

KM: What they've done, they've done it cleverly, I think. What they've done is, they've gone round what I used to call the hidey holes, all the little nooks and crannies. For example the battery bays, they don't have them any more. They have Calor, all the trucks are Calor now. There is no more maintenance on the trucks, they are all leased trucks, and the maintenance is going to get done by whoever leases them.

MW: All those forklift trucks, a lot of them are going to go.

KM: These days, what's come to fruition is, although you could see it to some extent in the early days, I think you can see it clearly now, the control that the company wants over all of its suppliers. It never had that control when it was internal.

Take the seats, for argument's sake; they never had the control that they wanted over them. I've seen that now with all the Lear [supplier] stuff that comes in, they just send it back; we're not paying you, end of story, if you're a supplier we're not paying you.

They have the supplier in and they all turn him over, you know what I mean? And they all do the supplier; publicly humiliate them, in order to get what they want out of them.

MW: They're gonna stop that. There is legislation coming in, where they've got to pay for goods delivered. You've had holes in this thing, where people go bankrupt, because he won't pay me.

KM: Yeah, so what's the next logical step? They won't deliver it to the plant; they'll deliver it to the logistics company that's taken over. It's down to them then, so then it's easy to get round, that's the next logical step for them, isn't it?

For me that's what I thought they were going to do with Lear. I thought Lear was going to be like the stop before the plant. Where everything would get delivered and they'd say, everything that's been delivered here is in perfect order, and now we're sending it to you. They're then responsible for the safe delivery of everything, and they'd just dolly it all up and send it on to us then.

MW: That's right, that's the concept, but you know and I know, you're always gonna get some problems, aren't you?

KM: Oh yeah, of course. Yeah, you're still gonna have them …. I hope so, it's my job. [Laughs]

JC: Can we bring in Tony [Lewis] here? Tony works for Commando [a contractor to GM-Vauxhall].

TL: The thing is, if I can give you this example recently. If Vauxhall have got a major dispute involving a strike, because we are contractors, there's a contract that if we go out, the firm is imposed with a hefty fine, a really hefty fine.

So last time for example with the Luton issue, we had a half-day dispute for Luton. We were actually told by the union that we couldn't support them, even though we wanted to support them. We couldn't support them. What you actually got was a lot of people … phoned in sick or what have you.

PS: Like the big sicky at British Airways?

TL: Yeah, but we were actually told, it's down to the individual's choice …. Some of us actually went to the gate and because they had pickets on it was our choice to turn round then, and go back, and that was more or less what happened. We were actually told by the union official, 'No, you can't come out in dispute or whatever.'

PS: So people actually went up to the gate and went back? What was the attitude of Commando then?

TL: The attitude of Commando management, because they don't want any dispute with us or with the union, should I say. They just accepted it, they just accepted the fact that Mick would go back to Mr Vauxhall and say, 'We told the lads to come in; we didn't say they could go out.'

PS: So in that case did Vauxhall fine them?

TL: No, they didn't fine them because we'd actually – well, we'd gone to the gate. We just wouldn't cross the picket, so it was individual choice. But because we turned around we lost a day's pay.

But to be fair the only reason the T&G didn't call us out was the fine. They didn't want to put the firm in jeopardy, you know? The amount of fine might actually put the firm out of business. We're in the game of keeping jobs. As I told you before, we've got very good support from the union in Vauxhall as contractors. We actually use, we are part of their stewards' body, we are invited to all their meetings. So instead of just being isolated as a contractor and on our own, we've actually got the backing of the T&G in Vauxhalls, which gives us a lot more strength. But I know on other sites they haven't got it, which is reflected in our wages.

UNION, SHOP STEWARDS AND LEAN: CAPTURING HEARTS AND MINDS

JC: The desire for Vauxhall certainly was to replace the shop steward by the team leader, which never worked, because we made sure it didn't. So they move on to the next level. We break the teams down to smaller independent units if we can, so we create this feeling of 'fourness' or 'fiveness' together, you know. And it's like a geographical line there, an imaginary line where that's another team, cause we've had it, haven't we?

The air of competition, the battle for hearts and minds, we've won that, it's a day on, day on battle.

GL: And it's going to come back, it definitely will, as you said there with the smaller teams. You've also got it – it's not just a case of team on team, it's within the team especially if, as John says there are eight people and they know it's going to split down to four. The competition then is to be the next team leader. 'Oh, I can do that', and the next thing they are coming in all smartly dressed. They're doing all they can so they can be the next team leader. It gets that ambition going as well within the team.

Demonstration against Luton closure, January 2001

Left to right, Davy Mac, Terry Griffin and John Fetherston at the demonstration against Luton closure, January 2001

JC: And you find people doing each other in, don't you? And that's another strand of lean production, what they'll use. Because no one is more knowledgeable than the feller on the job, we'll use his expertise to make this particular area more lean.

PS: That's the idea, but how much does that happen?

JC: It happens. Yeah, of course!

PS: What's the ideology behind it?

JC: The ideology? Well there's a book I read some time ago, *Jointness at GM* [Leary and Menaker nd]. Jointness was based on the incestuous relationship between the UAW [United Auto Workers] and General Motors, where for example Saginaw steering, when they send the steering racks out, it hasn't just got GM on the box, it's got UAW stamped on it. That was one of the examples they used for *Jointness at GM*. That's the trouble. If the unions buy into it feels OK for the guys on the shop floor to do it too, so they think it's fine to compete to be team leader and that. That's the hope anyway from management and unions committed to jointness. ... I'm loath to say the company don't have their successes because they do, they do, but in the battle for hearts and minds, if that's what we're talking about,

I think we win more than we lose. I mean only a fool would say we don't lose, but we win more than we lose. I believe the majority of people still identify themselves in the first instance with the trade union [more] than they do with the company.

PS: But why, John?

JC: Why? Because we care more about them than the company. People do identify with us first because there is also a belief – and I'm not just saying this, I'm saying this because this is true – we're good at what we do in Vauxhalls. We really are, and it comes home to people when they go outside and hear and understand the experiences that they have. I'll give you an example. I used to bring a lad to work and his son worked in a small woodyard in Liverpool, and he was late three times – he wasn't off, he was late three times – and they terminated him. Now this lad, who was a member of a trade union but not a trade unionist, all of a sudden realised, hang on, it wouldn't happen in Vauxhall Motors. Why wouldn't it happen in Vauxhall Motors? We must have a strong trade union. That's just one example of the realisation, when it dawns on people. It just underlines their belief that the best friend that they have got is the shop steward. The only bulwark if you like to the drive, the company's ever increasing drive to get more with less, is the shop steward, and I think that people are clever enough to understand that we can't win everything, but we'll win more than we'll lose.

PS: Can you give examples of that? Where you have won something significant? It might be a little detail, but significant in the company's terms. Or lost something, for example?

GL: It doesn't matter how minute?

PS: It's often the minute things that matter.

GL: What we've got at the moment, I think extended sick pay is one. I think that it's happening every day, where people have got to write a letter in and they're getting knocked back. That's where it comes to the people on the sick. They get so much sick pay and to get it extended they have to write a letter in, and it's just been, the last – I don't know, the last ten years – a formality. They write the letter in and the clerk pays it out, he'll get another 26 weeks, he'll pay it out. In just the last six weeks or so it's been the personnel manager saying, 'Hey, you know all these cutbacks? Everything comes through me.' But I know of about five who've rung our office after being knocked back, and have all been paid out in the end. One of them got £1,000. And that's it – people come up and say thanks very much.

PS: And that spreads?

GL: There are other examples recently, yeah.

JC: We have floating vacations, and we have this thing where it's only two per shift per section, and the foremen stick rigidly to that, and if you're the third one, me old mate, then you haven't got a chance. Until they speak to the shop steward, and then again, not every time but a lot of the time, we win the arguments and here's the reason why. He's got a genuine problem. He has a floating vacation and he gets it, and that's just run of the mill stuff to a shop steward. To the guy it's a major victory, and again it's back to the hearts and minds. It is a fact of life that we should expose our victories. We should say, 'Hang on, this is a result!' And we shouldn't be afraid of that.

GL: You'll find that everyone else knows about it on that section. They all know that he's battling for that lieu day, but you'll get people giving him stick: 'Aye, you haven't got your lieu day!' Next thing he comes back out of the office and goes, 'I've got it.' And they all know who got it for him; it breeds, as you said before.

JC: The company's agent on the section, the supervisor, has said, 'You're not having it, mate. I'm telling you you're not having it.' Then he comes along and he's got it. Hallelujah, the magic wand's come out.

PS: Why?

JC: Why? Because we're professional trade unionists.

PS: But you could say they were like that at Luton as well? The question implied then is, why keep Ellesmere Port open?

JC: Why keep us open? And why close Luton down? That is the question, isn't it? Perhaps it's because it's economically better. The reason Luton shut was in my opinion 50 per cent economical and 50 per cent political. I don't believe for one minute, if Ford hadn't closed Dagenham down Luton would have remained open on one shift.

PS: You think it would have stayed open?

JC: Yes, I believe Luton could have stayed open if there had been a stronger fight at Dagenham, and they'd have kept some semblance of car assembly at Dagenham.

Vauxhall, General Motors, looked at Ford. They've put their toe in the water; they never lost one car to sales in the UK, during all the furore at Dagenham, their sales stayed almost the same as what they were. The trade unions went to people, and the people who were getting finished up voted to accept the sack. It was turkeys voting for Christmas.

Vauxhalls through General Motors saw that and thought, hang

on, the political fear that we've got has been taken away now by the reaction from the Dagenham plant. The financial problem is still with us, Put them both together and what do we need to do? We'll close a plant down, and the plant that they chose was Luton, and it was purely and simply – and again this is only my view – if the model cycle had been the other way round, it would have been Ellesmere Port. That's my view.

PS: Despite the combativeness?

GL: Even so. Model cycle comes into it a lot. I honestly think that at Ellesmere Port they'd have kicked up a lot more stick, to put it nicely, if they'd tried to close it. Unemployment is high and all that, that's the political side of it, the north-west's high unemployment. You've also got that Nick Reilly [Chair of Vauxhall] – he was our plant manager.

PS: So that's another element of how management is more strategic in redundancies as well.

GL: You see, when they open redundancies, I don't know how many times, people say to us like, you should be negotiating to get it higher, but every time they put something down, there's queues around the block.

JC: Historically, that is so spot on. It's unbelievable. I can remember us having mass meetings about separation programmes, standing on the backs of wagons saying, 'Don't go, don't go! Give us the chance to negotiate a better deal.'

GL: 1983 and 1985.

JC: I remember it, as Gary says; the queues were round the block to sign up, because people wanted the less work-intensive work that there still was in the 1980s. People still wanted to get out of the car plant, and if there was a separation programme tomorrow at Ellesmere Port we'd have the same problem in preventing people from going.[5] So everywhere is bad now, but car work has got harder too!

GL: Even of people who have gone, I know two who have never worked since.

PS: Really?

GL: You could get jobs then, but not as well paid as what car plants are.

PS: And you could get jobs now?

GL: Yeah, stacking shelves and things like that.

PS: But the money ....

GL: Yeah. There are people who've gone, I spoke to them and they've said it's the worse thing they've ever done. And they've thought , 'Oh, I've got a good job on £4.80 per hour and I'm work-ing 42 hours per week. Gotta work 42 hours and I've gotta work overtime just to make a living wage. Sorry I ever left Vauxhalls.'

PS: So what about the future? How do you see the future developing, for lean and for trade unions?

GL: It comes back to basic stuff; it always does come back to basic stuff, where you win hearts and minds of people on the shopfloor.

JC: That means we fight around things like team leaders and teams, but you'll get more people battling to be the team leader, and that affects us. The management footsoldiers. Provided those footsoldiers are our footsoldiers, if you know what I mean. A lot of team leaders[6] now are still our team leaders, if you know what I mean? They're our people, in their own minds, and they've got this path they want to go down – and I could name half a dozen, you know, without thinking.

But the most important person in the battle for hearts and minds, how we combat lean production as it evolves, is the shop steward. It really, really is, and I know we said this, but you can't say it too much. We could have the

Demonstration against Luton closure, January 2001

best negotiator in the world, negotiating with the president of General Motors, but the most important person in how things are going to evolve and change is the shop steward.

How is capitalism going to evolve? I mean, I thought Karl Marx had it right, but I'm not that sure now.

PS: Oh, you pessimist!

JC: I honestly don't know. We don't know how things are going to go until afterwards, do we? The problem for us is, instead of pushing it, we're reacting, aren't we? We're reacting to events, or when they're about to happen – very late.

GL: We need to be proactive rather that reactive, although we do try.

JC: When for example they are designing the next car, we should have a role to play in how that car, the design of the car is put into practice, the build-ability if you like.

PS: That's obviously a crucial aspect, and getting into questions of how to control resources and planning, which impacts on staffing levels, for example. But then that's also about shopfloor strength. Can you say something about steward numbers and density, because that's obviously vital in terms of holding the line?

JC: We've actually got more stewards now in terms of coverage. We had an argument recently in the trim, where we've got four legs that make up the general assembly, but that's split into six sections. The company's desire was to move from six sections to four legs, and a corresponding reduction of shop stewards. We argued against it and won. ...

PS: How do you communicate? Through briefings then, word of mouth? How often would you have mass meetings? Is that normally around big issues?

GL: The stewards' meetings are every month, yeah. What happens is after stewards' meetings, all the stewards report back. That's where you keep your contact.

PS: How much time does the company give? Is that done in lunch break or ...?

GL: Tea break. Sometimes it runs over and we have a bit of a battle over that. It comes back again to the strength of the union. They'll [management will] ring up and say, 'Hey, they ran over their five minutes.' You'll tell them not to do it again and that's it. Now and again it goes a bit naughty, but most of the time it's done within tea breaks. But plenty of people would be active but they wouldn't, there's quite a lot who wouldn't like to be a steward. Sometimes this is because they've got to get up and speak in front of people, which 99 per cent of people don't like, and that's the only thing holding them back. You go and have a little conversation one to one with them, and a lot of them know more than you, they're really, really good. They're really active. You've got quite a lot of them in our place, to help you; they're the footsoldiers on your section.

PS: This raises another question about the basis of mobilising people, of your collectivism. How does it compare now with the past?

KM: In the old days – God blimey, I'm only 47 years of age. I'm not talking a hundred years ago, I'm talking about relatively recently in our industrial history – we used to have 40 on a section together. All have our tea breaks together, dinner together, all go out on the ale together, all go to each other's houses, you know? Weddings and so on – every section was like a community, they knew each other and they'd live in each other's pockets. Not any more. In the new body shop a feller will be working on his own. He may know one feller, he may talk to two people each day, because he's working in like what you call cells. So he's not going to have it like in the old days, where we used to get together and have a little camaraderie. All that's gone, that won't happen. It can't happen, because the manufacturing process doesn't lend itself to that. In the past it did. For example stewards' meetings: you'd go back from a shop stewards' meeting for a report back, there was 30 men. Not any more. He's gotta go round the cells now, one at a time.

PS: People would argue that's why it's impossible to create solidarity and trade union organisation in lean production companies.

KM: Yeah, but at the bottom of people's minds is the idea that they must belong to an organisation that is there to protect their interests, and people know that. Even though they might complain and moan and have a whinge, they know full well that in order to have their interests protected … they need to belong to an organisation that works on their behalf collectively. They know that, even people who may be right-wing in their views. People who go out and vote for the Tories every election for argument's sake, they still want to be in the union, because they want the protection that the union offers them.

PS: Is the union still able to get about and do the business though?

MW: Oh yes, I mean you've got a generation of people coming up out of the Thatcher era, and that's made a big, a major problem in the plant.

KM: Some of them had never worked in an organised workplace ever, never been in a union. And we won stuff for them like we said.

MW: They'd phone up and say, 'We get this, we get that sort of thing' – it was unbelievable.

KM: In some ways it spoilt them a bit because a lot of what we enjoy at work didn't just fall out of the sky; it was struggled for over a number of years …. Little things like a bit of respect, respect off the foreman, the manager, you earn that, but that takes a long period of time. Like a lot of them thought you could get that right away, this is how it is.

A lot of lads have come around, by the way. One or two decent people have floated to the top, but again it's for the same reason, because you are talking about people who were working in ware-houses, working in supermarkets, working on buildings on the lump. They'd never been in the union; never saw the need for it.

MW: Back to security: they want a job in Vauxhalls, because they see that as a secure job, a decent standard of living, a decent pension and all that.

KM: What they see is a three-bedroomed semi-detached, two weeks in Marbella and a car. That's it, and you can't blame them for that.

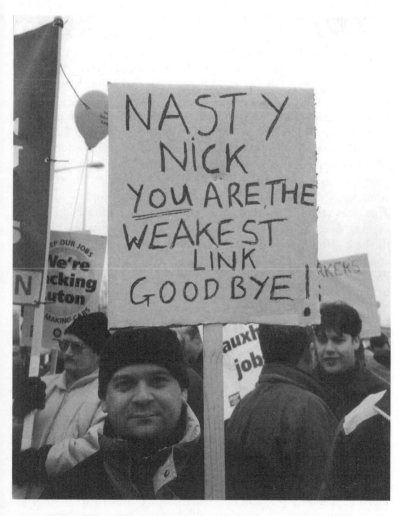

Demonstration against Luton closure, January 2001

PS: What do you think are the two or three big problems confronting union organisation today? In one respect your sense of doom that you often conveyed to me in the past hasn't been completely borne out. Lean's here and you're still around too.

KM: People have got to know that there is something there for them, that they can get something out of it. If you're gonna be a member of a union, you're buying a service. You're saying, I want to belong to your organisation because you're gonna provide me with this, this, this and this. Negotiating, accidents at work, wages and conditions, all the basic stuff, but people have got to know that. And it can be more than that. I mean a lot of the time, and Mick will tell you better than me, people decide to join the union through struggle, because they're in dispute or they're having a problem at work, not because they think it's the right thing to do, but because they are under pressure; and that's one of the reasons that forces them to join the union.

MW: When we had a shop stewards' conference in our region, the first one we believe in the country, people were saying 'Look, we don't want services, we don't want cheap mortgages, we don't want cheap insurance, discounts – we want representation.' They want people to go in there and negotiate right, whether it's for improved conditions, representation in discipline cases, and things like that. That was stark. That was really coming to the fore. People were saying, 'Aye, if I want insurance, I'll go to the Prudential; I'll go to the best. What I want the union to do is represent me, improve my conditions, get me more money, whatever.'

PS: Insurance companies look at problems, unions make things better.

MW: That's right. By the way, that is exactly the view that we hold.

KM: I was just saying to Paul, if you look around at the little places, since 1991 who embraced everything – I wouldn't say capitulate, that's not the right word – people who embraced what the company were offering, the likes of Fords, Cowley and Longbridge and places like that. They had a vibrant organisation, not as vibrant as we were; certainly they had well-organised organisations though. Ford at Halewood, their convener was a General Executive member. They had fellers on the National Trade Group Committee, and fellers on the Regional Committee. As soon as they embraced that, it all waned. It all started to go downhill for them. The same is true of Cowley. Just talking about 'John' at Cowley, I remember going to a meeting around 1991, and they were really hostile to what we were doing with the V6 Agreement. All I was saying was, 'Hang on, you've got to look ahead. You can't say, this is how it should be and have all your principles, you know? It's not going to be a Socialist democracy tomorrow, because it's not going to happen. You know what I mean? It's not going to happen.'

PS: It's not a good idea then? [Laughs]

KM: The idea is superb! You've gotta deal with the reality if you're a convener in a car plant and you've got, 4,000, 5,000 workers. That's your priority rather than your own personal politics. OK, your politics may have a say in that, but you're talking about people's livelihoods. That's what you've got to protect as best you can, as well as protecting your organisation that negotiates their wages and conditions. Cowley is a perfect example, they just capitulated and now they're blaming Tony Woodley for them capitulating in 1992. That's exactly what happened. If they'd ... had a structured and reasoned shop stewards' committee up till the present day, I'm not saying what happened wouldn't have happened, but they would've had a better idea of how it happened. [See Chapters 3 and 6.]

MW: What you said before, Paul, ... about lean production and all that. The easiest target to blame for lean production is the union. As soon as a plant closes or there's a threat of closure, it's 'What do we do to prevent closure? We'll do all the things that the company wanted to get in and couldn't get in.' Like Dagenham. Dagenham would've done anything to retain car assembly, Halewood did exactly the same. There's the threat, so going back to the point we made before, our priorities are job security.

PS: Does that mean you'd do anything as well?

MW: What you can do is, you can try and get a happy medium, get as much respite off the job as you possibly can, or argue your manning levels, or contingencies, like contingency time – more time off, holidays, shorter working week and things like that, you can do all that.

Once you've accepted that you can get on with it, but we've got to keep our eye on the likes of GM Europe. Because just say they come to us and say, 'Look, we've got half a billion pounds in investment and only one plant is going to get it. If you don't produce the quality and the volumes, don't waste my time.' What do we do? To turn the question to you, what do you do?

It's the whipsawing thing, it's there, so what you do is, you try and be as competitive as you can, in terms of safeguarding your plant. Some things – at this moment in time, we've got a problem with the company, we can see a head-to-head coming. They're saying, 'We want to outsource certain things.' We're saying, 'OK, fair enough, the seats are going,' but we knew that five years ago. I said to the workforce five years ago, that's gonna go, because they got out of the business. They got rid of all the design engineers, all the people connected with designing seats and all that, flogged it to Lear or Johnson Controls or whatever. They're gonna get out right, so now they want to say to us, 'Everyone's got a job, but they're all going on the conveyor.' The next thing is, they want to get rid of the forklift truck drivers. So that's the logic, right? We're saying, 'No, we're not having it.'

PS: How can you say no? How can you make sure that sticks? Can you say, 'We'll take action'? Will they say, 'Well, do it and we'll close you down'?

MW: It depends on the company and how badly they want it. If we turn round and draw a line in the sand and say, 'Look that's as far as you've gone, and you're not going to get any more', and they say, 'Look, we don't think we're gonna win it.' They can either back off or think they're gonna win it and persevere. Go to your members and say, 'We're not prepared to accept this and we want your support. Now you can give the support or if you don't, you let the

Demonstration against Luton closure, January 2001

company get on with it.' There are certain things, you'd say, we're not prepared to accept. Other things they can have. Logic tells you that – you know?

PS: So that's one crucial way in terms of actually confronting lean. And you're combining this with issues around age and dealing with the health and safety issues and questions of equity.

MW: If you look at Toyota, Toyota is starting to insource certain things back to keep control of that component. On the Toyota model, if you've got an older workforce they'll insource them into those component firms. What we said, 'We want – we would like to see our people with no loss of pension rights, no loss of money, if they get to an age where they can't physically do a job for GM, go to a contracting firm, and work for that contracting firm and carry on working there.' But what GM says is, once they go there, they are not our employees. We've got to make that happen. I think that is one of the things that we've got to do. Otherwise, fellers won't be able to physically work with their hands, can't do it, so we've got to make it a little bit more easier. I mean, when you say stackers, it's an easy job, you can jump on a truck and deliver and all that, it's a pretty easy job.

KM: It's not physically taxing.

MW: So the next thing, if that job goes, people will say, 'Hang on, I've got my name down for that! It means I can never get off the conveyer [assembly line].' I mean if all the other jobs have gone and there are no other jobs left for you to do, I know that once I'm on that job, I'm there for life. So what we've got to do as unions, I believe, if you've got like supplier parks around a particular manu-facturing plant, we've got to look at that and say, 'Hang on a minute, why can't our people do that job?' Sooner or later we've got to address ourselves to that.

PS: So the agenda has to be around, not just – what you're saying there, if I interpret it right – just defending conditions, but reinterpret-ing what those conditions are, which is different from the traditional approach?

Maybe this is where we can think about wrapping it up?

MW: Yeah, but just to add there, it's tied into that, about reinterpreting things. There's going to be a time when everything that can be, will be outsourced. We've got an agreement that it's incumbent upon the company to look after its restricted people, and medically unfit people. So we just say, 'Hey, that's an agreement, you've got to find him a job. We're not finding him a job, *you* find him a job.' Unless they insource work they can't do it. To find a job for eight hours, five days a week, the company are going to be snookered, they're going to have to make them redundant and bring other people in. So as unions we've got to explore other avenues, right, to make work available to our members, so they can do a job that's conducive. If they've got RSI, carpal tunnel syndrome and that, what we're saying now to the company is, in the last agreement that we had, we want insourcing. But obviously that's not finding favour with the company, although they understand what we're saying, you know? It's up to us to keep pushing to make it hard for the company for the reason that people are going to say, 'Have I got to go to work for the rest of my life on this bloody job?' That's what they're going to say, aren't they?

So I don't think the unions are staying still. It's finding the will with the company to turn round and say, 'OK then, too old to do it.' They do it in Japan. Right, they farmed them out to component supply, but they farmed them out on less wages and conditions. Now that wouldn't be acceptable to us because that has a big impact on your pension – you know, your earnings and all that. But that's what we work on.

So therefore it comes back to our priority, which is job security. Now you can turn round and say, in the early years we used to say, we want a job but not at any cost. And that was a good principle to stand by, but you know events overtake you. I mean, they can make the same model wherever – it's globalisation. You want to take the new model, of course you do, but then it's about keeping everything together. But on your terms if and where you can.

Comments from Ken Murphy, Vauxhall-GM (Ellesmere Port)

Over the last 28 years I have seen many changes in the workplace, a steady drift from Measured Day Work to 'lean production'. I would say it is difficult to accurately assess how the transition has occurred, because I believe that a lot of what has happened has been ad hoc and a desire to change for change's sake. There has however been some structure to the way management has implemented its agenda. For example we now have within General Motors what is called the Global Manufacturing System. This has allowed them to cherry-pick things that work for them – all the good things. This comes out of the global standardisation programme. Each plant is benchmarked against each other and all systems and procedures are the same, whether in the United States or in Germany.

That is to say, it is a way to shrink the direct workforce and contract out as much as possible, aligned with the new 'modular build', and GM will be competing realistically with its rivals, namely the Japanese rivals like Toyota. For us in Ellesmere Port, the process of change has been a constant one, and the thrust and pain has been felt by production workers, not in one go, but in a steady drip, a bite at a time. The first ten years I worked at Vauxhall were at a time when the company were still an offshoot of Vauxhall Luton and never really had a European identity, or at least this was the impression that I had. We did set up many links with trade unionists in Germany and Belgium, from our sister plants at Bochum and Antwerp. In the main the links were with trade unionists who were isolated by the works councils, but they were important links.

It would be fair to say that relations between Ellesmere Port and Luton were strained at this time as well, mainly because of the failure of the unions in Luton to support the wage dispute of 1979. I am making the point about these links because I feel there was not enough emphasis on strengthening what we had. There was a tendency to fight well in the plant, but not being able to take anyone with us. The V6 Agreement is a good example of this. The unions at Vauxhall were in some quarters scoffed at for their decision to try to negotiate a workable and acceptable agreement. What happened was that we did negotiate a new agreement, one that encompassed a lot of what the company was trying to achieve, mainly a switch to teamwork and teams, with team leaders taking a more positive role. The reality of this is that things carried on much as before and the team revolution never actually took place. Many years later however, the reverse is true: a reduction in the amount of white-collar supervisors and a different role for the team leaders, one which now takes in a lot of what the supervisors did.

When I first started in Vauxhall, everyone clocked in and out, morning, lunch, afternoon, etcetera. We now do not use clock cards and haven't for over 15 years, the result being the eradication of a whole department overnight. The responsibility then went to the supervisor, who took control of attendance directly. This will be the next package for the team leaders in my opinion: it will not be long before they are in control of attendance.

Another huge move was the eradication of the works study department and with it the end of another department, but more importantly the end of Measured Day Work as we knew it. While, from a blue-collar perspective, we feel threatened and fear for our livelihoods at each change at the helm, the white-collar workers have been most affected by the changes: that is, in terms of how many work here in relation to how many blue-collar workers there now are. I'm sure that in some workplaces, teamwork was something that took off and there were some benefits for workers. But in a car plant, this is nigh on impossible. The pace of work and the relentless push for more with less is mind-blowing. Couple this with short work breaks with less opportunity to interact with workmates, and the result is that workers feel less valued by the system, not more, as the propaganda might suggest.

I think the most noticeable tactic of GM over the years has been its relentless whipsawing (playing one plant off against another). For us this was most noticeable before the Luton plant was closed. We were told during wage negotiations that the only way to save the plant was to accept a pay deal that was to say the least not up to scratch. Given the past history of the two plants there were a lot of people unhappy at this, who thought that Luton was going to close whatever we did during wage negotiations. History shows of course that the company had every intention of closing Luton down, and used this as way of keeping the wage deal down to an acceptable level. This hardened a lot of people, and I would think that any similar threats in the future would be met with disdain, but who knows? Stranger things have happened.

The German workforce were told, as were the Swedish workforce, that one plant would have to close to make the business viable. The unions then accepted a catalogue of changes to work practices that would have been completely unacceptable at any previous time. Again history shows that not one plant did close in Germany or indeed in Sweden, and the company achieved all of its objectives with little loss of production. So the whipsawing goes on, and until we have a cohesive and more importantly trustworthy works council, it will go on for some time to come.

Another major innovation by the company has been its relentless push for independent parts suppliers. In the past this was mainly small parts and nuts and bolts. This then became panel pressings, and more latterly seats and cockpit manufacture. While this may look like a logical progression, its only objective was to force down the cost of the product by outsourcing. This of course meant lower wages and also a way of directly influencing the quality of the product. For example, the company would only pay for good parts and all scrap cost would then be borne by the supplier. It is now even more difficult for suppliers. They are measured by a matrix known as

Global Quality Tracking Systems (GQTS), an Internet-based system that is used by all GM plants worldwide. When there are parts from a supplier that are no good, a defect is entered in the system, so for example if there were ten bad parts from a supplier, this would form part of a calculation that penalised the supplier. This is the reason we have very few bad parts from suppliers, as the calculation is later used in the process of allotting contracts to suppliers. I know this isn't explained too well, but it is a bit difficult to say it in a few words as this is a major part of its supplier strategy.

The peaks and troughs of the industry, how many cars they sell, was in the past dealt with by an agreement whereby we were paid for any layoffs. This has been dismantled and replaced with a working time agreement, whereby we are laid off for say an eight-hour shift. Then we will work back the time at half an hour per shift when volume is needed. This as well as temporary labour has pushed the unions into a no-win fight with the company. On the one hand we object to temporary labour and would push hard for permanent labour, but the company could simply go public and announce that the unions were blocking jobs for people who wanted them.

I have noticed that many of the new people we have had are very much of a different generation, not just in terms of age, but in terms of what they expect from an employer. In a flash, many of the current or later new employees would accept performance-related pay, because they have come to expect this in modern industry.

I have felt that over the years, much of what has transpired here in Ellesmere Port has been done with the full understanding of what the company was about, and I still feel this is true today. We know that the company want to build all of its cars and vans all over the globe in exactly the same way, with standardised everything, not just management structures and procedures, but also in the engineering of its parts. The aim is to produce several models on the same platform, with only differing outer panels and some changes to suit different countries. One cost for technical development, but also parts that can be sourced from single global suppliers, who would have their own TDC departments and subsequently absorb these costs, the end result being the lean monster that the company has pursued for the past 15 or so years. I say 15 or so, even though this is probably where the company always wanted to be, but I think that they have only realised the potential in the past 15 years, since they have been pushed by the Japanese car plants and their system of manufacture. Where it will all end is anyone's guess, but it will not be for the betterment of the workforce, here or anywhere else in the world, but for the pursuit of profit at any price.

There is an air of resignation at the moment, where 900 people have elected to either retire or take a severance package. Retirement is a good option providing that one has the years in and has paid into the voluntary contributions. Even with my 28 years, and of course my young age, I never felt that I could afford to take any sort of retirement package, and I will be here till the place closes. But this is the new way of downsizing the workforce and replacing it with temporary workers: retire people with their own money and take on a new starter! Yes, daft as it sounds, from the company's point of view this makes perfect financial logic. If I were to retire and was replaced at a later date, the savings are quite extraordinary. No floating vacations (I have eight days that I can take over and above my holidays) and no pension. Less per hour, a short-term contract to fit in with peaks and troughs of the industry, not to mention modular build and more outside contractors, minimum wage and so on. The list goes on. The floating vacations are something the company has problems with. Of course only service people have them, starting at five years with from three days to a maximum of eight. So if 100 workers have eight days, then 800 absent workers need to be relieved for a day! From the point of view of the workers, things are on a downward slope and people are dispirited; from the point of view of the company, things are looking rosy and the achievement of 900 volunteers is a boost to our standing!

It is difficult to look back and try to reflect on how things might have been if we had done things any differently, but I am sure that we have done everything humanly possible to cushion the effects of lean on the workers at Ellesmere Port, although there are a lot of people who are working on the track that would not agree with this, not because it isn't true, but because they are bearing the full brunt of all the changes that the company has thrown at them. I think that people have semi-resigned themselves to the fact that Ellesmere Port will be like the Polish plant within the next five years: the only people that work for GM are the direct workforce, everyone else is a contractor. So in the short term there is a future for us here I believe, but in the long term, the way that GM operates and moves its options from country to country and contractor to contractor, who knows. This is the area that I believe that we should be concentrating on. If we can organise the suppliers in a realistic way, then the pendulum could very well swing closer to the middle. This is an area where I know the union is concentrating some resources, but in comparison to what the employers are doing, it is a drop in the ocean. If we can help to push up the wages and conditions of the supplier workers, then the economic argument to shift production is not there. This would also strengthen the hand of the direct workforce in the plant because one of the threats would have been removed.

I have alluded to the fact that the European Works Council (EWC) is a bit weak as it stands; they might disagree. This is an area that could be worked on, but not just at the level of direct representatives. There should be a better understanding on the shop floor of what the EWC stands for and what it does, who is on it and who they represent. Workers need to know that a German car worker is no different and is under the same threats as we are. After all as far as the Bochum worker is concerned, GM wants to close a plant. Will it be Bochum, Ellesmere Port or Antwerp!

A strategy for the unions must encompass all of the players in some way. It's a big ask, but it is in my opinion the way forward.

Comments from John Cooper, deputy convener, Ellesmere Port

I have been active in both the trade union and labour movement for the past 32 years, and started in Vauxhalls in 1967. I joined the Communist Party of Great Britain in 1970 and was elected as a shop steward in the same year. The Vauxhall plant in the 1970s was and still is the biggest employer in the area, but labour relations were typical of the era, and we moved from one dispute to the next.

The workforce was continually sent home without pay at all hours of the day and night if a dispute broke out anywhere in the plant, and for any given reason. This practice by the company resulted in a dispute in the mid-1970s for a guaranteed shift agreement. It was a dispute that the trade unions won, and an agreement that gave the membership the knowledge that they would never again be sent home without pay for any reason outside of their control. The consequences of the guaranteed shift agreement were that Vauxhalls became less keen to send our members home as they would have been sent home on full pay for the remainder of their shift.

Labour relations within the plant continued in a similar vein as we moved towards the end of the decade. The 1979 Wage and Conditions Claim, although justified, was resisted by the company and resulted in a long and bitter dispute. The dispute ran for eleven weeks and only ended with the realisation by both the union leadership and more importantly our members that it was unwinnable. The result of the dispute was a disaster for the trade unions, for on the return to work the company issued a 'Return to Work' document that for a number of years gave them the whip hand in all matters of working life for our members.

As we moved into the 1980s and with a change of leadership of the trade unions, labour relations improved from a trade union perspective, but the auto industry was in decline. We suffered a number of redundancies and moved from two-shift working to a one-shift setting.

In 1983 the plant returned to two-shift working as a result of the very successful 'S' car campaign organised by the TGWU. The main thrust of the campaign was to bring the production of the new Corsa to the United Kingdom. Although the Corsa was never to be built in the United Kingdom the success of the campaign ensured that the plant returned to two-shift production. There are many issues that will be of concern to our members in the coming months and years: never forget, the nature of the beast (capitalism) is always to seek more and more from our members for less and less reward.

The problems facing us today, including exit costs, globalisation and outsourcing, need our urgent attention, for if multinational companies are allowed to move across national borders or from continent to continent in the search for higher profits and cheaper labour, all workers from whatever nation will be the losers.

Comments from Gary Lindsay, former Safety Committee chairman

I started at Vauxhall in March 1978 as a junior operator, as a naïve but canny 16-year-old. Before I even started I came into contact with the TGWU. The reason was that I was having difficulty over passing my medical because of a problem with my left eye. This was sorted out when my father got the TGWU involved. Their intervention definitely helped me get a start at Vauxhall, and that is something that will always stay with me.

Ironically when I started as a junior operator on the engine line I had to join the AUEW because of a spheres of influence agreement that was in force at the time. I had two good years on the engine line, but in 1980 I had to move to another job in another part of the plant because the engine line was being run down. The last in, first out rule was applied, so I packed all my worldly goods and moved over to the mad house (vehicle assembly) in another block.

The spheres of influence rule applied again and so it came to pass that I joined the great TGWU. I was put into the body shop on the underbody line. This line was full of young lads – a far cry from the engine line which was predominantly middle-aged men. I fitted in right away. There were about 40 people on this line all working in very close proximity, so you can imagine the pranks and banter that went on there. The work was heavy, pulling the components from one workstation to the next and then spot welding with guns that were as big as me. But the shifts passed quite well because of the camaraderie between the people who worked on the line.

In August 1980 the plant went on to one-shift working as opposed to two shifts. This meant there was a huge overcapacity of people. To alleviate this problem the company did a number of things. They asked for volunteers to go to our sister plant in Luton to alleviate the problem of turnover of labour they had there. The company also laid people off on a week on, week off basis, on pay under the wage security agreement that we had in place.

I actually opted for a change of scenery and packed my bags and moved to sunny Luton. The first thing I noticed when I got into the Luton plant was the number of women working on the line there. It was a bit of a shock because at Ellesmere Port there were only a handful of women on the line, whereas at Luton it was about 50 : 50. I was put to work in the hard trim, where again it was very labour-intensive, so the shifts passed fairly easily. It was also a change working with both males and females.

After 13 months at the Luton plant I was recalled to Ellesmere Port and went back to the underbody line. I became the deputy steward after being asked by the then steward, Kenny Murphy, if I was interested in taking up the position. Kenny took me under his wing for the next 18 months, showing me the ropes.

In April 1983 the company wanted us back on a two-shift setting. I was originally from the A shift and Kenny was from the B shift. This gave me the opportunity to take up the shop steward's role in earnest on the A shift.

I have been the shop steward on the underbodies ever since – some 19 years – and what an experience it has been. I became a safety rep in 1987 and Safety Committee chairperson in 1993. In 1995 I also became the member-nominated pensions trustee for the TGWU at Vauxhall Motors. I have enjoyed every minute of each of my jobs, even the bad times, which are far outweighed by the good. I have seen the introduction of four new models and all that they have entailed. The change that impacted the most was the introduction of robotics. There have been other changes as well, like new management practices such as teamworking and *kaizen*.

The introduction of robotics greatly reduced the amount of people that were required to build the cars. To give you some idea of the effect robotics has had, the body shop used to employ over 300 people per shift in 1980; this year the new body shop will employ just over 100 per shift. The new management techniques have also had an effect on the labour force. We are told that these new practices are making us work 'smarter not harder' when in fact the latter is closer to the truth. Teamwork puts pressure on the weakest member of the team to keep up with their team mates. It also creates a competitive atmosphere because people are vying for the position of team leader and more pay.

Although I understand the need for robotics and updating work practices, the lean production philosophy for me goes too far. In my opinion it puts unnecessary pressure on people and isolates individuals. People are working on their own with no human contact at all for hours at a time. The constant pressure of job security weighs heavily on the shoulders of our members.

There is a clear link between stress, working time and working practices. Stress is a topic for trade union policy and should enter the field of collective bargaining. Constantly changing organisation of work and its corollary stress and burnout are challenges for trade unions. New attitudes and strategies are needed to tackle this new area of worker protection. Trade unions must promote understanding of the stress syndrome, its causes and the problems that result from it. Trade unions must explain the need for early intervention, as prevention is better than cure.

To try to prevent stress-related illness at Vauxhall we have started by making some basic changes, the first being the introduction of a lifestyle nurse in our surgery. This gives people the opportunity to take a series of examinations and take advice from a professional person. Another small but helpful change was the introduction of job rotation, so people were not left isolated for long periods of time. We also got the company to install radio systems at lineside, breaking the monotony of working alone. This is not an exhaustive list of remedies and others are always being sought.

See Appendix 3, Working on the line 'after Fordism'.

6 ROVER-BMW: FROM *ROVER TOMORROW* TO THE LONGBRIDGE CLOSURE AND THE BITTER FRUITS OF LEAN PRODUCTION

INTRODUCTION

When we look at the rise and subsequent advance of lean production in the automotive industry in the United Kingdom during the last two decades of the twentieth century, there are three aspects that need to be taken into consideration. These are, first, the economic situation of the industry; second, government measures taken specifically to weaken trade union resistance to employers' restructuring plans; and third, the response by labour. By labour we mean

The demonstration against the closure of Longbridge, April 2000

national and local union leaderships and workers themselves, including their responses to the impact of lean on the labour process. In terms of the question of the role of organised labour, there is an argument that at a number of levels trade unions found themselves in a position of having to more or less buy into the employer's productivity agenda for survival. If this is understandable, the role of trade unions has often been understated in analysis of new management practices. As we shall see, while lean was having a negative impact on workers' health, its development at Rover was indelibly tied to the restructuring of the company. Various strategies were introduced to bring about a regime that could survive in the new lean-driven competitive environment.

It is crucial that we begin to understand lean as a new corporatist fix to the problems posed by the crisis of profitability in the UK automobile industry. In this case the question arises of the role of organised labour in the strategic choices posed by capital, and this has to be placed at the heart of our analysis. As we argue in Chapter 3, at least two possible routes were discernible in union responses at Rover and Vauxhall. While of course neither would challenge the terms of the debate about the importance of profitability to the rule of capital, one arguably risked subordinating trade union autonomy while the other sought to protect it, albeit in a different environment.

Here we look at the history of Rover from the perspective of Cowley workers, from the introduction of lean to the eventual sale of Longbridge in 2000 to the Phoenix Four, for a symbolic figure of £10. Although union choices were limited and have to be seen in the context of a long struggle to defend the gains built up during the fight against Measured Day Work (MDW), the story here highlights the role played by both national and local unions. While a minute part of what in 1966 had been the world's fourth largest producer (Whisler 1999: 4) survived at Cowley, as BMW's 'new' Mini facility, every management strategy accepted by organised labour – and sometimes anticipated by it – failed to protect anything more than a minority of the jobs that had existed prior to *Rover Tomorrow* in 1992. Moreover, and perhaps ironically, survival resulted from cut-throat competition between workers who had previously been working for the same firm. In the United States the game of plant playoffs, 'whipsawing', was at Rover a game to which labour was tragically committed.

It is true that after 2000 BMW created a vibrant assembly plant at what was once a major manufacturing facility of the state-owned auto industry at Cowley-Oxford, but this arguably depended precisely on the elimination of the pre-existing practices and management–union cultures. BMW had tinkered with these after its buy-out in 1994, but it was only with the transformation of Cowley-Oxford into a neo-greenfield plant in 2000 that the past was buried, or so the company might have hoped. While it might have introduced the BMW way of working, as our data illustrates in Chapter 7, it has far from eliminated the impact of its form of lean production on the quality of working life.

THE RECENT ORIGINS OF THE CRISIS: LEAN PRODUCTION AND THE RISE OF A NEW MANAGEMENT REGIME

While people might accept that the path to a viable future in the automobile industry was very narrow in the face of increased global competition, particularly from Japanese producers, some media commentators, and many academics, exploited this situation to argue in favour of the integrity of the employers' proposals for survival. This especially helped to give respectability to the impression that workers would have no choice but to accept the employer agenda for change based on the imperatives of new management practices, and particularly the adoption of lean production as an organisational model.

The execution and effects of radical change at Rover were manifest in four key episodes:

- the implementation of *Rover Tomorrow* in 1992
- the plant implementations following the 1997 wage review
- the 1998 Longbridge crisis
- the 2000 BMW deal.

We consider each of these in turn.

THE BACKGROUND TO THE IMPLEMENTATION OF *ROVER TOMORROW*

The media constantly refer back to the 'bad old days' when trade unions were too strong and people were constantly on strike. As well as misrepresenting past events, they omit from this picture the role of management, who at Cowley, for instance, moved to end the piecework system in 1971 and replaced it with MDW. While this strategy entailed giving concessions on work effort to shopfloor workers, enshrined in a mutuality agreement, it bought management time to establish the new MDW system. Once achieved, however, there was constant pressure by management to speed up, reduce breaks and keep lines running at all costs.

Essentially every type of industrial engineering technique was used to create speed-ups. 'Thou shall not stop' was the order of the day, so rectification and other problems were left unresolved, and tracks that used to run less than 80 per cent of the day were now running at nearly 100 per cent. Costs were also being kept down by contracting out cleaning and catering operations, despite strong shopfloor opposition, and keeping a tight lid on wages at a time of high inflation. So every year there was a battle over wages. Even when the 37-hour-week agreement was reached in June 1990, breaks were cut and work effort was increased from 100 to 105 per cent. Also almost all inspectors were removed, increasing the pressure for self-inspection. The critical point here is that these changes were implemented without full consultation with the workforce. The curtailment of employee voice reinforced the perception, widely held, that management was dictatorial and determined to squeeze more value from its workforce through work intensification. It was not difficult to predict that this would see a strengthening of shop stewards' legitimacy. Their organisation was seen as the most democratic institution in the company.

Michael Edwardes' appointment as chairman of British Leyland, by the Labour government at the end of 1977, was specifically seen as a warning to labour, both organised and unorganised, and indeed this could fairly be said to have been borne out by his actions. The workforce was reduced from 186,000 in 1978 to 46,000 by 1988. To some, his reign could justly be termed a form of management dictatorship. To eradicate opposition, first came the sacking in November 1979 of Derek Robinson, a leading convener at Longbridge. By creating a climate of fear, this paved the way for the distribution of the so-called 'Blue newspaper' in April 1980. This document, sent directly to each employee, pronounced that management would take greater control in the use of labour with respect to flexibility, in terms of not just increased job loading but also mobility around the plant. The era of mutuality was brought to a close, and shop stewards' ability to represent their members further eroded.

In response there was some industrial action, but it was brief. Shopfloor organisation at the Cowley plant was further weakened when in November 1982 Alan Thornett, a leading steward, was sacked. Yet despite this loss of a leading militant, and the balance of power with management so clearly weighted against them, Cowley workers were still prepared to take strike action in an attempt to preserve existing union–management agreements. However, strike action taken at the end of March 1983 in defence of the three-minute hand wash time at the end of each shift ended in defeat after two weeks. Another victimisation followed when immediately after a company-wide strike on wages, in November 1984, the deputy senior steward, Bob Cullen, was sacked. His dismissal, and that of other militant stewards in the company, at both Cowley and Long-bridge, inevitably helped to create a mood of defeatism amongst the Cowley workforce.

The problem for the workforce was that the company was able to close plants, despite being state-owned, because government investment was channelled into the company's rationalisation programme, directed by Edwardes. This point is sometimes overlooked. To a significant extent this investment assisted rationalisation in the form of job reduction and plant closure programmes. And when the inevitable disputes arose, the government threw massive amounts of cash into the war chest to defeat them. Moreover, Edwardes developed a collaborative relationship with Honda, exposing BL workers to Japanese management techniques. The first joint model appeared in May 1979, and the first Triumph Acclaim was produced in autumn 1981. The Metro aside, future models were produced jointly until 1988, when shared production was abandoned.

Edwardes' main task, however, was to prepare the company for privatisation, and the strategy he followed to this end was large-scale rationalisation and taming the unions. This was further pursued under Graham Day, appointed by Margaret Thatcher as executive chair of Austin-Rover. He broadened the rationalisation process by selling off parts of the business (Unipart, Leyland Bus) before overseeing the sale to British Aerospace (BAe) on 14 July 1988.

Within a few days of acquiring Austin-Rover and Land Rover (renaming the company the Rover Group), BAe announced the closure of Cowley Assembly together with the Llanelli plant in South Wales. Over the next three years all assembly work in Cowley was moved to the site of the adjacent body plant. The chance of any broad opposition to closure was stymied when the two senior stewards in the body plant opposed any attempt to spread resistance throughout the Rover Group. Thus, despite powerful in-plant and community opposition, the company was able to achieve its closure agenda.[1] Closure allowed the company to forge ahead with what became known as its Japanisation agenda, which sought to build upon a number of existing social and organisational (and political) features of the labour process. The new approach tended to take arrangements for drawing workers into the production process, such as quality circles, which had been tried in the past but with limited success. Typically these had been pushed quite strongly during the Honda period.

However, at the turn of the decade there were attempts by the local union leadership to forge better relationships with the company. In January 1990, for instance, the union leaderships in both the assembly and body plant put forward a proposal to the company designed to convince it of the union's commitment to improving industrial relations. The proposal was that in local disputes the union would be willing to agree to binding arbitration. The idea was to get more work from the Rover–Honda relationship by demonstrating that the union leadership was serious in its attempt to forge a better working relationship with the company. However, in the body plant it took three shop stewards' meetings before this was finally agreed, which indicates something of the scepticism of the membership.

In the run-up to the 1992 *Rover Tomorrow* deal, more serious attempts were made in relation to introducing team leaders. Membership meetings held in 1990 at Longbridge and the Cowley assembly plant accepted the principle of elected team leaders. However, in October 1990 Cowley body plant workers voted to oppose the introduction of team leaders. Resistance continued for several months. The company failed to gather enough support from its employees to legitimise the introduction of team leaders by holding elections for these roles. Eventually, the company was forced to appoint rather than elect team leaders, because when elections did take place very few people voted. Sometimes it was only the nominees and their nominators who voted, and often in the case of the assembly plant the box that said 'None of the above' got the most votes. Second, team leaders' job description excluded disciplinary matters: when one team leader in the body plant was found to have a list of late or absent workers, a dispute ensued. In Cowley, any stewards applying for team leader jobs were expected to resign their union position, unlike Longbridge where both functions could be performed. Essentially, at Cowley they were treated as first-line managers but with very limited powers.

As far as team briefings were concerned, nobody listened to team leaders: at first briefings were conducted by foremen, but so few people attended that managers started to take control of them, to very little effect. When the company representative read out from a brief about quality or productivity, shopfloor workers raised questions concerning their pensions or working conditions. Eventually the briefings were abandoned. The company tried to resurrect them on several occasions without success. Periodically the company held road-shows, at which the plant director would present the need for greater productivity. Questions were allowed, and they became one of the few places where workers could display their feelings towards the management. For example, at one of these in the body plant, just after the closure announcement, all the shopfloor workers walked out. It was becoming clear that these piecemeal efforts to control the workforce were unsuccessful, despite the fact that thousands of workers had left the company between 1988 and 1991, largely under the voluntary redundancy scheme.

In 1991 around 325 compulsory redundancies were carried through in Cowley, with the agreement of the union leadership. Although compulsory redundancy was against union policy, the union leadership nationally found itself in a difficult position, and at Cowley workers were persuaded to accept it on the basis of 'last in first out'. The union was bereft of ideas. It was a case of saving the jobs of the longest serving employees first.

ROVER TOMORROW

With the trade unions at Rover severely weakened, and the workforce demoralised, the company took advantage of its strengthened position to dictate another raft of changes, aimed at intensifying the labour process, and introducing new ways in conducting labour relations. The first *Rover Tomorrow* document was presented on 16 September 1991. The details of *Rover Tomorrow* covered:

- Single status: a sick-pay scheme, the same workwear, the end of clocking in, wages paid by credit transfer, and a single grade structure (with staff in the highest grades).
- Continuous improvement: a 'requirement for everyone', with reduced levels of staffing – 'working smarter not harder'.
- Flexibility: people were 'expected to be flexible subject to their ability' and to follow 'safe working practices'.
- Teams: were to be consulted over work planning changes, to satisfy customer demands. Amongst other things they were made

responsible for 'routine maintenance', 'housekeeping', process improvements, cost reduction, work allocation, job rotation and the training of each other.

- Bonus: all other schemes removed, and their replacement by a scheme related to the performance of the company, within which managers received higher payment.
- Jobs for life: 'employees who want to work for Rover will be able to stay with Rover'. Labour would then be cut by workers being moved, natural wastage, voluntary redundancy or early retirement.
- Briefings: 'the process of daily, weekly, monthly and annual employee briefings will be strengthened'.
- Discussion groups: 'all of us will be expected to participate in discussion groups, quality action teams, suggestion schemes'.
- Joint negotiations: there was to be a single Joint Negotiating Committee (JNC). 'Consultation with representatives of recognised trade unions will be enhanced, to insure maximum of company performance, competitive practices and standards.'
- Disputes procedure: there was to be a full procedure ending with the JNC. In addition, 'if both parties agree, it will be referred to arbitration, the outcome of which will be binding'.
- Further negotiations: to take place on a timekeeping agreement, and at local level, agreements over time and movement of labour.

Seven months of negotiations on the contents of the document followed, but there were no reports back to the shopfloor, and thus no limits were placed on what union representatives could negotiate. Considering that this involved many issues, such as teams and the new bonus scheme, which were fiercely contested on the shopfloor, and which involved a transformation of working conditions, this lack of consultation with union members was a major step backwards in union democracy. The argument was that in the end the members would be able to vote on the agreement, but this meant a vote of yes or no to a complete document, and that the vote would take place under conditions designed to be favourable to achieving a yes vote.

Jack Adams, then senior union negotiator, reported that the managing director of Rover, John Towers, had said the company was prepared to introduce the document with or without the union's assistance. This could only mean the threat of derecognition, as the company would be operating an agreement directly with its workforce. This was seen as a real threat, and was certainly used as leverage in attempting to persuade the plant leaderships to vote in favour of the final document. In addition, as the final document included the objective that Rover would become a single-status company (harmonisation of working conditions), for the first time white-collar staff were included in a vote, tempering the traditional militancy of shopfloor workers.

However, the decisive factor was that the Longbridge delegation voted en bloc for the deal. When the deal was first reported back to the shop stewards' committee at Longbridge, they voted against it. After some small changes were made to the proposed agreement, especially on clocking-in procedure, the stewards changed their minds. At Cowley the shop stewards were not allowed a vote, and were told no shop stewards could vote or speak against the deal – it was now regarded as union policy. Thus when the membership came to vote on the deal they were presented with a solid union position in its favour.

One of the clauses in the document specified that anybody who wanted to continue working for Rover would be able to do so. This was interpreted as meaning 'jobs for life'. So when the membership did come to vote, the media presented this as a great step forward. No alternative views were expressed. The count first showed a 25 majority to reject. A recount put the vote at 11,961–11,793 in favour of the deal: still marginal, yet no further recount was taken. Considering the odds stacked in favour of a yes vote, and the fact that the notoriously less militant white-collar staff were included, the vote shows the strength of feeling against the deal, and the instinctive realisation by many workers that the effects would be detrimental to their working conditions.

The Transport and General Workers Union (TGWU) had only recently changed its policy on employee involvement,[2] at the 1989 Biannual Delegate Conference, at the request of Bill Morris before he became general secretary of the union in 1991. From a policy of opposition it moved to one where, to paraphrase, 'if its introduction was inevitable then the best deal should be negotiated'. This inevitably placed the union – the TGWU in fairness was not the only union faced with this dilemma – in a difficult position. It was against new management techniques such as employee involvement, but in practice it was sometimes able to do little other than limit their impact.

Management was glad to see the speedy introduction of *Rover Tomorrow,* with the inclusion of practices such as employee involvement, but the workforce latched on to every limitation. After the vote, the TGWU organised a number of events and seminars about how to cope with the new management techniques in *Rover Tomorrow.* After just a few years these events were abandoned by the union, as it became rather less able to oppose the techniques in practice.

On 3 November 1992, in the Coventry office, a meeting of officers and conveners discussed the pros and cons of the *Rover Tomorrow* agreement. On 23 November a one-day seminar, organised by the unions, was held at Longbridge. At this seminar Bill Morris, then general secretary of the TGWU, spoke in favour of the *Rover Tomorrow* deal. John Towers also addressed the gathering, putting the company's position. Another of the speakers was Dan Jones, from Cardiff Business School and one of the authors of *The Machine that Changed the World* (Womack, Jones and Roos 1990). who argued that the union had no choice but to accept the new management techniques behind *Rover Tomorrow* in order to survive. Tony Woodley, TGWU national automotive secretary, also spoke at the meeting, indicating qualified support for the agreement.

The audience in the main was made up of Rover shop stewards who were given documentation and articles by Paul Stewart and Phil Garrahan, authors of the book *The Nissan Enigma* (1992), arguing that the lean production philosophy disregards the effects on workers and promotes new management techniques as uniformly desirable, and that the Massachusetts Institute of Technology (MIT) International Motor Vehicle Program, which backed the new techniques, ignored the 'human costs'. They made the point that rushing to accept these new practices would result in huge job losses and an attack on the quality of working life in the plants.

The TGWU held another seminar examining lean production from the 6 to 11 December 1992, with speakers for and against new management techniques. The personnel directors of Vauxhall Motors, Nissan UK and Rover Cars addressed the conference, as did Dan Jones and Bill Morris. David Robertson of the Canadian Auto Workers' union strongly condemned the techniques. In attendance were representatives from almost every car plant in the United Kingdom, from the components sector, and from many plants across Europe. This was a major step forward in the sense that a wide-ranging and representative conference of car workers from across Europe, officially called by a major trade union, discussed common problems. This was an important initiative by the TGWU, but unfortunately it proved to be the last such event.

Tony Woodley called for EU cooperation, while admitting that the TGWU had been slow in preparing, educating and assisting. He argued that the union had now started this process, but that there was no short-term solution to the employers' long-term strategy: no quick fix. Woodley recognised that the employers' long-term aim was to maximise efficiencies, to maximise effort, and to pick workers' brains, in order to maximise control. He also ridiculed the idea of benchmarking, as suggested by Jones.

IMPLEMENTATION OF *ROVER TOMORROW*

Some parts of *Rover Tomorrow* were not negotiated and left for later, while others were to be sorted out at local level. The company first presented a sick pay scheme based on the 'Bradford' principles for measuring and monitoring absence from work, which unions found unacceptable because it allowed in some cases the disciplining of people with a doctor's medical certificate. Nevertheless, the company implemented it without agreement in May 1993. It was so unsuccessful that they were forced to return to the negotiating table. A new agreement was formulated on 21 March 1994, although it was not a great deal better. The agreement stipulated that anybody with more than three single absences in 58 weeks would be disciplined. This was a points system that penalised separate absences. It was possible to have disciplinary points removed, but only through periods of perfect timekeeping. Although absence authorised by a doctor's medical certificate was not included in the points system, it was covered by a clause referring to patterns of absence, as the agreement made clear: 'absenteeism can occur for unacceptable reasons and when unacceptable patterns of absence are identified and there are no excusing circumstances … procedures will be initiated'. The individual would then go before a manager to be warned that change was necessary, and to reach an agreement that their absence record would improve by the end of a fixed period. If change had not taken place after the third such 'time', the individual could be dismissed. As a result large numbers of people at Longbridge and Swindon were sacked.

The key clauses of *Rover Tomorrow* at local level were related to the fairness of overtime and the movement of labour in relation to seniority, and as the deal continued, the limitation on short-term contract labour. The shopfloor was able to utilise these clauses to prevent the facilitators dividing them up and creating favourites, and they also maintained a role for the shop stewards.

Although BMW took over the company in 1994, and cooperation with Honda quickly ended, this did not immediately affect the way in which Rover proceeded. In April 1994 the company proposed to put skilled workers in selected production jobs, as part of the flexibility agreement. At first production workers objected because of the wage differential between skilled workers and semi-skilled production workers. An agreement was reached whereby skilled workers could only fill vacancies, and would be the first to be removed if team numbers were reduced. In practice this arrangement was short-lived, as the skilled workers affected were found work within their own trade. Nonetheless, on some occasions skilled workers continued to be used to fill in for absentees. This form of flexibility is extremely contentious, as production workers were averse to working side by side with skilled workers doing the same job on higher rates of pay, so it proved difficult to implement.

In principle, after the signing of the *Rover Tomorrow* agreement, workers were deemed to be willing to move between jobs if so required. In practice some were more willing than others. The main concern of employees was fairness. Some were asked to move more than others. Labour shortages meant that very little training was given to ensure flexibility, as time was too short. Perhaps the most significant change was the much wider range of work employees were expected to cover than previously. So 'stores' people had to be able to drive fork-lift trucks when required, and more importantly most production workers had to carry out self-inspection of their work. This entailed a quality check by the operator at each stage of production. This creates great pressure in case a mistake is overlooked, and is perhaps the most important aspect of the new management techniques which were designed to maintain workers' concentration on their jobs.

The other form of flexibility the company sought, particularly after BMW took over, was movement between plants. This only occurred where workers received payment to compensate for the costs involved, for example where workers from Cowley moved to Swindon or Solihull.

As the implementation of the various clauses of *Rover Tomorrow* gathered pace, workers began to realise that the new arrangements were having a detrimental effect on working conditions.

John Towers was sacked as managing director of Rover in August 1996. It was said that BMW were angry because the true picture of the state of the company had been concealed from them. It is very difficult for any worker to understand these figures: the 1996 profit of £29 million was turned into a £119 million loss and the 1997 profit of £31 million was turned into a £91 million loss. BMW was already making moves to squeeze more concessions out of the work-force via the National JNC. Delegations of senior stewards were being dispatched all over the world by BMW on a benchmarking exercise, and it was clear that they were not seeking better working conditions or wages. The company was trying to get shop stewards on side by parading some of the newer techniques they wanted to implement. What occurred next in many ways revealed yet again the uncomfortable, paradoxical role in which the union found itself.

On 29 August 1996 the union and the company issued a joint statement emphasising the need for benchmarking visits in order to meet, and indeed overcome, competition in the sector. It was issued at about the same time as the TGWU *Auto Bulletin* special issue about the trade group (promoted at a national industrial policy conference). Under the headline, 'Deadly game of world competition blasted', the *Bulletin* reviewed the union's policy for strengthening international links between car workers. The Cowley delegate moved a resolution calling for independent links between all European trade unions and a block on the transfer of work from one country to another without the agreement of both workforces. Yet again the union was arguing for one stance on a – very critical – issue, while on the ground it went along with the employer's change agenda. While this was hardly new in the auto sector and is fairly common in other industries, it meant that a clear, unambiguous and independent union strategy, in Rover at least, was difficult to attain.

In March 1997, the TGWU national secretary issued a joint letter with Dunlevy (a company industrial relations manager) attempting to explain why BMW required mobility between plants. The letter concluded by stating that for Rover to continue to win high levels of investment in order to compete, workers must continually strive for ways to become more effective. As well as requiring significant changes in work practices, BMW made future investment dependent on the acceptance of 'an early positive conclusion to the "partner-ship principles" discussions'. These principles drew heavily on the co-determination model of cooperation between labour and management practised by BMW and other large companies in Germany and elsewhere in Europe.

In the April-May edition of the company magazine *Torque*, Dunlevy emphasised the fact that '[i]ssues being covered in one wide ranging discussion with trade unions include flexibility, mobility, flexible working time, including flexible holidays, short term support and supplier delivery to line'. In order to persuade the company to build its new engine plant at Hams Hall, near Birming-ham, full-time officials and the senior stewards from Longbridge and Solihull engaged in negotiations on working time accounts (annualised hours), shift patterns, including Saturdays, and changes in work practices before consulting with their members. It was these conditions that local plant managements were pushing from June 1997 onwards. Management obviously realised that in the end these changes could be achieved provided the threat of closure or job reductions was sufficiently real to worry the work force.

This was an important change: for the first time, negotiations over changes in working conditions were taking place separately from negotiations over wages, a strategy that served management in achieving its original objective. That is, it could attack working conditions and impose productivity norms including staffing levels (all tied in with new forms of flexibility) with little union resistance. Arguably, it could be said that the union, perhaps unwittingly, played into management's hands. From the union's perspective, these negotiations were driven by the wish to maintain the 1992 guarantee of no enforced redundancies, known as jobs for life. No one seemed to want to argue that the *Rover Tomorrow* agreement could not amount to much if it was continually necessary to renegotiate it.

THE 1998 COWLEY AGREEMENT

A new car, the Rover 75, was scheduled for Cowley. On the back of this the company wanted to implement new working conditions. It wanted negotiations over proposed changes to working conditions to be completed by May 1998. There were no reports back to the membership during this period. The negotiators were sworn to secrecy until the negotiations were completed. In fact the company had said in April 1997 that it would sack anybody divulging information from within the plant to outside sources. This was to make sure that nobody on the negotiating body gave information to those people who were regularly issuing critical leaflets on the factory gates.

In May 1998 the shop stewards were finally given details of what the plant committee had negotiated. The final deal involved flexible holidays and volume protection, whereby if the company felt it necessary, it became compulsory to work an extra half-hour a day, in order make up lost production resulting from breakdowns in the production process. In addition contract workers would be hired on short-term contracts. Most contentious of all was a shift system termed 'four/five', which included working on Friday nights until 2.00 am. Most workers had not worked such a shift for 30 years. While workers were presented with the facts as interpreted by the union leadership, and were able to ask questions, no alternative was discussed and their only choice was to vote 'yes' or 'no'. The vote was 70 per cent in favour of the deal and 27 per cent against. Local deals were also negotiated in other plants, but these did not include the contentious Friday evening shift.

THE WORKING TIME ACCOUNT

When the company failed at national level to achieve agreement on a working time account (in July 1998), BMW approached the union at local level in Cowley. It proposed a system of plus or minus 200 banked hours per annum. Annualised hours systems enable employers to deal with uneven demand by the flexible arrangement of working hours across a 12-month period. Under previous Rover agreements, if workers were laid off, they were paid. However, under a working time account agreement, if they were laid off and paid, they subsequently had to work additional hours to compensate. This would be achieved by overtime work, and under this proposed agreement they would not receive overtime pay. The national officers declared that as this affected wages, the proposed working-time account system could not be negotiated outside a wage review.[3]

A NEW MODEL, THE ROVER 75

For the manufacture of the Rover 75 at Cowley all production workers were moved into new buildings. The company always attempted to use such situations to introduce new working arrangements. First it brought in a large number of new managers, most of whom had never worked before in the motor industry. Because of their background they had a set plan which took little account of the problems of car workers or of car production. The company told the managers how they would like the new production facilities to run, based on a guiding principle termed PRIDE. At first no worker was to be allowed in the new facilities without attending a three-day induction programme, although this was soon reduced to one day. PRIDE had never been agreed with the trade unions, and therefore was presented as simply company policy. Its provisions were:

- No bags, coats or other personal items, including newspapers, books, food and drink to be kept trackside. Each individual was responsible for the housekeeping in their area. No unauthorised seating, benches or lockers were permissible within the work area. All items dropped during the work process had to be picked up and put in the appropriate place. There were to be no posters and the like, and no personal stereos. Smoking was allowed in designated areas only. Tables in the rest area were to be cleared after each break.

- Correct work wear had to be worn at all times in the correct manner, with buttons done up etcetera. No metal badges or buckled belts could be worn. Rings, watches and jewellery were to be covered.
- Individual ownership of equipment and processes. All associates (that is, workers) should be punctual. All associates should understand and work to approve the process. All associates should take an active part in process validation. Involvement of all in ongoing improvements to processes, to involve measuring their processes where applicable and completing them prior to leaving a workstation.

The reaction to some of these conditions was immediate, while to others, which often involved extra work, it was delayed by the fact that at the beginning of all new model introductions there is only a small amount of work, as the volume on the line is much reduced. The conditions outlined in the first point, for example, are not so contentious when workers are able to leave the area to have a sandwich or cup of tea outside their break time, or sweep up when there are no jobs. However, when production finally got underway workers stopped responding to what they interpreted as mindless imperatives, arguing that it was impossible to follow PRIDE since it had not taken into consideration the studies of industrial engineers in their work to improve the manufacturing process.

THE LONGBRIDGE CRISIS, OCTOBER 1998

On 20 October 1998 the Rover 75 was launched at the Birmingham International Motor show. At this launch Bernd Pischetsrieder, BMW's executive chairman, declared that 'short term actions are required for the long-term future of the Rover Group'. His announcement completely overshadowed the unveiling of the Rover 75, undermining its promotion. His objective was to pressurise the workforce and the unions to accept job losses and changes to work practices. Development work at Longbridge was stopped while the company, as part of its survival plan, placed demands on the union, including a 30 per cent increase in productivity, and called on the UK government to provide a large subsidy for the development of a new small car.

The trade unions at national level responded immediately, but from a position of relative weakness. The TGWU through the pages of its journal maintained that management sought to terminate all existing contracts, which would have required in effect dismissing the entire workforce and re-employing them on inferior wages and conditions. The threat of union derecognition loomed menacingly if an agreement could not be reached.

After discussions with the German unions, and negotiations with the British unions, the company agreed to the scheduled November pay deal, but to compensate for a freeze on pay for the next two years there would be a reduction in the working week of one hour each year. The union recommended acceptance of this deal even though it conceded the working time account – which it had always claimed it would oppose – the loss of the next year's holiday bonus and new shifts in both the Land Rover and Longbridge plants. All of this fed into the union argument of embracing Rover's competitiveness.

The position of the unions throughout was intriguing. A communication issued to the membership stated that 'we have to inform you that the situation is far worse than you may have appreciated. The very future of the Rover cars, if not the whole company, is in question.' While negotiations continued, the company pumped out the inevitable literature extolling the benefits of working time flexibility – and it was the company that produced the final draft of the agreement. In the period leading up to the vote Labour ministers, such as Peter Mandelson, argued that the workforce 'had to sharpen up their act'. and the local MP for Oxford East, Andrew Smith, pushed for the deal to be accepted. The media campaign was almost unprecedented, with headlines in the *Daily Mirror* such as 'Car industry must change gear ... or die', and the local paper, the *Oxford Mail*, pushing for a yes vote for survival.

A final delegate conference took place in November. At this conference the leadership argued that if the deal was not accepted, BMW would close Longbridge. Only Cowley's delegates spoke against the deal, reflecting the feeling of their members, arguing that the blackmailing would never end, and that a stand had to be taken. The leadership said that this meant that they were in favour closing Longbridge! For many stewards this did indeed look like a form of blackmail, but in the end only the Cowley delegates voted against. How much the other delegates understood what they had voted for was not clear. It is one thing for the leadership to obtain the support of stewards away from the assembly line, at a delegate conference, and another thing entirely to garner support on the shopfloor. Workers will not willingly, or easily, agree to drastically worsen their working conditions.

However, this is what the TGWU leadership managed to do, by taking the unprecedented step of addressing all Rover workers together in the one place. Workers from Longbridge and Solihull were bussed to the National Exhibition Centre in Birmingham. Union leaders, supported by the local and national media, argued forcibly that this deal was the only way to save Longbridge. When the ballot was counted on 11 December there were 17,784 votes in favour of the deal and 7,045 against. It was clear that only Cowley had delivered a heavy 'no' vote.

One of the biggest problems with the deal was that it set a precedent, and the negotiators realised this. The union's argument, to the effect that it was being realistic in trying to save the Longbridge plant from closure, and protect the no compulsory redundancies agreement, was persuasive. However, the problem was that more and more jobs were being lost and conditions worsened throughout the industry as the unions – not just the TGWU – abstained from any alternative strategy. A fight was effectively avoided. And tragically, the threat to close Longbridge was subsequently realised. This downward spiral should have been resisted. The TGWU, which represented workers in every car and component company, had international union links, detached and distinct from European Works Council (EWC) representatives, willing to support the union in making a stand. Yet the union failed to utilise these links, missing the opportunity to form a strong alliance to oppose job losses and the deterioration of working conditions across international boundaries. Instead the TGWU chose to form an alliance with Germany's BMW EWC representatives in supporting the Rover survival plan.

IMPLEMENTATION OF THE 1998 AGREEMENT

Almost immediately the company began laying workers off in each plant, until most Rover workers were 200 hours in deficit, which was the limit under the working time agreement. At Cowley, layoffs ensued in February 1999 because of problems with the quality of the Rover 75. In March 1999, 300 Cowley workers volunteered to go to work in Regensburg in Bavaria for three months. While this was a very expensive episode, it was nevertheless part of the creation of a culture of moving from plant to plant at times of production problems. When production of the Rover 75 began in August, Cowley workers were called on to work the deficit hours they had accumulated under the working time agreement. Meanwhile large numbers of workers from

Longbridge had volunteered for temporary work at Cowley, during which period they were paid three hours' daily travel overtime allowance. The company also employed several hundred agency workers, so there were almost as many irregular as regular Cowley employees, which was clearly the kind of flexibility BMW was looking for. At the same time as the company was implementing the deal, it was clearly not committed to its part of the bargain: that is, the guarantee of jobs.

Throughout 1999 there were threats of job losses, of closures, and to the future of the company as a whole. The agreement that was supposed to have meant security led to Rover workers' most insecure year in history. On 31 January Professor Werner Seamen, who had replaced Walter Hasselkus as head of Rover, warned that thousands more Rover jobs would have to go if survival was to be ensured. On Friday 5 February the BMW board met, and a row erupted over whether to continue with Rover. As a result both major protagonists, Pischetsrieder and the hard-line Wolfgang Reitzle, were forced out. It was decided to continue with Rover under Professor Joachim Milberg, BMW's production chief.

On 14 February the *Observer* anticipated that Rover would seek 1,000 more job losses as a step towards restoring profitability. It would seem that the only people who were showing much confidence were the unions who had negotiated the deal. In a statement issued to the workforce, immediately after the departure of Reitzle and Pischetsrieder, they said, 'The agreement of last December stands.' There was logic in promoting the small-car option – legal commitment to emissions reductions and the lower cost of redeveloping the Longbridge complex. Nevertheless, given that no government aid was yet forthcoming, the *Guardian* was able to pose the question on 10 March, 'Is it over for Rover?' The *Observer* claimed on 14 March that the government had agreed a £150 million subsidy for the R30, the replacement for the Rover 200 and 400, but that BMW was comparing this offer with offers from Hungary. The saga over the government subsidy continued. The *Guardian* pointed out on 31 March that the new chairman Milberg had warned the government that BMW would build its new Rover car outside Britain if it continued to drag its feet over aid for Longbridge. It is important to remember at this juncture that the agreement with the trade unions in November was supposed to have guaranteed this model for Longbridge.

The company's paper, *Torque*, presented the picture of a Rover crisis in its March-April issue: £650 million losses as a result of currency factors, market conditions and restructuring. On the same front page it was reported that 'BMW group has successful year', 'BMW automobiles achieved their best ever results with a 25 per cent increase in profit, before tax, of £1,355 million' and 'The financial services division of the BMW group increased its profit to £60 million.' How much of this latter money came from Rover? On 1 April the *Guardian* carried the headline, 'Longbridge: safe at last'. Trade secretary Stephen Byers had agreed £180 million in state aid with Milberg, yet three days later the *Observer* quoted the chairman of BMW's supervisory board to the effect that the future of Rover's car division was by no means certain.

Still the union had to make sure that the workforce carried through the agreement on working conditions. On 9 June at Land Rover, 1,500 workers stopped work because they were told that in five weeks' time they would be working a shift on Friday evenings from 5:30 pm to 11.30 pm for no extra money as part of the working-time account scheme. These workers had previously not normally worked on a Friday evening, and most had not realised that this was part of the deal. In the end minor changes were made and Friday evening working was enforced.

Manfred Schoch, the representative of IG-Metall (the German Metal Workers' union) on the BMW supervisory board and the board's vice-chairman, felt it necessary to scotch the rumours circulating about the future of the Rover Group and that BMW intended to sell its UK subsidiary. In a statement on 12 November he said scare stories were inappropriate and unhelpful:

> During the last weeks there have been a lot of news items about BMW and Rover. Most of them were totally wrong and caused a great damage to the image of BMW group, even though BMW published denials. BMW believes in the future of Rover and it keeps on running the turnaround process.

Whether Schoch was privy to the talks that had taken place the previous month, about the possible sale of Rover to Alchemy, a venture capital company, is unclear. The reference to turnaround in Schoch's statement was in relation to a cost-saving exercise that BMW had instituted in September throughout the Rover Group. Not only were managers drawn from the German plants, but outside consultants were brought in at huge cost. Processes were changed, often leading to increased workloads. Work gangs had their numbers reduced, with the rest expected to cover their work. The company tried to involve the trade unions at local level in these turnaround committees, but shop stewards at both Longbridge and Cowley refused to be involved, and the process went ahead.

In January 2000 workers from all over Rover were taken, in batches, to Longbridge to be shown a huge model of the proposed transformation of the Longbridge site ready for the new R30. Directors spoke glowingly of the future of Longbridge. Who could seriously believe that BMW were already negotiating its sale? After this, back at Cowley, phase two of the turnaround process began. More jobs were cut to meet financial targets. Workers on loan from Longbridge were sent back, the number of temporary workers employed was reduced, and pressure intensified to increase productivity.

At this point a surprising development occurred. The company called a business review meeting with the National JNC, at which the company declared it was in crisis. At this meeting a union national officer suggested that one way of saving the company would be to move the Rover 75 to Longbridge and close down Cowley. When this was reported back to the Cowley workforce there was uproar. It has to be remembered that the union's trade group centre had pushed the working time account deal against the hostility of Cowley workers. The other national officers explained their position to a shop stewards' committee at Cowley on 29 February, where they argued that they had only been anticipating company options for which members would require time to respond, and that this would require thinking about a new model, possibly for Cowley. This response from the centre was to have a significant effect on Cowley workers when the crisis finally broke.

CRISIS 2000 – WHAT FUTURE FOR LONGBRIDGE?

On Tuesday 14 March 2000 the *Suddeutsche Zeitung* revealed that the agenda for the BMW board meeting on 16 March contained a proposal for the sale of Rover. The company issued a statement to the workforce saying that the company was looking at several scenarios. On 16 March the *Financial Times* announced that BMW was negotiating to sell Rover to Alchemy, and it later transpired that these negotiations had been going on since October of the previous year. The supervisory board meeting voted to give Alchemy, as sole prospective purchaser, six weeks to finalise the deal. It was to receive a large sum of money to take Longbridge off BMW's hands. Ford would buy Land Rover; BMW would keep Swindon and Cowley, which would build the new Mini and the Rover 75 under licence for Alchemy. Alchemy had no intention of

continuing Longbridge as a producer in the volume market, and therefore had no plans for replacing the Rover 25 and 45. As the facilities
for the new Mini were already at Longbridge, the loss of these as well
as an absence of future new models was a catastrophe for the plant. All
that Alchemy offered was the development of small-scale specialist
production utilising the MG brand.

Following this shock news, Rover's workers received another
demoralising blow when the lG-Metall representative on the supervisory board, Manfred Schoch, voted in favour of the company's plan by
signing the declaration of intent for negotiations on the sale. He
argued, in an interview in *Die Welt* on 20 March, that he did this
because 'Rover would have dragged in BMW with it'. Yet he had just
recently reported to an extraordinary general meeting of the workforce on 17 March that BMW was 'able to show new record pre-tax
profits of 4.1 billion Marks'. Asked why he had not told the British
trade unions about the planned sale when he received the agenda for
the meeting, all he would say was that he was bound by boardroom
secrecy. The British unions did not call for a EWC meeting to bring
him to account. In this way British workers were isolated from the
German workforce. From the outset the policy of the employer was to
divide and rule both between and within plants. The plan was that
Solihull would be part of a separate company, Cowley would be part
of BMW, and at Longbridge, while some workers would be retained to
produce the MG, as many 3–4,000 other jobs would go.

The government and local MPs presented a similar position.
Stephen Byers, for example, toured Longbridge on 18 March,
declaring that 'there are two groups of workers at Longbridge.
There are people who will lose their jobs, which we bitterly regret
but that is inevitable,' and there was 'another group of workers who
will have greater opportunities and they will not be staring over
their shoulders fearing redundancy'. The Oxford East MP, Andrew
Smith, said that the achievement of the Cowley workforce had
beyond any doubt convinced BMW to keep the Oxford plant. This
was the immediate reaction of Labour politicians, since they realised
that the biggest chance of action from the workforce was at the time
of announcement of closure or mass redundancy. So in their initial
statements they expressed their regrets at not having been informed
earlier, hoped that something better might develop, but insisted that
workers could do nothing about it and anyway, at least some of
them would be all right. Lay-offs at Longbridge began immediately:
half the plant for a week, then the other half for a week, then the
whole plant for four weeks, weakening any will to fight back.

On Tuesday 21 March Rover shop stewards were called to a meeting at Gaydon. The national officials' position was that if they could not persuade BMW to reverse its decision to break with and break up the Rover Group, they would call for the company to be nationalised. It was also decided, unanimously by the shop stewards, to hold a national demonstration in Birmingham on 1 April. One alternative course of action, proposed from the shopfloor, called for the immediate occupation of the plant, but it was not put to the vote.

In effect, by settling on a demonstration and avoiding direct action, the union left the fate of the company in the hands of BMW, hoping that either moral pressure would prevail or the UK government would step in. Given that workers were being laid off, occupation of the Longbridge plant would have been the only viable action to stop the company's reorganisation strategy. In the end, Longbridge did not even hold a mass meeting. Although the leadership at Cowley had voted for the Gaydon resolution, they clearly did not really believe in it. An Oxford joint union statement dated 26 March cited Professor Milberg's comment that BMW will 'commit to investment in the Oxford plant,' and continued, 'The new Mini was given to Oxford as a reward to our members for producing the best car ever, the award-winning Rover 75.' In other words, the union leadership at Cowley was in effect saying, 'We are safe, we are better workers than Longbridge, and this is why the tracks are being pulled out of that plant and put into Cowley.'

Some in the Cowley plant leadership argued that even though some might believe that the new Mini should be a Longbridge car, they were forgetting that the Mini had originally been built at Oxford in 1959 and only later moved to Longbridge. There was also talk of negotiating separate conditions at Cowley at a time when workers there were supposed to be part of a national fight to keep the whole of Rover together. The implication of the latter fight was that new models should be shared and not all concentrated in Cowley, yet the message was that Cowley must try to secure agreement on the future of the Oxford plant. The message from the local leadership was clear: without the new Mini at Oxford, the plant would have no future. It should be remembered that this car was being produced at Longbridge at the time the statement was made. It was the only new car Longbridge had, and Cowley, a much smaller plant, already had the Rover 75.

The company continued to take advantage of this situation by constantly pledging Cowley's security. Under the headlines 'BMW makes pledge over Cowley jobs' and 'Cowley pledge by BMW', the *Oxford Mail* and the *Oxford Times* quoted company sources as saying they were 'looking to retain the whole of the workforce at Oxford'. This was on 31 March, the day before the large demonstration in Birmingham. It was not surprising, therefore, that only half a coachload of workers went from Cowley to that demonstration.

Meanwhile a huge crisis was developing in the motor and component industry. The *Sunday Times* suggested on 19 March that Ford was set to close its Dagenham plant with the loss of 4,000 jobs. The paper claimed that executives had decided to stop production of the Ford Fiesta in Dagenham and produce it in Cologne, Germany. This turned out to be entirely accurate. This decision, like the Rover decision, would affect tens of thousands of other jobs in the distribution, component and supplier sector. On 26 March the *Observer* pointed to the imminent closure of the Goodyear tyre factory which employed 2,500 workers. Other firms were already laying workers off, including Excel, next to the Cowley plant, which finally laid off nearly 200. Within Cowley itself, the last 150 agency workers were paid off. Yet despite these savage job losses, at no point was there any attempt to unify the opposition. Rover workers were isolated not only within the company but also outside of it. Nevertheless, messages of support were arriving, from the Canadian Auto Workers' union, from the BMW Berlin plant and some workers in BMW Munich. A Transnational Information Exchange (TIE) conference in Cologne involving many car workers called for delegations from BMW-Rover plants to meet together to discuss the crisis and call for a meeting of the EWC. None of this support was used, apart from a show of solidarity at the demonstration on 1 April.

THE DEMONSTRATION FOR LONGBRIDGE, 1 APRIL 2000

The demonstration in Birmingham was 100,000 strong, mainly workers and their families, and included support from all over the country. Many of the leaflets given out on the demonstration called for the occupation of Longbridge and the renationalisation of Rover. The feeling among the demonstrators was for action but the speeches at the end of the rally, though critical of BMW, proposed no form of action. So there was no talk of the nationalisation that the national secretary had spoken of at the Gaydon meeting only ten days previously. Tony Blair was later to declare that he had resisted calls for nationalisation. He considered that the government's role was not to intervene in the market but merely to use taxpayers' money to retrain the workers and return them to the labour market to compete with other unemployed workers for the limited opportunities available. He did not put it as crudely as this. According to the *Sunday Business* (2 April 2000), Blair said, 'Governments have been drawn towards rescuing a company in difficulty; we see our role now as helping to equip people and business for the new economy.'

It later transpired that the TGWU had not been actively pushing the government to nationalise the Rover Group because it had been hoping for a rival capitalist takeover. The union's journal reported the prospect of a late bidder for the

The death of the British car industry: the demonstration against the closure of Longbridge, April 2000

company headed by former Rover chief executive, John Towers. The last-minute bid, backed by a consortium of financiers, was being encouraged by union negotiators even as thousands marched through the centre of Birmingham. But even though the Phoenix consortium had held talks with the union three days before the demonstration, there was no mention of this by any of the union representatives on the platform. The only speech at the rally that called for any form of action was by a local historian, Dr Carl Chinn, who argued for blocking the gates of the plant if the company attempted to move the Mini assembly facilities. None of the shop stewards from Longbridge spoke at the rally.

The government's response to the demonstration was to say that it did not believe in rescuing the company since it saw its role as 'managing transition'. Tony Blair himself said the government 'would make sure that everyone who lost their job would get help in finding a new one' (TGWU journal *The Record*). The media response was similar. In the days following the demonstration they painted a picture of worker powerlessness. Headlines such as one in the *Daily Express* on 6 April caught the attitude of the time. 'New hope for car workers' referred to the possibility of a new buyer, and indeed it was on the same day that Towers' bid was revealed. From then on the media focused solely on two issues; whether BMW had lied to Byers, and whether John Towers' bid would be allowed. Workers laid off at Cowley, and those about to be laid off at Longbridge, in the absence of a national fight-back strategy had little choice but to sit at home.

THE UNION POSITION CHANGES

On 19 April another meeting of all Rover stewards took place at Gaydon. This was to formally change the position adopted by the stewards at the previous Gaydon conference. On arrival the stewards were presented with a joint trade unions' briefing spelling out the new Towers' bid:

> This bid has the support of the trade unions both at national and JNC levels as it will result in less job losses than under the

Demonstration against the closure of Longbridge, April 2000

Demonstration against the closure of Longbridge, April 2000

Alchemy proposals. The bid however, does not include Cowley or Mini as BMW categorically refused to include them in any transaction.

Furthermore, as the briefing went on to point out:

> Our original objective was to keep the whole of Rover Group together but we have to acknowledge the fact that the finance gained from the sale of Land-Rover is in the main being utilised by BMW in their disposal of Rover cars. In view of the current circumstances, the JNC have had to adopt a policy of damage limitation and to attempt to secure the best possible conditions for the many thousands who will be affected by this disaster. We are attempting to improve redundancy terms with BMW prior to the break-up of the company.

Tony Woodley, addressing the shop stewards, made it clear that ministers had told him there was no way that Rover would be nationalised, and that therefore there would be no national demonstration arguing for this policy. He said that he had been unsuccessful in attempts to persuade other car companies to take over Rover. He went on to say that he had persuaded John Towers to become involved with the bid, and that this could only be positive since Towers was 'a car man' who believed in mass production. However, it soon became evident that Towers had no plans for the replacement of the Rover 25 or 45, and so the TGWU could only hope that he would forge a partnership with another car company in the not too distant future. As regards the criticism that a previously united workforce was ironically being divided by union policy, the response was that realism had to prevail. A sense of realism was also the tenor of the reply given to the suggestion that without a new model there was little difference between the Alchemy and Phoenix bids. (In later months this was to prove accurate because Phoenix adopted Alchemy's policy of badging cars as MGs.)

When Longbridge stewards queried the absence of a fall-back plan the response was that none existed – the union believed in 'successful outcomes'. Longbridge stewards revealed that the company was already planning to apportion workers to different divisions of the organisation. The Mini workers at Longbridge were assigned to stay with BMW, although Mini production was to be transferred to Oxford. Other workers at Longbridge were allotted to the Rover division that BMW was in the process of selling. This was the tactic adopted throughout the company, and was intended to make some workers feel secure and others not. It surely worked.

Unsurprisingly, the shop stewards left the Gaydon conference divided. The Land Rover stewards went off to negotiate with Ford, the Cowley stewards went off to negotiate with BMW and the Longbridge stewards were left hoping that things would turn out all right with Phoenix. When, two days later, national TGWU officers addressed a mass meeting of Ford workers about the threat to close Dagenham, it was obvious after what had taken place at Rover that any united action by car workers would now be most unlikely.

As the date set by BMW for settlement with Alchemy neared (Friday 28 April), the union's entire efforts were concentrated on ensuring that BMW listened to the Phoenix bid. At an EWC meeting it was argued that members should persuade BMW to listen to the Phoenix bid. Meanwhile, in their Easter layoff, Longbridge shop stewards organised a demonstration of 1,000 workers opposing both Towers (Phoenix) and Alchemy. On Friday 28 April Alchemy pulled out and BMW started negotiations with Phoenix. Now, ironically, some workers again demonstrated outside the Longbridge gates, but this time in support of the Towers bid; workers were desperate and latching onto anyone apparently offering the chance of survival. At the same time, workers at Cowley were sitting at home reading reports, such as one in the *Independent on Sunday* on 30 April that

BMW, 'Wants to pull out of UK entirely', or in the *Observer* on the same day that 'Now BMW set to axe Mini plant'. How could workers act independently in such a climate, and against this backdrop of uncertainty? At one moment they were told that the union would go for the Phoenix bid and that this was the only game in town, while at the next the media was informing them that BMW wanted to pull out of the United Kingdom entirely: no Longbridge, no Cowley.

On May Day, TUC general secretary John Monks called on the government to plough cash into the Phoenix bid – 'I think that the challenge to the government is to find imaginative ways of helping' – while Stephen Byers, according to the *Daily Mail*, talked of committing £100 million. The problem was that other capitalists, particularly the British banks, were not willing to put up any more money. According to the *Guardian* on 3 May, 'The banks suspect that the government only wants a political fix for Longbridge, one that would see it through the next election.'

On 3 May BMW said it would allow the Rover 75 to be moved to Longbridge, and finally, on 10 May, Phoenix bought the company for £10. Two days later Ford officially announced the closure of Dagenham.

For Longbridge, which was to receive the Rover 75 in exchange for the Cowley Mini, Towers immediately said, 'There won't be any area of this business that won't have to reduce costs.' Moreover, the bleak outlook for the components sector was underlined when Ford indicated it would begin sourcing Land Rover parts from outside the United Kingdom, as Rover already did. BMW made it clear that it would take advantage of the long period of no work up until April that year, when production of the Mini was planned to commence, to try to force through new, more arduous, working conditions than those adopted at the time of the first Longbridge crisis. In June, when redundancy was offered to workers aged over 50, the vast majority accepted, fearful of the kind of working conditions BMW would seek to impose. So with work at a standstill, with many workers laid off, accumulating negative hours which would have to be paid back, the company entered into negotiations with the union leadership at the Cowley plant.

The document the company produced, for the proposed Mini production, was an assault on working conditions. There was no limit on the number of agency workers the company could employ. It also included new shifts that would establish virtually round the clock production. By a narrow majority, however, the union leadership voted to accept the conditions for producing the Mini at Cowley. When the deal was outlined and recommended at a mass meeting of the membership, it was the first time workers had heard any of the details. So strong was the hostility of the workforce that they voted against it in a ballot. This was especially surprising given the fact that the ballot was held at a time when workers were laid off and the plant was at a standstill.

At hastily reconvened mass meetings, the union officials told them they had a choice between rescinding their decision or going on an immediate all-out strike. This time the union leadership finally obtained a vote for acceptance. So although there was great opposition to the employer's offensive, hopes that any substantial opposition to the attacks on labour standards could be mounted, in this new era of lean production, evaporated when the union leadership capitulated to company demands.

A cadre of shop stewards able to resist the employers' tactics and give firm leadership to workers was clearly needed. This would be difficult in just one firm. We return to this theme in our concluding chapter, where we wish to consider the possible responses to the myriad structural changes that have taken place over the last two decades. Short-term agency working is now structurally central to lean, and we only have to look at the situation at Cowley, an important focus of this chapter, to understand some of the obstacles to trade union mobilisation: more than 30 per cent of the workforce at Cowley are now agency workers. The proportion is higher still at Hams Hall, the engine plant.

In the next chapter we focus on the way in which GM continued its drive to deepen lean production. This can be seen in its accelerating Europeanisation and the consequent impact on workers' ability to resist changes to the production regime. The chapter also considers developments at BMW (Oxford-Cowley), examining the period from 2000 when production of BMW's new Mini took off. In both companies we were especially concerned with workers' experiences of the way in which lean production impacts on the quality of their lives on the assembly tracks. Despite significant differences in lean production at GM-Vauxhall and BMW, workers at both companies reported stress, excessive work pace and bullying. Their different responses, while in part reflecting the different management methods of lean production, can also be attributed to the role of unions. This reinforces to an important extent our previous distinction between the 'Embrace and Change' and 'Engage and Change' legacies at Rover and GM-Vauxhall respectively. Nonetheless, whatever the early saliency of the latter, the time has now come for the development of new workplace agendas, an issue to which we return in the Conclusion.

7 LEAN PRODUCTION: FROM 'ENGAGE AND CHANGE' TO ENDLESS CHANGE

INTRODUCTION

Vauxhall yesterday unveiled plans to axe 2,000 jobs and cease car production at Luton, one of the country's more efficient car plants, sending shock waves through British manufacturing .... The unions reacted with fury to what they called a 'bolt out of the blue' .... They vowed to fight the closure ... where the new Vectra model was expected to be built .... Overcapacity in Europe was the main reason for the restructuring.

(*Guardian* 13/12/2000)

Surprise, fighting back and overcapacity: if only it were so straightforward. While the *Financial Times* (17/12/00) might have been surprised, the same could hardly be said of those who worked for Vauxhall-GM. As for fighting back, there were a number of reasons, as we shall argue, why existing attempts to deal with lean production, some of which had been reasonably successful until the late 1990s (at GM-Vauxhall), were now less effective. Yet we now know for sure that the company rationale – 'overcapacity' – bore only a semblance of reality. And of course, all of this was only a matter of months after the threatened closure of Rover-Longbridge (which eventually closed in April 2005). What tied the plight of both firms together was the deepening impact of lean production. This chapter is particularly concerned with the impact of lean on workers at GM-Vauxhall and BMW one year after the events at Vauxhall-Luton and Rover-Longbridge, in 2001.

In this chapter we examine responses by workers at GM-Vauxhall and BMW to lean production in the context of company commitments to positively transform work and employment relations. In Chapter 6 we followed the travails of BMW-Rover, and the first section of this chapter focuses mostly on GM-Vauxhall's institutional and workplace evolution of lean production. The politics of lean production at GM-Vauxhall were marked by two phases, each of which comprised processes leading to two pay and conditions agreements. The first phase covered the implementation of the 1989–92 and the 1995–96 agreements. The second phase was marked by the 1997–98 and 2001 agreements.

We would take issue with Arrowsmith's (2002) use of the term 'security and flexibility agreements' to describe the agreements up to and including 1997–98, but it does reflect the misleading rhetoric employed, at least in the promise of job protection. There have been many presumptions along the way to lean production's Holy Grail of job enhancement and security, but if ever a phrase concealed the real character of a management agenda it is surely this. As critics of lean production have shown time and again, flexibility offers little by way of workplace outcomes that could be understood as beneficial to employees, while job security is precisely what lean production can never guarantee, since it undermines one of its primary imperatives – continuous improvement. As a Vauxhall worker with over 25 years' experience recently noted:

> There will never be a security of work agreement – how can there be? The unions will always find it hard to reach an agreement that actually protects, while at the same time the company is building more capacity into the eastern European plants – there is no agreement here as far as I know. They have just announced 700,000 capacity for two plants in Poland and in Russia …. Are the two plants for the eastern market only or for Europe as a whole? This is the contradiction in it all – take a shift out of Ellesmere Port because of overcapacity and at the same time build more capacity into the market! Scary stuff.
>
> (JM, 4/6/2006)

The first agreement in 1989–90 (Ellesmere Port Wages and Conditions Agreement, known by the TGWU as the V6 Agreement) incorporated a robust TGWU response. This was followed in 1992 with the Luton Agreement (*Working Together to Win* – WTW), the substance of which was examined in Chapter 3, and which we characterised as a strategy of bargained dissent which could be summarised as 'Engage and Change'. (For present purposes V6 and WTW are taken together as one agreement.) In each of the agreements there was a discernible sequence of debate, then agreement on organisational and plant changes, followed by an unsatisfactory pay

Table 7.1 Significant processes and events at GM-Vauxhall and BMW (1989–2001)

Period	GM-Vauxhall	BMW
1989–92	'V6' & 'WTW' Agreements Beginning of integration (Europeanisation) of Vauxhall-UK into General Motors Europe (GME)	
1994		BMW take over Rover
1995–96	Dispute and unofficial strike over Pay and Conditions Agreement	
1997–98	Pay and Conditions Agreement	'Concerns' over fate of Rover
2000–01	Luton closure process 'Project Olympia'	Sale by BMW of Rover (Longbridge)to Phoenix for £10. Oxford Mini plant remains with BMW – 2001 Agreement Plant Oxford (APO).

deal. In this regard, job security was 'guaranteed', notwithstanding our scepticism above, in so far as it was not yet seen in apocalyptic terms. The apocalyptic spin on the need for flexibility and security could bide its time.

To be sure, until the debate around the 1997–98 agreement, there was no general threat to either Luton or Ellesmere Port, and concerns over security were not part of the company's managerial and ideological arsenal. The options for labour control were still restricted by UK company and labour traditions, which remained in part because of the still relatively febrile nature of GM's Europeanisation strategy, as we argue below.[1] However, after the 1995–96 agreement, the issue of conditions became calculatedly tied not simply to the notion of job improvements and functional flexibility, as had initially been understood by – and sold to – the unions, but to broader job, and even plant, security (Joint Trade Union document, 1998).

As we saw in Chapter 3, the period 1989 to 1992 witnessed what was really the first agreement in the UK auto sector on lean production. It was thrashed out after a vociferous union campaign which saw the retention of significant job controls and vital elements, by the standards of lean, of shopfloor autonomy. This was indeed impressive since it represented a critical and reasonably successful labour response to management arguments for lean production. It was especially distinctive in that the union response to the impact of lean production on the quality of work life on the assembly lines found a deep resonance in workers' experiences. The measured success of 'Engage and Change' arguably held until the 1995–96 agreement (see Chapter 4) had pretty well run its course, after which GM's strategy was irrevocably transformed. By the time of the 1998 agreement, the unions found it increasingly difficult to hold the line established between 1989 and 1995–96.

Two factors gradually eroded labour's ability to engage robustly with management's agenda. First, beginning in 1989, we can observe the increasing drive by GM to Europeanise Vauxhall, as witnessed by the development of a lean organisational strategy, which certainly fed into, and was part of, the new production logic of GM's global rationalisation agenda. One outcome was that GM was now no longer interested in the increasingly costly niceties of separate research and development facilities in Britain and on the European mainland. Moreover, and as part of this key objective, reduced capacity would allow for no more than two locations for the same model.

At the same time, however, GM wanted to see all facilities transformed into flexi-plants[2] capable of running a multiplicity of models, or variants thereof, on a limited range of platforms. In fact, what the lean changes really presaged was the company's attempt to have it all ways, as the concept of the flexi-plant envisages. In other words, reduced capacity is not, nor could it sensibly be, the only logic of lean. (It is not just about the performance of one plant.) Lean is so vital because it leads automatically not to capacity reduction but rather to greater capacity utilisation, including the reduction in the time taken to introduce changes within and beyond existing plant capacity. That is to say, having one model produced in just two sites while at the same time increasing plant flexibility is about management making swift strategic production choices and resource-allocation choices (which plants get investment) in anticipation of market changes.[3]

There is a second and overarching factor that placed increasing strain on the V6 'Engage and Change' agenda, which can be summed up as the progressively corrosive impact of neoliberalism. As we argued in Chapter 1, the political and social character of lean is a vital logic of the current period of neoliberal hegemony. Lean has often been understood in terms of either production strategies, with their attendant logic of inevitability – who can be against the 'best' way to do things? – or its offer of democratic and thereby participative social engagement. And who could oppose that either? But this would be to miss the bigger picture, which is that lean production is in fact logically premised, from a social and political point of view, on the need to shift the political balance in the workplace in favour of capital. In its strategic imperatives, in its operational logic, this is precisely what it sets out to achieve. The drive here is for labour subordination, especially in the context of a new pattern of global competition with its new division of social and economic labour. To the extent that the state focuses on social control, control of labour (economic relations including both the internal and external labour markets) becomes increasingly the privilege of the lean corporation, or work organisation more broadly conceived, since today lean is the philosophy of workplace control *par excellence* (see Durand 2007). Assessing the so-called 'security and flexibility agreements' will allow us to track the embedding of lean at GM-Vauxhall.

EMBEDDING LEAN PRODUCTION AT VAUXHALL-GM, 1989–2001

To reiterate, the four tri-annual agreements at GM-Vauxhall should be understood as forming part of the warp and weft of a 'new politics of production' (Martinez Lucio and Stewart 1998). It can also be seen as constituting two phases of the new politics of lean. The first phase, covering the 1989–92 and 1995–96 agreements, was still driven by the peculiarities of UK national bargaining, including the ability of the unions to exert significant leverage over the outcome of informal shopfloor and other forms of more institutionalised bargaining. While it is true, as Arrowsmith (2002) points out, that the V6 (Wages and Conditions Agreement) signalled Vauxhall's integration into GM Europe (GME), this was nevertheless only the beginning of a process that would take almost a decade to achieve, especially in terms of labour relations. The second phase of lean, ushered in with the 1997–98 Pay and Conditions Agreement and marked by debate over the future of Luton, was completed in October 2001 with the pan-European management–union corporate agreement, Project Olympia (signed on 1 October 2001 – see the Project Olympia Framework document (*PO* 2001), reproduced on page 198). Since 2001 issues around pay and conditions have merely consolidated this phase of Europeanisation.

From 1989 onwards, GM's Europe agenda was to be achieved primarily by reducing local vehicle component content and vertical integration, which would lead eventually to Ellesmere Port and Luton becoming screwdriver facilities.[4] This would be a far cry from the kind of vertically integrated operations described by Robert H. Guest in his visit to the two plants in 1974.[5] In the 1989 V6 Agreement, the TGWU, the leading union, retained considerable autonomy and strength on the ground because of its ability to respond to members' interests (see worker responses in Chapters 3 and 4), notably on critical issues such as health and safety. While in many respects this continued to be the case over the next decade, despite Project Olympia[6] (see worker responses below), it is nevertheless fair to argue that organised labour is now at a crossroads.[7] Despite GM-Vauxhall's rhetoric in 1995 that the firm and its unions (and employees in the form of intra-company competition) were now performing on a wider European playing field, it was only really with the signing of the 1998 Agreement on Pay and Conditions that this finally began to reap rewards in terms of the logics of production and employment relations. This was because for the first time the UK unions committed themselves to a Europe-wide concession bargaining programme of an unusually pernicious kind, known in North America as whipsawing – although it would seem they had little choice, since the whole agenda was loaded in favour of Opel (GME) and its industrial relations institutions.

Whipsawing has been interpreted in a number of ways, and more usually from the point of view of anti-competitive business practices. However the usage here, and the one commonly adopted in the labour movement, refers to the situation whereby workers in different plants of the same company are encouraged to bid against one another by reducing their social and labour costs in the hope of investment preferment.

At this time – until Project Olympia – there was as yet no pan-European formal agreement, although the ability of plants in the United Kingdom and elsewhere to manoeuvre separately was in any event severely reduced. The terms of debate, all talk of job security and compensation for currency fluctuations aside, were really about the extent to which unions could be compelled, perhaps for the first time in the sector in Europe, to ratify formally a whipsawing agreement promoting intra-worker competition on wages and social conditions. To achieve this in the United Kingdom, GM-Vauxhall was eventually able to extract an agreement allowing labour flexibility (temporary workers), a working time corridor clause (the beginning of annualised hours) and a three-shift system. The notion of adaptation on the basis of local conditions – in other words, workers could be shed according to how difficult this would prove to be under the rubric of specific national legislation – would have to wait another three years for Project Olympia to become a factor of major prominence.

The 1997–98 negotiations on workplace change were critical because they were ostensibly predicated on the usual job security guarantees, and notably on promises that Luton was to get investment for the Corsa. Yet tragically, while the unions made the commitment, and obtained shopfloor support, GME announced that investment would not be forthcoming, committing instead to Saragossa in Spain. The problem for labour was that GME was already pushing the unions in other Vectra and Astra plants in Belgium and Germany to cut a deal which they subsequently delivered (GME Works Council Papers, 1997, 1998). The TGWU was so alarmed by this turn of events that the national secretary, Tony Woodley, wrote to Nick Reilly, the chairman and managing director of Vauxhall, to express his concern:

> The recent announcement that the Corsa is not to be built in Britain, coupled with the further announcement of an agreement between the German unions and the Company, ratified no doubt by the Strategy Board, concerning investment, capacity and employment protection for all the German plants lead us to believe the UK will be disadvantaged by the effect of both these agreements if they remain unchanged. In short, it is our genuine belief and fear that one of the two British plants may be down for closure by mid-2000.
>
> (Woodley, 5/2/98)

This fear was indeed to be cruelly borne out by the year's end.

While the UK unions fretted over what Mike Parker of *Labor Notes* describes as a 'lights out' scenario for Luton in the event of failure to land investment for the Corsa, the discussion across GME, including the different national unions, appeared to be couched in less pessimistic terms. If anyone was to take the hit of what GME euphemistically termed 'capacity adjustment' – as if this was simply a technical problem without human cost – the implicit, if not overt, assumption was that as in the past this would be achieved through 'natural wastage'. (Later, in Project Olympia, it would be known as 'rightsizing of capacity'. See *PO* 2001.)

While 'capacity adjustment' obviously should have been understood as anticipating plant closure, we have to look at it in terms of people's experiences at GM-Vauxhall up until that time. Of course, as was pointed out above (Joint Trade Union document, 1998) the various UK union responses addressed this fear very directly, but there was also the feeling among many that despite the fearful logic of 'capacity adjustment', negotiated job loss could be made to prevail over plant closure. In the 1980s, for workers at Vauxhall, while 'capacity adjustment' might mean job loss, usually for example via early retirement, it had never before implied total plant closure. In practice, many remained convinced that the strategy of the past – 'Engage and Change' as we have termed it – would win through in the end. Yet the playing field had changed, and unions found it difficult to know how best to respond to a situation where GM-Vauxhall was merely one item on the wider GME balance sheet.

So in fairness, Woodley did raise the issue of closure when it became obvious that the German and Belgian unions had made secret pathbreaking deals, which basically undermined many of their previous conditions. Although this would allow the German and Belgian unions to believe they could save their own plants if plant closure was threatened, another promise that at least the new Vectra would come to Luton was sufficient to obtain an agreement and stymie opposition.[8] But if GME could renege on its promise of the Corsa, why not also on the Vectra? Nevertheless, by the end of April that year, most people assumed that with a signed deal the new Vectra, codenamed Epsilon, would be coming to Luton, shored up by a massive government grant.

To try to keep the unions onside, it could be argued that one bright management tactic was to create an alliance of national solidarity between Vauxhall management and the labour force, as if this allowed some scope to act independently as a force to be reckoned with inside GME. In *Update* no. 2 on 30 March 1998, a month after Woodley's letter, GM-Vauxhall spelled out the necessity for this joint management–union approach to GME as if the big bad corporation lived in a place called Europe, and as if the decisions on investment could somehow be tailor-made for an idiosyncratic UK programme. As if, that is, something distinctive called Vauxhall Motors could operate semi-autonomously within the GM empire. This surely could be seen to be a fiction since management had been driving forward GME's Europeanisation agenda – an agenda that had been sold precisely as the precondition of survival.

> There is substantial overcapacity in the West European car market .... That is why the closure of one plant is seen as one

possible means of dealing with over-capacity and improving competitiveness and financial viability. Our task is to provide a better alternative.

(*Update* no. 2, 30 March 1998)[9]

Of course, replacement of the Luton Vectra was one of the many management 'guarantees' unions and workers could be certain of once a settlement had been reached – except that this promise proved to be about as watertight as the earlier certainty over the Corsa. History was repeating itself in just a matter of months. As previously, there was the usual rhetoric and agreement on conditions (on overtime, outsourcing and this time on lower pay for new starts) in order to obtain the new Vectra. This was tied to the future of Ellesmere Port and its continued production of the Astra: if the two plants whose destinies were inextricably linked did not accept the deal as a whole, not only might Luton disappear but the future of Ellesmere Port, which might have looked safe, would also be jeopardised. Welcome to inter-company competition with a vengeance. Welcome to whipsawing.

Whipsawing would not have been possible, nor was it easily deliverable, on a national, or at any rate regional, basis in the absence of plant and model duplication. Inspired by the strategic options of lean production, one plant–one model represented one of the key sources of production inflexibility supposedly lying at the heart of GME's product and facilities frailties. The solution, as was pointed out above, was for the development of flexi-plants, and this would eventually be proffered as the solution to Ellesmere Port's woes (see note 2). However that has not solved anything for around 1,000 workers whose jobs (one-third of the total) have disappeared since the knight in shining armour of security through flexibilisation (flexiplantisation) came galloping out of the propaganda machine.

At a pan-European level inter-plant competition looked to be unstoppable. With unions as well as plants now fighting to attract investment, in the case of Ellesmere Port for the Astra, the terms of the debate have so far not been well addressed by organised labour. (We return to this in the Conclusion.) Although we do not want to pre-empt the discussion later, it is clear where the source of a range of antagonisms lie, it is clear how these are sustained, and we may possibly be able to say something about the ways in which these could provide the wellspring for new strategic alternatives to lean production. For the survey reported here, together with our previous surveys, highlights the vital independent factor of worker antipathy to lean production. It is moreover the factor to which we are forced to return repeatedly: that is, the effects of lean production on workers' physical and emotional lives, both at home and at work.

GM'S PROJECT OLYMPIA 2001, BMW AND PARTNERSHIP

> Another thing about production on the line you've got to understand, and I don't care what you're doing, even if you're welding, I don't give a fuck, because you switch off. I tell you honestly if you don't switch off and do it on autopilot you won't survive the day.
>
> (BMW worker, trim shop, 28/9/00)

In the light of the BMW and GM-Vauxhall totems of flexibility, rationalisation and 'partnership', albeit with differing histories and agendas, our survey examined employee responses by concentrating on three broad themes: consultation (including attitudes to union and company performance when it comes to involvement); working conditions, work load and work speed; and workplace stress (employee autonomy, stress and bullying – issues associated with the quality of working life). When we conducted our survey, production of the new Mini was ramping up at the BMW plant,[10] while workers at Vauxhall-Ellesmere Port were still coming to terms with the Luton closure decision of December 2000 (the last Vectra would roll off the assembly line in March 2002). The survey was conducted just after GME's announcement of Project Olympia in October, after it had gone through a number of revisions during the previous months. Project Olympia was vital to the corporation essentially because it was a critical indicator of how far labour unions would be committed to the greater GM project of lean production.

By committing to Project Olympia, GM unions throughout Europe effectively tied themselves into a form of concession-bargaining partnership, and nowhere more obviously so than with the clause ensuring commitment to what GME euphemistically termed 'rightsizing of capacity'. Yet it would not be the usual concession-bargaining agenda characteristic of so many labour agreements in the auto sector and elsewhere in the 1990s. In fact, arguably for the first time, caveats and niceties aside, the agreement institutionalised whipsawing, and the European context was the vital arena in which this came to fruition. This is important when we recall our characterisation of the pattern of agreements at Rover and GM-Vauxhall in the period 1989–92. At GM-Vauxhall (V6, Ellesmere Port, 1989 and *Working Together to Win*, Luton, 1992), labour cooperation was seen to derive from union autonomy and vitality on the basis of 'bargained dissent'. In the case of Rover it was found that a pattern of compliance was established in the context of union commitments which we termed 'cooperation in the context of compliance' – eventually codified in the period between BMW's takeover in 1994 and the sale of Longbridge in 2000 to Phoenix as a fully fledged form of subordinate partnership.[11]

Project Olympia 2001

The context and agenda were different at GM-Vauxhall, and initially it would appear as if union organisation might benefit from a stronger Europe-based organisation and trade union agenda, including European Works Council (EWC) initiatives. However, it soon become clear that GME would now seek to use the strength of the EWC to tie unions into an intra-company – intra-worker – whipsawing competition on wages and conditions. It was a competition moreover which would be hierarchical, with the strongest union – IG-Metall –in the driving seat. Indeed, Project Olympia effectively conceded that the social agenda, including company responses to what it perceived to be overcapacity, would necessarily defer to social and national protocol on redundancies – 'depending on individual custom and national legislation' (*PO* 2001).

As *PO* spelled out, 'Management and employee representatives have the joint goal to institute actions leading to company profitability and sustainable growth, thus achieving the turnaround of GME to competitiveness and a successful future of the employees.' 'Rightsizing' would entail cost-cutting, including the elimination of 350,000 units in all production areas – stamping, powertrain and components. The agreement went on to promise that 'Management agrees that the outcome of the implementation of the Olympia initiatives will not include a site closure' in any of its European operations (*PO* 2001). Thankfully, Luton had by now been dealt with, no doubt acting as a warning of GME's ruthlessness. This was important, necessary so as to:

> move the productivity levels to world-class benchmark standards, e.g. leanfield principles. Necessary measures to increase overall productivity and gain efficiencies will occur at

all locations. Best practices and adjustments in the area of salaried staff have to be implemented as well to obtain efficiencies and cost reductions.

(*PO* 2001)

How was this to be achieved successfully? Arguably there were four critical items in the agreement relating to the usual promises on job security. Flexibility – not just in terms of plant and equipment – would be achieved 'through alternative efficient and innovative working time and staffing models'. Early in 2001 GM-Vauxhall had already announced that the introduction of a third shift would safeguard over 700 jobs at Ellesmere Port, thus allowing the facility to become a flexi-plant. Second, GME was keen to promote the decade-old partnership accord but this time reinforced by pan-European commitment from all unions within its European facilities – 'Priority must be to maintain or grow employment at the respective locations' (*PO* 2001). Now appeared the third, possibly killer, element in the agreement; 'Manpower adjustments'. These are sensible; 'manpower adjustments' are an intelligent response to the interminable rise and fall in market share. Anyone can understand the necessity for them, which means that no rational person could possibly dissent:

> Manpower adjustments, where necessary will be handled in socially responsible ways, which depending on individual custom and national legislation may include early retirements, separation programs, transfers to other National and International GM locations to available openings, outplacement assistance etc. These measures will enable us to avoid forced redundancies while implementing the necessary restructuring. Efforts to place workers in reasonable positions will require an increased willingness of employees with regard to mobility and flexibility for the work location as well as for working time and practices. It is also necessary to ensure that the required numbers of employees are placed in facilities that have urgent start-up needs and requirements due to market conditions.
>
> (*PO* 2001)

That this neither precludes nor admits the scope for site 'closure' is clear enough, except that given the politics, including the pedantic nature of all such agreements, the absence of the word is itself revealing.

The final promise or inclusion was that implementation of the framework would derive from 'continuing inclusion and consultation during this process with the intention to reach mutually agreed solutions. This process will include dialogue at a national level and will be performed according to the respective national legislation and practice.' As we shall see, our survey results can hardly be said to offer much support for this promise of inclusive consultation. (For the questionnaire see Appendix 2.) Finally of course we have the usual touching of the forelock to legal process – that solemn and binding thing, that 'concrete abstraction', as Marx called it, which allows the self-interested business of the powerful to be legitimised as the interests of all: 'Implementation of this framework shall occur at the national level. According to European legislation and national laws Management and employee representatives will ensure that the agreed provisions will become legally binding for individual employees as well as negotiating partners' (*PO* 2001).

While this new dispensation did indeed signal a qualitative turn in the road of labour–management relations both in GME and more especially for unions at GM-Vauxhall, its precedent had been in the making for nearly a decade, and most recently since the debate in the United Kingdom around the 1998 Wages and Conditions Agreement.

WORKER ATTRIBUTES

Table 7.2 provides a summary of the attributes of the workers who participated in the survey. A number of these reflect core workforce characteristics of brownfield manufacturing plants in the United Kingdom. For example, both plants had an ageing workforce. The combined average age was 42 years (only 10 per cent of respondents were aged under 30), while average length of employment at the plants was 18 years. The gender profile of these shopfloor workforces also reflected the deeply entrenched gender segmentation in UK automotive manufacture (the number of women respondents in the survey amounted to little more than one in 20). Recruitment practices corresponded to the traditions associated with paternalism and the close cultural bonds between the plants and their local communities, in that many workers had family members and other relatives who also worked in the plant. Nearly three-quarters of respondents were classed as direct workers, mainly assembly and body shop workers, while the remainder were classed as indirect workers, mostly forklift drivers and other shopfloor labourers. Finally, high proportions of workers in both plants classed them-

Table 7.2 Attributes of survey respondents

Average age	42 years
Average experience	18 years
Men	94%
Women	6%
Direct workers	72%
Indirect workers	28%
Relations in plant	49%
Active in union (BMW)	65%
Active in union (GM)	78%

selves as being active in the union – active in the sense of regularly attending union meetings, discussing issues with shop stewards, reading union newsletters and so on.

Workplace Partnership, and Management and Union Performance

In Chapter 3, we described a form of workplace partnership developed at Rover – and then BMW – in the aftermath of the company's *Rover Tomorrow* initiative in 1992. In the context of company crisis, and in the interests of 'factory survival' concerns, the national leadership of the TGWU endorsed management's attempt to impose a raft of lean production techniques. It also attempted to foster among its senior activists a less adversarial culture of 'Embrace and Change' at the factory level. Although the development of partnership relations between management and workplace unions was incomplete and subject to some contestation by less senior stewards, the underlying trajectory towards greater cooperation was made easier by the relatively close relationship between Rover plant senior stewards and the TGWU's regional and national automotive officials.

By contrast, a pattern of managerial caution at GM, and indeed the constraints imposed by a form of 'micro-corporatism' in management–union relations, acted against any impulse to impose new production techniques without local negotiations at GM's UK plants. Moreover, a greater distance in relations between plant activists and the TGWU bureaucracy, and extant traditions of inter-plant autonomy, gave GM's shop stewards much greater leeway to adopt oppositional positions in these negotiations. Unlike Rover, what developed was a partnership-sceptic strategy based on 'Engage and Change'.

In this context of different industrial relations at the two plants, our questionnaire survey first explored the extent to which employees felt that their managers were providing them with opportunities to participate in decisions governing organisational change, and whether they felt they were treated with respect. These are central themes in the supposed shift from control to commitment in new management philosophy (Gallie, Felstead and Green 2001, Hodson 2001). They also take on a particular resonance in the light of the supposed importance of these issues for the development of partnership in contemporary workplace relations (Coupar and Stevens 1998, Heery 2002).

The results are shown in Tables 7.3 and 7.4. There were two different pairs of questions. The first asked whether management had been involved in consulting employees about new work practices and reorganisation, and to what extent employees felt

Table 7.3 Workers' assessment of consultation and respect at work (row percentages)

How involved has management been in telling you about new practices and work reorganisation?

	Very involved	Involved	Not very involved	Not involved at all
All	4	40	37	19
BMW	3	47	33	17
GM	5	35	41	19

To what extent do you feel consulted over company policy?

	Great deal	A lot	Some	A little	None
All	3	5	24	24	44
BMW	1	3	29	24	43
GM	5	6	21	24	45

Are management policies reasonable and fair at this workplace?

	Very fair	Fair	Neither	Unfair	Very unfair
All	1	31	31	30	7
BMW	1	38	23	31	7
GM	1	27	37	29	6

How interested is management in your welfare?

	Very interested	Interested	Not sure	Not interested	Not interested at all
All	2	22	28	27	22
BMW	3	27	23	27	20
GM	2	18	31	26	23

Table 7.4 Management performance scale

	Management performance Mean score: Max 12–Min 0
BMW	4.57
GM	4.33
Aged 18–30	4.07
Aged 31–40	4.52
Aged 41–50	4.46
Aged 51–65	4.82
Direct workers	4.17
Indirect workers	4.93
Active union members	4.35
Non-active union members	4.50

consulted over company policy. Table 7.3 suggests a pattern of some management activity in employee consultation but predominant worker dissatisfaction with the results. Overall, nearly half of respondents felt that management had been involved in consulting them about work organisational change. As we might expect, the proportion was higher in BMW's partnership setting. However, when asked whether they felt consulted over company policy, a more negative pattern emerged. Of all respondents, 68 per cent responded either 'a little' or 'none', and there was no obvious difference between the two plants.

The second pair of questions related to the issue of respect, asking employees whether they felt management policies at their workplace were reasonable and fair, and whether management was interested in their welfare. Responses were more polarised in their assessment of whether management policies were reasonable and fair. For instance, BMW workers were more likely than their partnership-sceptic GM counterparts to indicate positively, but equally likely to indicate negatively. As for management interest in employee welfare, although there were inter-plant differences, the clearest pattern was one of worker cynicism – in both cases nearly 50 per cent of respondents felt that their managers were not interested in their welfare.

We explored further facets of these employee responses by creating a 'management performance' summative scale based on the four questions presented in Table 7.3.[12] The first point to note is that these workers' ratings of management performance were generally low, and well below the mid-point of 6 on the scale. The results show some differences between employee groups, although none of these were substantial. Workers at BMW's partnership plant were slightly more likely than their GM counterparts to provide a positive assessment of management performance. Combining both plants, the same applies to indirect workers compared with direct workers on the production lines, and to those union members who showed little interest in participating in union affairs compared with their more active colleagues. There was a more obvious age-related pattern, in that younger workers seemed to hold more cynical attitudes in their assessment of management performance.

The survey also explored employee assessments of trade union performance at the two workplaces. In this case, three related questions were asked. Mirroring the 'management involvement' question, respondents were asked how involved their unions had been in communicating about work organisational change. They were asked how involved their unions had been in getting management to modify work practices and in trying to improve health and safety conditions. Taken together, the questions provided a rudimentary index of union engagement with the 'micro-politics' of lean production.

The first pattern to emerge from the results (presented in Table 7.5) is that workers at both plants rated their trade unions' performance significantly higher than management's. Overall, 54 per cent of workers felt that their union had been involved in communicating about work organisational change compared with 44 per cent who felt that management had been involved. Moreover, very large proportions of employees at both plants rated union involvement highly with regard to modifying work practices and improving health and safety. Interestingly, however, there were some differences between the two plants. Workers in the partnership-sceptic GM plant were far more likely to indicate that their unions had been very involved on all three counts.

As with management performance, we explored inter-plant difference and other factors by creating a 'union performance' summative scale based on the three questions.[13] Unlike the management performance scale there was a large (and statistically significant) difference between employees' assessment of union performance in the two plants. The data suggest that the GM unions (which rejected partnership and engaged more critically with new management initiatives) were more likely to garner rank and file support.

Table 7.6 also highlights a number of differences between subgroups of employees. In line with their ratings of management performance, younger workers tended to view the extent of union

Table 7.5 Workers' assessment of union performance at work (row percentages)

How involved has the union been in telling you about new practices and work reorganisation?

	Very involved	Involved	Not very involved	Not involved at all
All	18	36	30	15
BMW	7	38	35	21
GM	26	35	27	11

How involved has the union been in getting management to modify work practices?

	Very involved	Involved	Not very involved	Not involved at all
All	30	49	15	5
BMW	20	53	20	7
GM	38	47	11	4

How involved has the union been in trying to improve health and safety conditions?

	Very involved	Involved	Not very involved	Not involved at all
All	42	42	11	5
BMW	21	58	13	9
GM	57	31	9	3

involvement less positively than older workers, perhaps a reflection of a youth-related alienation from the rigour and monotony of life on the shopfloor under lean production regimes. There was also a substantial

Table 7.6 Union performance scale

	Union performance Mean score: Max 9–Min 0
BMW	5.08
GM	6.35
Aged 18–30	5.36
Aged 31–40	5.57
Aged 41–50	5.96
Aged 51–65	6.40
Direct workers	6.07
Indirect workers	5.56
Active union members	6.30
Non-active union members	4.60

(and statistically significant) difference between active and non-active union members. A statement that active members (who were larger in number than non-active members: see Table 7.2) were more likely to indicate feelings of higher union involvement in the politics of work organisation might be regarded as a truism. However, the difference is interesting in that active members were more likely to be based in the partnership-sceptic GM plant (78 per cent) than at BMW (65 per cent). In other words, these data raise the possibility that partnership relations between employers and unions may be acting gradually to undermine the traditions of independent workplace unionism based on grassroots member participation, traditions that were core characteristics of the history of union relations in both plants.

Working Conditions and Workload

The dominant managerial discourse governing the labour productivity benefits that accrue from lean production is underpinned by a belief in the potential of a more sophisticated management of the indeterminacy of labour. Compared with conventional Fordist work organisation, the technological and supervisory architecture of lean production is assumed to engender high trust relations and processes of empowerment on the shopfloor. In the 1980s and 1990s, this was summarised through the trite maxim 'working smarter not harder', and exemplified by the IMVP research (Womack, Jones and Roos 1990; see also MacDuffie 1995, MacDuffie and Pil 1999). In more refined form, it was also embodied in the work of Kenney and Florida (1993), who argued that the competitive edge of Japanese forms of lean production lay in what they termed 'innovation-mediated production'. Essentially, this was a relational framework that attempted to harness the job knowledge of design and production engineers and shopfloor workers.

In this section (and the next) we provide an alternative – and more problematic – picture to this, an analysis of line workers' own experiences of the automotive lean production line. We consider in turn basic conditions on the line, workload and work speed, before moving on to different dimensions of quality of working life, such as employee autonomy, workplace stress and bullying. While it is not difficult to find evidence of workplace harassment, or bullying, in the good old, bad old days, there is certainly evidence for its persistence under the various manifestations of lean. As one BMW steward pointed out, the way in which workers cope with it is different today since exit options are limited:

Well, the management styles have changed considerably because 20 years ago things that the management are doing now wouldn't have been tolerated. People, you know, would have just got their coats on and gone home. But now I mean they treat you ... [looks away resigned] I wouldn't treat a dog like some managers treat people.

(28/9/00)

In our sample, three-quarters of employees reported that they worked in some form of production team (of which two-thirds reported the practice of job rotation). Despite the optimistic claims of those management gurus who proclaim a new, post-Taylorist manufacturing environment, few workers had any delusions over the skill content of work on the new team-based lean production assembly line. At both plants, three-quarters of workers felt that it would take less than a month to train someone to do their job, and nearly 40 cent felt it would take a few days or less. At the GM plant, as many as 25 per cent of workers felt that it would take just a few hours. At BMW, in spite of, or maybe because of, the innovation in work techniques introduced for the production of the new Mini, the perception of need for increased skills was also limited. According to one body shop worker:

It's not really skill as such like even with the new car. I mean yeah, you do get a lot of different new things to do, but taken on their own they're pretty simple jobs. It's not skill, it's like you are really a robot. For me that's easy, I can switch off and I'm sitting on a beach in Barbados. It's bloody boring.

(28/9/00)

Also, nearly 50 per cent (and three-quarters of GM workers) reported that they worked rotating shifts of one week of days and one week of nights. This is a high proportion given that such shift patterns are likely to be a causal risk factor in the stress–coronary heart disease mechanism (Mayhew 2003).

Another facet of the labour process of these employees was the high degree of management surveillance reported, something that has recently been shown to be an increasingly pervasive and powerful aspect of management control in British workplaces (White et al. 2004). Again this stands in contrast to the 'independent', 'working smarter' idiom of lean management discourse. As Table 7.7 shows, and with little difference between the two plants, 72 per cent of

Table 7.7 Management surveillance (row percentages)

How closely is your work performance monitored by management?			
	Very closely	Closely	Some	Not closely
---	---	---	---	---
All	33	40	22	5
BMW	32	41	24	3
GM	33	39	21	7
Direct	32	46	18	4
Indirect workers	33	29	29	9
Secure workers	38	28	28	6
Insecure workers	31	45	19	5
Bullied by managers	52	33	11	4
Rarely bullied	26	43	25	6

employees indicated that their work performance was either closely or very closely monitored by management. Not surprisingly, this was higher among direct production workers. It was also higher both for employees who felt insecure in their jobs and for those who had been subjected to bullying by their managers (both variables are analysed in the next section). We are not able to provide evidence of direction of causation here. However, these associations do suggest that as well as remaining a source of work degradation and a pervasive alternative management strategy to a more enlightened 'responsible autonomy' (Friedman 1977), direct control can also impair the psychological and material well-being of workers who are subject to its managerial gaze.

We now turn to employee evaluations of the intensity of their work by considering staffing levels, workload factors and the pace of production. We assessed staffing level concerns by asking whether respondents felt there were sufficient people in their work area to cover the work assigned, and whether there were adequate relief staff to enable them to leave the job to attend to personal matters, such as going to the toilet. The results are presented in Table 7.8.

The first pattern to emerge is that although substantial numbers of respondents felt that staffing levels were about right (though very few felt they were generous), the majority of employees believed they were understaffed in their work areas. As one trim shop worker observed:

The pace has changed a lot. When we were producing – 20 years ago – say 39,000 cars with 10,000 people, we're now producing 39,000 cars with 3,000 people. You know, so I mean it's not all in the technology, and of course that's part of it, that's reduced manning levels but the 3,000 still have to manage the machines that are producing all of that lot. The trouble is that 20 years ago in some cases the lines were running faster than they are now! But you had more people, you had less to do. You've got more to do in less time now.

(28/9/2000)

This is not surprising, given lean production's imperative of 'waste' elimination. Nevertheless, it does suggest that many workers did not endorse this principle. Overall, more than half felt that staffing levels were insufficient (particularly at BMW), and similar numbers indicated inadequate provision of relief staff.

The data also suggested that the most experienced employees

Table 7.8 Workers' assessment of staffing levels (row percentages)

Enough people in your work area to cover the work assigned?

	Too many or far too many	About right	Too few or far too few
All	4	43	53
BMW	3	37	60
GM	5	47	48
<5 yrs experience	0	37	63
6–10 yrs experience	0	39	61
11–20 yrs experience	9	36	56
>20 yrs experience	3	49	48
Direct	4	35	61
Indirect workers	4	60	36

Adequate relief staff in your area?

	Too many or far too many	About right	Too few or far too few
All	1	43	56
BMW	3	42	55
GM	0	44	56
<5 yrs experience	0	26	74
6–10 yrs experience	0	50	50
11–20 yrs experience	5	46	49
>20 yrs experience	0	49	51
Direct	2	43	55
Indirect workers	0	43	57

regarded staffing levels as less of a problem (although we found that this was not age-related), while direct production workers were more likely to experience understaffing than indirect labourers.

Significant minorities of employees also reported work overload. We first used the crude dimension of 'weight' of work responsibilities by asking respondents whether their current manual workload – for example, positioning and fastening pieces, moving and lifting subassemblies and use of air tool torque – was too light, too heavy or about right. Around a quarter of employees felt that their workload was too heavy, although the figure was higher at GM (Table 7.9). Another question used to measure workload intensity generated more negative patterns: over 40 per cent of employees felt that they had too little time to complete their work assignments (nearly 45 per cent of BMW workers indicated this). Similar proportions of respondents in both plants felt that their current work speed was too fast. For one worker in the paint shop at BMW,

> It's mental pressure all the fuckin' time. I mean I'd say it's more that than the physical, especially in paint and trim where I've worked. The company says we're going to give you more responsibility, we're going to give you more info so's you've got more control over your job. It's not! It's more pressure. It's more to think about. For example, he's missed something in the car, whoever he is –right, then you should fuckin' point it out to him and put it right. That's a small thing I'm telling you, but let me tell you something else. If your cycle time is one minute and you have got 59.9 seconds work in it, then you please tell me how that guy's gonna cope helping me or pointing out to me what I've missed.
> (28/9/2000)

These patterns were also mediated by age and task. On all three measures younger workers were more likely to report overload and excessive work speed than their older colleagues, especially in the direct worker group. One reason might be that while it took a relatively small amount of time to learn the routines required for each job, it took much longer to become accustomed to the arduous nature and intensity of lean production work. Another is the effect of the traditions of informal seniority arrangements in British automotive production, where in some plants, there is still a tendency for older workers to gravitate towards easier jobs (Danford 1999; Jurgens, Malsch and Dohse 1993; Tolliday and Zeitlin 1992).

We explored the problem of work intensity further by asking

Table 7.9 Workers' evaluation of workload and pace of work (row percentages)

Is your current manual workload:

	Too heavy or much too heavy	About right	Too light or much too light
All	25	69	5
BMW	19	72	9
GM	30	68	2
Aged 18–30	38	56	6
Aged 31–40	22	74	4
Aged 41–50	27	68	5
Aged 51–65	13	82	5
Direct	30	67	3
Indirect workers	14	77	9

How much time do you have to do the work currently assigned to you?

	Too much or far too much	About right	Too little or Far too little
All	7	51	42
BMW	9	47	44
GM	6	54	40
Aged 18–30	0	37	63
Aged 31–40	4	50	46
Aged 41–50	9	50	41
Aged 51–65	9	65	26
Direct	8	44	48
Indirect workers	4	68	28

Is your current work speed or work pace:

	Too fast or much too fast	About right	Too slow or much too slow
All	43	55	2
BMW	43	54	3
GM	44	55	1
Aged 18–30	56	31	13
Aged 31–40	37	61	2
Aged 41–50	46	54	0
Aged 51–65	32	68	0
Direct	48	50	2
Indirect workers	32	68	0

employees what proportion of each day they had to work as fast as they could to keep up with the rhythm of production, and whether they felt they could maintain their current work pace until the age of 60

(Table 7.10). The results showed that overall, as many as two-thirds of employees (although a lower proportion of younger workers) had to work at full speed at least half the time to keep up with the pace of production; nearly half had to work at full speed for three-quarters of the time. At BMW's partnership plant over a third of employees indicated that they had to work at full speed for the whole day. Not surprisingly, nearly two-thirds felt that they would be unlikely to be able to maintain the current pace of work until the age of 60.

Finally, we investigated evidence of association between some of these work conditions and workload variables.[14] As Table 7.11 shows, the analysis found that there were statistically significant associations. For example, in our sample of workers, those who indicated understaffing in their areas were more likely to report excessive work speeds and inability to keep pace until the age of 60;

Table 7.10 Workers' views on maintaining the pace of production (row percentages)

For what part of each day do you work as fast as you can so you don't fall behind?

	All day	75 per cent of the time	50 per cent of the time	25 per cent of the time or less
All	27	18	21	34
BMW	34	13	24	29
GM	22	22	19	37
Aged 18–30	13	19	12	56
Aged 31–40	16	23	22	39
Aged 41–50	36	15	20	29
Aged 51–65	35	17	22	26
Direct workers	29	19	19	33
Indirect workers	20	17	28	35

Could you work at the pace of your current job until the age of 60?

	Yes	Likely	Not likely	No
All	18	18	27	36
BMW	20	15	20	45
GM	17	21	32	30
Aged 18–30	6	19	25	50
Aged 31–40	18	20	39	22
Aged 41–50	16	16	22	45
Aged 51–65	39	22	13	26
Direct	13	18	30	39
Indirect workers	30	19	23	28

employees who indicated excessive work speeds were more likely to report excessive workload and again, an inability to keep pace until the age of 60. Employees who reported high managerial surveillance (who were the majority in our sample) were more likely to indicate that their work areas were understaffed, that their work speed was too fast and that they would be unable to keep up the pace until the age of 60. Working in teams had mostly no significant association with these variables. This suggested that for these workers, the intense rhythm of production, along with lean staffing levels, had a greater impact on effort rates than work organisation itself.

Table 7.11 Correlations between selected work conditions and workload variables

Variable	1	2	3	4	5	6
1. Enough people in work area	1					
2. Current manual workload	0.006	2				
3. Current work speed	0.236**	0.285**	3			
4. Keeping pace until 60	0.166**	0.106	0.307**	4		
5. Performance closely monitored	0.153*	0.004	0.264**	0.245**	5	
6. Work in a team	0.085	0.084	0.085	-0.180*	0.064	6

WORKPLACE STRESS

Workload and effort intensification are likely to increase levels of workplace stress when task and job demands become excessive (Cooper, Dewe and O'Driscol 2001; Macdonald 2003). For automotive workers, so are insufficient job control, or a lack of autonomy, since higher levels of control enable them to take actions that shield them from the incessant pressure of the production line. The rhetoric of lean production might refer to this autonomy as 'empowerment', conditions that allow workers to make decisions that make jobs easier – provided, of course, that the efficiency of the line is enhanced. By contrast, a critical labour process account would consider autonomy in more prosaic terms, as a worker's right to create parcels of time, to take a breather, or an informal break when required. Whichever way this is considered, it is clear that the balance between work demands and worker autonomy is a core quality of working life issue for workers deployed on the lean production line. Our survey explored this by adopting a series of measures of employee influence and workplace stress (which were used to create autonomy and stress scales). These were then used for an exploratory multivariate analysis of stress, to consider the interplay between workload, autonomy and other variables.

Employee Autonomy

Employee autonomy was operationalised by asking respondents how much influence they exerted over the way they carried out their work, how much they were able to vary the pace of their work over the course of the day, how much control they had over resolving problems that prevented them doing their job, and how easy it was to change the things they did not like about their jobs. The results are shown in Table 7.12.

Table 7.12 Workers' views on job influence and autonomy (row percentages)

How much influence do you have over the way you do your job?

	A great deal	A fair amount	Some	Very little	None at all
All	10	21	29	23	17
BMW	10	20	37	14	19
GM	10	22	22	31	15

Over the course of a day, how much can you vary the pace of your work?

	A great deal	A fair amount	Some	Very little	None at all
All	8	7	23	21	41
BMW	7	10	22	25	36
GM	9	6	23	18	44

How much control do you have sorting out problems that prevent you from doing your job?

	A great deal	A fair amount	Some	Very little	None at all
All	12	22	28	29	9
BMW	6	22	35	29	8
GM	17	22	23	28	9

How easy is it for you to change the things you do not like about your job?

	Very easy	Easy	Neither	Difficult	Very difficult
All	1	6	20	42	31
BMW	0	7	21	47	25
GM	1	5	19	40	35

The first point to note is a general pattern of relatively weak job control amongst these semi-skilled production line workers and unskilled labourers, far lower than is generally the case for skilled production workers (see, for example, Danford et al. 2005). Only one-third of respondents felt that they exerted either a great deal or a fair amount of influence over the way they carried out their work; a similar proportion indicated the same for control over sorting out problems that prevented them from doing their jobs. Moreover, in both plants large proportions of our sample felt that they could vary the pace of their work very little or not at all, and three-quarters found it difficult to change the things they did not like about their jobs. A body shop worker at GM argued that:

> They say we have more leeway, but whoever 'they' are, they want to get down here and try it! You cannot do that – everything's fixed. OK, the odd time you can take a blow, and you've seen it and worked there, but everything that was our time has been engineered out.
>
> (2000 Field notes GM)[15]

At BMW, an interesting point was made regarding job rotation, where it was understood largely as a way of coping with the tedium of monotonous jobs with little or no scope for variation of content. The boring nature of the job is made worse by the pace of job routines and understaffing, all of which add up to constant pressure and unremitting stress.

> Well, what's made the job boring is that the work is constant now, whereas before you had the work spread between more people so that can give you time to communicate, to have a laugh or a joke. Because there's less people now you're doing the work of say four people now, you just don't have the time to communicate, to have a laugh or whatever. It's isolating too, and even though you're in a team it doesn't matter because people don't talk any more. It's so difficult – well, like not difficult … just constant.
>
> (24/9/01)

The mean score results in Table 7.13[16] show a negligible difference between the BMW and GM plant and indeed between workers of different ages. Active union members tended to report higher autonomy than their less active colleagues, as did workers who felt secure in their jobs compared with the more insecure. A much

Table 7.13 Employee autonomy scale

	Employee autonomy Mean score: Max 16–Min 0
BMW	6.12
GM	5.97
Aged 18–30	6.14
Aged 31–40	5.89
Aged 41–50	6.03
Aged 51–65	6.29
Direct workers	5.56
Indirect workers	7.04
Active union members	6.12
Non-active union members	5.59
Secure workers	6.40
Insecure workers	5.81

greater (and statistically significant) difference existed between direct (semi-skilled) and indirect (predominantly unskilled) production workers. In this case, while autonomy is normally associated with higher skill, this result is consistent with other differences between these two groups in that, quite predictably, the degradation of work under lean manufacturing regimes is more acute for those whose labour power is consumed directly on the production line.

Worker Stress

Arduous, repetitive and monotonous work of the type associated with the automotive production line is always likely to be stressful for workers. Research has shown that repetitive work characterised by short cycle times and determined by production process time or speed of the assembly line is likely to have a negative impact on employees' physical and psychological well-being (Macdonald 2003). One of the core claims of the IMVP researchers was that lean production offered something better for workers, in that 'working smarter' provided them with the space and management techniques to establish a more participative (and less stressful) work environment:

> While the mass-production plant is often filled with mind-numbing stress, as workers struggle to assemble unmanufacturable products and have no way to improve their working environment, lean production offers a creative tension in which workers have many ways to address challenges. This creative

tension involved in solving complex problems is precisely what has separated manual factory work from professional 'think' work in the age of mass production.

(Womack et al. 1990: 101)

There is now a good deal of critical research that refutes this claim. For example, case study work such as that by Graham (1995) and Rinehart, Huxley and Robertson (1997) found that the core features of worker experience involved job rationalisation, work overload and constant 'speed-up' of the production line. Survey work has found relatively high levels of worker stress in car plants in Canada, Japan and the United Kingdom (Stewart et al. 2004), while multi-sectoral survey work in the United States has found clear evidence that the use of such lean techniques as just-in-time and quality circles increases the risk of cumulative trauma disorders (Brenner, Fairris and Ruser 2004).

Our survey investigated patterns of workplace stress by asking a number of questions governing the negative features of auto assembly work and workers' ability to cope with this. The first set of questions is shown in Table 7.14. When asked how often over the previous month they had worked in physical pain or discomfort, a third of workers indicated at least half the time. Over a quarter indicated 'every day or most days'. Similar proportions of workers reported working in physically awkward positions at least half of the time. There were differences between the two plants, in that GM workers were more likely to report these conditions than their BMW counterparts. Rather than the impact of any relational change under partnership, this is more likely to be attributable to the quality of investment in new production technology for the BMW Mini, together with the fact that at the time of the survey Mini production was still being ramped up.

A greater proportion of respondents described much of their work as boring or monotonous. Nearly three-quarters of workers felt that their work was monotonous for at least half of each working day. Again GM workers were more likely to indicate this. Two-thirds of workers reported feelings of exhaustion after their shift, with little difference between the two plants.

The data presented in Table 7.15 cover questions exploring how well the surveyed employees were able to cope with the demands of production. They seem to suggest that these demands were causing patterns of psychological ill-health. When asked if they ever felt that 'things are getting on top of you during your shift', two-thirds indicated that this was the case at least some of the time; one-third

Table 7.14 Workers' evaluation of work demands (row percentages)

In the last month at work, how often have you worked with physical pain or discomfort?

	Every day or most days	Half the time	A few days/never
All	28	6	66
BMW	23	4	73
GM	31	8	61

What part of each day do you work in physically awkward positions?

	All to ¾ of the time	Half of the time	¼ of the time or less
All	22	10	68
BMW	18	8	74
GM	25	12	63

What part of each day would you describe your work as boring or monotonous?

	All to ¾ of the time	Half of the time	¼ of the time or less
All	54	19	27
BMW	44	17	39
GM	61	20	19

In the last month, how often have you felt exhausted after your shift?

	Every day or most days	Half the time	A few days or never
All	49	15	36
BMW	45	17	38
GM	52	13	35

indicated a great deal or a fair amount of the time. One worker described this:

> When you think of how it's now changed, even for me that's only in his 30s, it's tough, you know? You worry a lot at home. My daughter says when I come home I just sit there and then it's like at breakfast, 'Oh, you're off again,' and you know she means you don't even talk at home. I worry a lot outside about the job, how to keep up and that.
>
> (BMW body shop welder and health and safety rep, 28/9/2000)

And at GM, a paint shop worker of ten years wondered about the long-term and wider effects of stress when he said:

> When you compare this survey now with maybe 20 years ago

if you could, I know the company wouldn't admit it but, it would make you think how it's all got to us, if you could compare that, and even more if you looked at problems here and at home, or like, local problems.

(2000 Field notes GM[17])

When asked how tense they were at work during the last month, nearly two-thirds indicated either very tense or somewhat tense (the pattern was stronger at BMW). A related question concerned the link between work intensification, stress and the quality of life outside of work. We could not consider this in any depth, but workers were asked whether tiredness at work had restricted their participation in family and social activities during the previous month. Nearly half of our respondents indicated that this was indeed the case for at least half the time; a very sizeable minority (over one-third) indicated that this was the case most days or every day.

If we place these results in the context of the work intensification data presented in the previous section, there does seem to be a link between working harder under lean production and the impairment of both physical and psychological health. Our survey

Table 7.15 Workers' evaluation of the impact of work demands (row percentages)

Do you ever feel that things are getting on top of you during your shift?

	A great deal	A fair amount	Some	Very little	None at all
All	16	18	31	21	14
BMW	15	15	36	21	13
GM	16	20	28	21	15

In the last month at work, how tense and wound up were you?

	Very tense	Somewhat tense	Not very tense	Not tense at all
All	21	41	21	17
BMW	24	42	21	14
GM	18	41	21	20

In the last month, how often has tiredness due to work restricted your participation in family and social activities?

	Every day	Most days	Half the time	A few days	Never
All	14	22	11	34	19
BMW	19	20	10	26	25
GM	10	23	12	40	15

also operationalised an additional stress factor that might be expected to have a more acute effect on employees' sense of well-being: workplace bullying. Although managerial harassment in its different forms has long been regarded as a defining feature of the process of direct management control, it is only relatively recently that this has been problematised as a discrete feature of workplace relations. Moreover, in the new world of lean production, respect is supposed to have superseded condescension. The International Labour Organization (ILO) (1998) defined bullying as a form of workplace violence in which a person is threatened or assaulted, and that can originate from customers and co-workers at any level of the organisation. The survey asked respondents whether they had ever felt bullied by a fellow worker, a team leader or a manager. The results are shown in Table 7.16.

The results suggest that although the experience of bullying by co-workers, including team leaders, was not pervasive, neither was it unknown. Overall, 10 per cent of workers had experienced some form of bullying by co-workers and 14 per cent by team leaders

Table 7.16 Workers' experience of bullying at work (row percentages)

Do you feel bullied at work?

	A great deal	A fair amount	Some	Very little	Never
Bullied by a fellow worker	2	2	6	17	73
Bullied by a team leader	3	2	9	16	70
Bullied by a manager	9	9	18	22	42

How closely is your work performance monitored by management?

	Very closely	Closely	Some	Not closely
Bullied by a manager	53	33	10	4
Rarely or never bullied	26	43	25	6

Do you ever feel that things are getting on top of you during your shift?

	A great deal	A fair amount	Some	Very little	Not at all
Bullied by a manager	31	19	29	8	13
Rarely or never bullied	9	19	30	25	17

In the last month at work, how tense and wound up were you?

	Very tense	Somewhat tense	Not very tense	Not tense at all
Bullied by a manager	35	51	6	8
Rarely or never bullied	12	40	26	23

(with little difference between plants). We cannot say whether this was a result of individual factors or of peer pressure. The data also show that a more significant proportion of workers, over a third, reported feeling some form of bullying by their managers. There is nothing unusual in this statistic, and it is reflected in the response from a number of shopfloor workers.

> Managers don't really show a lot of respect nowadays. It's a different culture because managers may be under pressure too. I mean I'm not making excuses for them, because they take their pressure out on the shopfloor. We've had instances where people have been spoken to in terrible situations, where people have got sworn at, and apart from physically hitting some-body, it's the worse kind of abuse that you can get – you know, harassment. They don't even get rapped over the knuckles. If it was you or me you'd lose your job. But see, it's like a class system.
>
> (BMW worker, 24/9/2001)

Billy, a BMW worker from trim, said, 'They're bullies, the managers here, if something goes wrong, like at school – if you don't stand up to them. It's a sad reflection, it is' (24/9/2001). Notwithstanding the currently fashionable interest in bullying and other features of the 'overwork culture' (Bunting 2004), in recent decades workplace case studies have provided abundant evidence of managerial harassment of manual workers (for example, Beynon 1984, Garrahan and Stewart 1992, Nichols and Beynon 1977, Roberts 1993). Also of note is the effect that such treatment might have on workers' sense of well-being and security. Table 7.16 shows that there is a close – if predictable – relationship between the extent of managerial surveillance of this sample of workers and their experience of bullying. Those who felt that their work was very closely monitored by management were also very likely to have experienced some, a fair amount or a great deal of managerial bullying. Moreover, those workers who felt bullied were more likely to have experienced stress indicators of 'things getting on top of you at work' and feeling 'tense and wound up'.

We created a summative scale of workplace stress based on the questions, 'In the last month how often have you worked with physical pain or discomfort?', 'How tense and wound up were you at work?', 'How often have you felt exhausted after your shift?', and lastly, 'Do you ever feel that things are getting on top of you during your shift?'[18] The mean

Table 7.17 Workplace stress scale

	Workplace stress Mean score: Max 15–Min 0
BMW	7.68
GM	8.12
Aged 18–30	7.53
Aged 31–40	7.45
Aged 41–50	8.40
Aged 51–65	7.38
Direct workers	8.01
Indirect workers	7.88
Bullied by manager	9.67
Rarely or never bullied	7.11
Workers closely monitored	8.26
Not closely monitored	6.94
Secure workers	7.77
Insecure workers	8.02

scores are shown in Table 7.17. There was little difference in the stress scores between workers at BMW and GM, or between different age groups, or direct and indirect production workers. There were differences, however, dependent on whether workers had felt bullied by their managers at work, whether they felt closely monitored by management, and whether they felt secure in their jobs. The latter variable was based on a question that asked employees whether or not they were concerned about losing their job in the next three years: 64 per cent indicated they were either concerned or very concerned. As a paint shop steward at GM pointed out:

> What do you do? I mean it's the uncertainty of not having a job in the society we live in today that keeps getting to you. I mean you know once you buy a house you're committed financially to the system and you can't get out of that system, and it's compounded by not knowing if you've got a regular job in the future – it causes all sorts of problems.
>
> (28/9/2000)

Table 7.17 shows that these insecure workers had a higher stress score than those who felt more secure. There were also large and significant stress score differences for workers who had felt bullied by their managers at work and for those who felt that their work performance was closely monitored by their managers. Although these differences are in some respects predictable, they do provide further evidence of the deleterious impact on workers of lean techniques which, notwithstanding the discourse of 'empowerment', may well intensify rather than loosen the processes of direct management control on the assembly line.

Evidence of association between some of the workload/work environment variables and the different indicators of workplace stress was then investigated. Our analysis highlighted significant associations between both work speed and workload and virtually every one of our stress variables (Table 7.18).[19] However, there was no association between stress and teamworking, and only one significant association with job security. In accordance with our predictions there was a significant negative relationship between autonomy and stress. We also found a negative relationship between stress and the management performance scale (which incorporated questions governing employee assessment of how well managers consulted with and treated employees: see above). Using this simple bivariate analysis, therefore, a pattern of association between high work demands and higher workplace stress can be discerned, as can an association between lower stress and both higher worker autonomy and higher worker evaluation of management performance in its treatment of employees.

Finally, multivariate regression analysis was carried out on the 15-point stress scale to investigate the significance of these intervening variables.[20] We add the caveat that because of the small size of the sample we present this as exploratory analysis only, with the purpose of generating hypotheses for further research.

The model (Table 7.19) shows that after we control for any plant effect, working in teams, employee autonomy and management performance governing employee consultation and welfare had no significant effect on the stress scale. Neither did job insecurity or management surveillance. The three variables that were positively related to worker stress were managerial bullying, excessive speed of work, and to a lesser extent excessive workload. Given the bulk of research that has highlighted the salience of such 'stressors' as speed of the assembly line and other production process drivers (Macdonald 2003), this result does seem predictable. For this sample of workers, the results suggest that the so-called 'empowerment' dimension of lean production, involving ideas such as increasing employee autonomy and participation, matters little for quality of working life on the shopfloor compared with the negative impact of the lean imperative to drive labour ever harder.

Table 7.18 Correlations between selected workload/work environment and stress variables

	Physical pain	Exhausted	Things getting on top	Tense and wound up	Family and social activity	Workplace stress scale
Work speed	0.290**	0.433**	0.298**	0.305**	0.227**	0.405**
Workload	0.216**	0.308**	0.206**	0.146	0.170*	0.255**
Work in a team	-0.021	-0.072	-0.142	-0.093	-0.036	0.085
Bullied by managers	0.223**	0.250**	0.255**	0.353**	0.183*	0.302**
Job security	-0.06	0.161*	0.050	0.126	0.071	0.098
Performance closely monitored	0.044	0.274**	0.206**	0.238**	0.125	0.225**
Autonomy scale	-0.229**	-0.333**	-0.274**	-0.171*	-0.194*	-0.301**
Management performance scale	-0.241**	-0.331**	-0.225**	-0.181*	-0.246**	-0.312**

* p = 0.05 ** p = 0.01

Table 7.19 Regression of workplace stress scale on plant, workload and other work environment determinants

	Stress scale Standardised B coefficients	Significance
Constant	14.613	0.000
BMW/GM	-0.377	0.647
Teamworkers	-0.111	0.901
Speed of work	1.969	0.036
Workload	1.849	0.074
Bullied by managers	1.928	0.030
Job insecurity	1.054	0.220
Management surveillance	1.078	0.245
Autonomy scale	-0.127	0.323
Management performance scale	-0.194	0.232

Adjusted R^2 = 0.285
N = 173

CONCLUSION

Having looked in detail at the history of the development of lean at Rover-BMW in Chapter 5, we began this chapter with a tour of the significant details of GM-Vauxhall's version of 'class struggle from above'. These form the context to the particular nature of attempted social subordination whose imprint is reflected by our results here. Critical conclusions to be drawn from our findings are that despite repeated claims to 'empowerment' deriving from promised worker involvement, at neither company can this be claimed to have occurred. Moreover, we would argue quite the contrary, that as a vital part of the armoury of 'class struggle from above', lean production drives down workers' perceptions of forms of involvement and participation.

Reassuringly, workers' reported experiences indicate the continued salience of collectivist (in this instance, trade union) forms of organisation to the maintenance of representation and, we would maintain, their feelings of autonomy. Reassuring too is the finding that workers give partnership-sceptic unions a higher union performance rating. Active members also give union performance a higher rating than do inactive members (and they were more common in partnership-sceptic Vauxhall-GM).

Another central finding is that lean production is the critically important variable in driving workers' stress, excessive workpace and bullying by management, as our quality of working life results indicate. But we are arguing for an even stronger case to be made, that these outcomes should be understood as centrally part of the democratic deficit which lean production is determined to drive through. In other words – we return to this in the Conclusion – the challenge to the technological and physical practices of lean production will require in the first place, a challenge to the rhetoric of representativeness, inclusiveness and mutual benefit that this vital management strategy has advanced so convincingly. Lean strategies present an upside world in which bullying, stress and powerlessness are simply unwanted hangovers of the old world of Fordism, which it is transforming for the obvious good of all.

APPENDIX: PROJECT OLYMPIA FRAMEWORK

PROJECT OLYMPIA

Zürich/Rüsselsheim, 1 October 2001

Framework

Regarding 'Project Olympia' initiatives, as partially presented in the meetings on August 15th and October 2nd, employee representatives and management, supplementary to the document signed on the 20th August 2001, agree on the following framework document. Details are to be solved at the respective national level with the inclusion of national unions and/or employee representation bodies according to national legislation and practice.

Preamble

Employee representatives, in general, support the Olympia objectives as presented in the meeting of the European Employee Forum (Manufacturing Committee) on August 15th, 2001. Management and employee representatives have the joint goal to institute actions leading to company profitability and sustainable growth, thus achieving the turnaround of GME to competitiveness and a successful future of the employees. Both parties agree that the strengthening of the Opel, Vauxhall and Saab brands and bringing them to leadership positions in the European automotive industry is first priority. It is the joint understanding that all initiatives of Project Olympia affect all brands, sites, plants and functions of GME. Management commits to the implementation of these initiatives with continuing inclusion and consultation during this process with the intention to reach mutually agreed solutions.

Rightsizing of capacity

Overall in the area of manufacturing, GME has to achieve significant structural cost reductions in conjunction with the reduction of 350,000 units installed capacity to contribute to the turnaround of the company. Necessary capacity adjustments in the areas of assembly, stamping, powertrain and components will be solved an a national level. With regard to placement of powertrain products and rightsizing of capacity according to newly adjusted requirements in the powertrain assembly area, necessary changes and adjustments of existing contracts are mutually possible while maintaining their substance. Initiatives will be implemented to meet GME required turnaround goals across all of its European operations. Management agrees that the outcome of the implementation of the Olympia initiatives will not include a site closure.

Productivity

It is the joint understanding of management and employee representatives that immediate action has to be taken to move the productivity levels to world-class benchmark standards, e.g. lean-field principles. Necessary measures to increase overall productivity and gain efficiencies will occur at all locations. Best practices and adjustments in the area of salaried staff have to be implemented as well to obtain efficiencies and cost reductions.

Flexibility

In order to increase the flexibility to react to changing customer demands and lifecycle variations (building more customer specified cars and fewer cars for stock) volume flexibility has to be enabled in different ways e.g. through alternative efficient and innovative working time and staffing models.

New business opportunities

New business and product opportunities for future growth, including export opportunities for all European brands outside of the European market, where competitiveness is ensured, will also be sought.

Partnerships

Management and employee representatives have a general joint understanding that resources and investment have to be focused in our situation. Therefore, increased efforts to find external partners for possible alternative business models will be taken. Both parties acknowledge that this depends on the nature of the business in general. Priority must be to maintain or grow employment at the respective locations. In the case of partnerships, Joint ventures will be established. Exceptions may be agreed at a national level. In both cases, the contents of the EEF framework signed on July 6th, 2000, will be honored. Exceptions to the contents may be agreed on a national level.

Manpower adjustments

Manpower adjustments, where necessary will be handled in socially responsible ways, which depending on individual custom and national legislation may include early retirements, separation programs, transfers to other National and International GM locations to available openings, outplacement assistance etc. These measures will enable us to avoid forced redundancies while implementing the necessary restructuring. Efforts to place workers in reasonable positions will require an increased willingness of employees with regard to mobility and flexibility for the work location as well as for working time and practices. It is also necessary to ensure that the required numbers of employees are placed in facilities that have urgent start-up needs and requirements due to market conditions.

Information and consultation

Management commits to the implementation of this framework with continuing inclusion and consultation during this process with the intention to reach mutually agreed solutions. This process will include dialogue at a national level and will be performed according to the respective national legislation and practice.

Implementation

Implementation of this framework shall occur at the national level. According to European legislation and national laws Management and employee representatives will ensure that the agreed provisions will become legally binding for individual employees as well as negotiating partners.

Unterzeichnet von:
Klaus Franz/Cheri L. Alexander/Dr. Thomas Klebe/Holger Kimmes/
John Jack/Bruce Warman/Peter Jaszczyk/Norbert Küpper/Rudy
Kennes/Bob Schelfhaut/Paul Akerlund/Allan Rothlind/Fernnando
Bolea/Pedro Esccudero.

CONCLUSION

LEAN PRODUCTION AND THE INDIVIDUALISATION OF WORKPLACE STRESS: THE NEW CLASS STRUGGLE FROM ABOVE

If our concern has been to expose the realities of the political economy of lean production, that great, supposedly anodyne term for more efficient and safer work, we have concentrated rather less on its promotion as a superior way to enhance an individual's development. One aspect to its broader rationale has been the claim by its protagonists that it inevitably enhances the development of the individual and makes for a less profligate society. There are to be no downsides to the superior way of living under lean. This is interesting and it is important, rather like the beliefs of those who argue that 'our' way is the best, the only 'one best way'. It is difficult to argue with this self-referential view of life and work. It must be one of the few management strategies that is at ease with itself. But the problem is that there are too many disconnects, too many instances of worker antipathy and opposition, too many instances of a gap between rhetoric and reality. Lean production as the great saviour of human time and effort?

> The firm that employed a man who killed himself years after suffering an injury at work is liable for his death, the Court of Appeal has ruled. Thomas Corr, then aged 31, had almost all his right ear severed at the Luton IBC van factory while fixing a machine. Six years later, in May 2002, he took his own life after suffering headaches, tinnitus and severe depression. The High Court originally ruled IBC Vehicles were not responsible for his death but that ruling has now been overturned.... IBC Vehicles, which produces vans for Vauxhall Motors in Luton, admitted liability for the workplace

accident but denied that its responsibility extended to him taking his own life six years later. This was accepted in the High Court when Deputy Judge Nigel Baker QC ruled against Mrs Corr, awarding her just £82,520 after finding IBC could not be held responsible for her husband's suicide. This High Court decision was overturned on a majority ruling at the Appeal Court. Lord Justice Sedley said all the evidence suggested there was no other cause of Mr Corr's suicide other than the injury he suffered at work, and he was previously a 'rational man'. He said: 'The suicide was proved to have been a function of the depression and so formed part of the damage for which IBC were liable.' He added that to treat Mr Corr as responsible for his own death was an 'unjustified exception' to modern views on the links between accidents and their causes.

('Employer to blame for suicide', *Hazards*, 8/4/2006)

The full reporting of the legal outcome to this tragic death is revealing of a political aspect of contemporary employment that usually eludes most attempts to explain the wider character of lean production. The terrible result of this worker's long fight against depression brought on by an industrial accident is certainly an unusual, though not unique,[1] instance of the consequences of contemporary, highly pressured employment. Intensity of effort, one of the drivers of lean production leading to stress, is now pervasive across many aspects of work and employment, and while there are many occupations where lean may be marginal, even here the necessary link across employment chains and networks means there are many fewer hiding places from management today.

One of the consequences of this is that lean will be persistently present in the job of someone to whom your job is related, even if it is not directly dependent on them. This means that work in contemporary society is increasingly governed by what the French sociologist Jean-Pierre Durand (2007) refers to as a 'tight flow' (*flux tendu*) in an 'invisible chain' of tight work organisation and labour subordination. Accepting the value of this perspective, we would add that there is an antagonistic relationship at the heart of this new form of production, which some commentators on occasion overlook. Borrowing Miliband's concept of 'class struggle from above' (1989: 115–66), we argue that lean production forms a major management tool in the political economy of neoliberalism, and as such is an essential tenet of the new class struggle from above. While it is not the only one, it is increasingly the most pervasive feature of class struggle from above in the advanced economies in the control and subjugation of labour at work.[2]

Class struggle from above is, in our view, what lies behind the rise of the stressed-out ('tight flow' for Durand) society. Getting to grips with the notion of 'tight flow' is important, especially because we find its origins in the automotive sector, in Toyota's management of production. Indeed, so pervasive has it become across so many sectors of the economy, and its consequent impact on individuals is so enveloping, including in their private lives, that it is unsurprising that the pressures of labour control lead to the kinds of outcome described above. In our own research, described throughout this book, we have seen how lean produces the kinds of worker responses that illustrate highly pressured work environments. While the occurrence of suicide is fortunately rare, the relatively high reporting of stress, overwork, dissatisfaction with work and the employment regime more broadly, should give policymakers and management cause for concern.

But as the quotation above highlights, one difficulty is the depoliticisation of the link between work regime, stress and accidents, including fatalities. *This depoliticisation is in fact a very important political aspect of lean production.*[3] Management might be forced to accept liability when it comes to 'individual' accidents, but deaths outside the workplace, whether by suicide or other causes, typically are seen to be unrelated to employment. Moreover, work-related deaths aside, accepting that stress, workload and bullying, among other forms of workplace pressure, are in any way related to work regime, as opposed to individual mistakes or inadequacies, will obviously not be part of management's conscious mind set. This complacency is inevitably at odds with our findings here, which can be summed up in Theo Nichols' memorable injunction that 'if men make accidents they do not do so under conditions of their own choosing' (1997: 117). For should we have not made the point sufficiently clear already, stress and 'hard' work are supposed to be part of lean production, as was pointed out so trenchantly in the late 1980s by Mike Parker and Jane Slaughter (see especially 1988, 1994).

While it is unsurprising that management is keen on this individualised view, it is imperative that unions address this more urgently, for it is at the heart of the contemporary politics of production which lies at the root of lean production. Unions can address this, as we suggest below, but the agenda will need to be central to a rejection of the individualising of worker experiences of poor and damaging work. This agenda will need to be centred upon workers' interests and concerns, and based upon collective responses to a continuing assault upon their attempts to restrain management in the workplace. And in any case, even when management is responsive to the consequences of lean working, while not admitting that lean itself is the issue, a typical response at best seeks a quick-fix palliative to patch up the worker ready for the next shift. We see this illustrated exquisitely in Peugeot-Citroen's response following a fourth suicide at the company's Mulhouse plant in 2007, the sixth such death at the company that year: counselling was offered to those experiencing stress. This was an important response indeed, since suicide is 'bad for business'. After the most recent death, the series of suicides was made public and shares in Peugeot Citroën nosedived immediately. Something had to be done:

> Despite Peugeot's introduction of measures earlier this year such as an emergency telephone helpline and counselling for those suffering from stress, the situation clearly remains worrying .... Peugeot Chief Executive Christian Streiff launched the 'Cap 2010' cost-cutting program on February 6, which aims to prune overheads by 30% over the next three years by slashing 4,800 jobs in France this year. Six new vehicle projects are to be added to the product plan by 2010, mainly through shortening the development cycle and bringing projects forward by three to six months. A representative for French Labor Minister Xavier Bertrand said the suicide was a 'human drama' and that a conference between employers, workers and trade unions slated for October would tackle the subject of labor conditions.
>
> (Laurent 2007)

Whereas it may indeed be an unexpected but positive reaction to offer counselling in the face of workplace stress, it is vital that unions defend workers in a manner that challenges production:[4]

> The trade union Solidaires Industrie on Tuesday blamed the 'isolation of workers, widespread suppression of breaks, work stress, job cuts generating heavier workloads for those remaining and competition between employees for meager raises' for the desperate state of some employees in the auto industry.
>
> (Laurent 2007)

Unsurprisingly, suicide is seen by management (when not explicitly denied) as a personal response by individual workers. Companies offer therapy in coping with hard work and the consequences it induces while inevitably ignoring the role of new management strategies in creating problems in the first place.

However, in our view, even attempting to ameliorate the consequences of lean necessarily draws us to a critique of its fundamentally systemic nature, which itself has to be confronted. The question is not only about the immediate impact of workplace reforms, but perhaps more significantly, about where they might end up. What is the long-term goal of union attempts to challenge the impact of lean production on workers' social and personal lives? This system is centrally dependent on attacking workers' conditions and protections to the extent that unlike previous regimes of labour control, a proper response requires measures that would actually challenge it head on at the workplace, on both the industrial and ideological levels.

This is for the reason that since Fordism was built upon a regime of pluralistic compromise, lean production is built upon defying workers' autonomous interests: the possibility of structural, worker-centred reform is anathema to management. We might briefly remind ourselves of Peter Titherington's comment in Chapter 2 that 'Under Measured Day Work we sold our time. Under lean we sell our time no more. Under lean, management determine our labour input and our time with a vengeance.' He also made the point that 'at least, that's their aim'. While management may attempt to eschew worker-centred views, workers, have always attempted to challenge this, individually or collectively, in ways that depend on their history and circumstances, (See discussions on this theme in Ackroyd and Thompson 1999, Martinez Lucio and Stewart 1997, Stewart 2006.)

Astra production halted by walkout

Hundreds of workers at a Vauxhall car plant staged an unofficial walkout yesterday in a dispute over temporary staff, halting production of the Astra. Workers at Ellesmere Port took part in the strike in protest at the ending of contracts for 46 temporary employees. Vauxhall said it was extremely disappointed at the walkout and said the contracts were due to run out yesterday. A spokesman said: 'It is extremely important that everyone at Ellesmere Port works together to ensure we can meet demand for the new Astra.' The company said parent General Motors could not afford to lose any production of the car. Members of the Transport and General Workers' Union at the plant will vote next week for industrial action. Since the temporary workers involved had been at the factory for two-and-a-half years, the union said they had been made compulsorily redundant.

(*Newsquest*, Media Group Newspapers, 27/11/2004)

As a contemporary form of Miliband's class struggle from above, lean production is built precisely upon the denial that workers' views might make sense, since management argue that alternatives would slow down or otherwise inhibit production and thereby undermine efficiency.[5] In this class struggle from above, line speeds, labour utility, time off for recovery: none of these should be of any concern to workers except to the extent that they can help to keep production regulated, and to augment quality and effort where demanded by the company in its desire to properly operationalise plant and equipment in line with the corporate plan. (In GM this goes under the auspices of the General Motors Global Manufacturing System – GM-GMS.[6]) It is true, as our reference to Renault highlights, that companies may on occasion respond in a positive way to individual worker concerns, but of course this will not be allowed to contaminate the company nostrums on the organisation and allocation of labour, and in any case, the company response on this occasion is the exception to the rule. People will still have to work hard for the greater good of the corporation.

Recognising the systemic character of lean as a form of class struggle from above allows a broader critique of lean production as an aspect of the constraining character of the lean society. The reason we argue this is because it is difficult to imagine how we might challenge the main tenets of lean production and its attack on working conditions without recognising the reason for this historic assault on labour. It is firmly part of the need to recast the political economy of contemporary capitalism. Lean is about getting rid of 'waste' – or about making sure others carry it (pay for it) in one form or another. This is an important aspect of the contemporary political economy, and lean is one of its key drivers.

Bauman (2004) argues that behind the obsession with waste is the fear that this might be our future. This fear drives us, and it is a fear primarily of rejection, which in turn encourages contemporary consumer society. The desire for the new, the fear of the old or the washed-up (which could be us), provides the compulsion behind the ever-increasing push for newer (often only superficially different) commodities.[7] While Bauman does not refer to it as such, lean production can in part be viewed this way. For just as the rubbish tip must be hidden and got rid off, so must 'waste', or *muda*, be eliminated in the context of the lean environment – and normally it is passed on to someone else. One view is that lean prevents waste in the first place, but this is entirely to ignore the whole squandering of resources, the character of the chains in commodity production leading to valorisation, including the waste of workers' time and their health, for the next, the latest commodity – as illustrated by our stark exemplar of Renault.

Waste, in other words, is really the term capital likes to use to describe an unnecessary pull on resources. But since it is impossible to control it entirely, what effectively happens is that another part of the process constrained by the tight flow – the 'invisible chain' – will take the slack and carry the inventory. In terms of physical effects, it is the worker who will have to work longer hours (without adequate overtime pay), and work more intensively. All this is made possible by means of the great innovations of *kaizen*, quality circles and team agendas. And of course, all is pressured by just-in-time (JIT). Zero inventories, zero defects, zero absence and zero tolerance of those who are not 'on message' are paid for in the currency of workers' health and the quality of their working lives. The assembly worker will be the one to put in the extra effort or become expendable. The waste in lean production, *muda*, takes bodily form in the shape of the unnecessary, unwanted workers. So herein lies the great irony: lean production, far from being 'lean', is actually incredibly wasteful of resources in the drive towards faster reductions in the time taken to bring through model changes.[8]

The encouragement of overconsumption and the consequent impact of an ever-reduced commodity lifespan are taking an extraordinary toll on workers and their families as we have seen, not to mention the impact on society more generally. Nevertheless workers do often manage to fight back, against the best efforts of the ideologues of lean, together with the institutions established to make it increasingly difficult for workers to resist. In March 2008 over 500 workers in the press shop at Vauxhall-GM staged a wildcat strike after a rumour that GM was about to cut over 400 posts. For the second time in two years workers took wildcat action. The first time was following the announcement (June 2006) of 900 job cuts. It is important to note that Amicus and the TGWU condemned the actions and encouraged what they termed 'restraint' to help with negotiation, but the fact is that in the end the jobs went and the unions ended up calling for a 'buy British' campaign. This was a major setback, but our point here is not so much what we can assume would be the position of the union leadership, but the fact that despite the years of lean organisation strategies and its attendant propaganda, workers still fought back – and in a very powerful manner.

WORKER AND UNION RESPONSES TO LEAN

One of our central themes in this book has been the character of actually existing lean production in its effects upon workers' lives on the line. Among other things, including increased corporate profits, the advocates of lean promised that it would generate improvements to worker experience of new forms of work in the automotive assembly industry. However, we illustrated the extent to which lean production has, by degrees, eroded the condition of labour in the sector – but in a path-dependent, company-specific way. Our analysis showed the fallacy of 'working smarter not harder', which is a hymn to management dominance, as opposed to a song of worker sovereignty. We know this because our various sets of data have illustrated the extent to which employee well-being has been eroded by lean manufacturing and lean organisational techniques. Worker autonomy has been reduced, and management control and surveillance has increased along with workloads, stress and the intensive character of work on the line. We have, in other words, shown up the gap between the reality and the rhetoric of actually existing lean production strategies. However, we have also given voice to those articulating opposition in various ways to lean.

More especially, the critical factor influencing the ability of management to push back the postwar gains of labour has been the strategic agenda adopted by trade unions in the companies. Nevertheless, we have to accept that whatever spaces for union-centred agendas have been created, capital has been able to drive home the lean agenda. The era of neoliberalism has allowed management to pursue this 'class struggle from above'.

Two related questions remain pertinent. First, we need to consider how, in the context of two decades of the qualitative erosion of labour standards and job loss, workers and their unions might still respond to management assaults on their ability to at least contain some of the consequences of lean on their working conditions. The second is more difficult, and will require an extended debate because it confronts our observations above concerning the nature of the lean society itself. If we can restrain –

shackle – lean production, if in other words we can begin to extend a new class struggle from below to counter that waged by capital from above, what shape might this take, and how deep must it go to push back the gains made by corporations over the last period at the expense of labour? While the two are obviously closely related, since apparently minor attempts to control capital can have quite extensive ramifications, it is not always possible to know whether apparently limited reforms will lead to larger and more sustainable social gains, although when they remain at the level of the factory this is unlikely, as we know. But at least the obvious lineaments of a strategy to mobilise to extend the various social and physical protections against lean production are eminently desirable and possible.

Below we set out what we take to be the basis for a worker-centred response to lean production. Some of what we have to say has been made in a different context by a number of critical labour movement writers, including Steve Babson (1995), Kim Moody (1997) and Rinehart, Huxley and Robertson (1997). Rather than offering a reprise of their respective agendas and prospects for change, we offer a number of arguments and suggestions as the basis for an international fight back against lean production.

CHALLENGING LEAN PRODUCTION AS A STRATEGY AND IDEOLOGY

While we can identify a number of areas in which lean production attacks labour standards, we have focused on two which we perceive as directly affecting workers in their daily lives at work, and which if confronted can begin to the lay the basis for a challenge to lean production. These are, one, lean production and outsourcing, and two, trade union and shopfloor organisation and activity, and the importance of the quality of working life.

Lean Production and Outsourcing

As multinational companies continue to spread the lean religion, we must continue to make the point that one of the major parts of this strategy is outsourcing of non-core business. The aim of this is to increase corporate profitability, and an attack on workers' pay and conditions is critical to this. The company's aim is to move outside the main assembly plant to smaller satellite areas located in close proximity to the main assembly area.

The trade union position should be total opposition to mainstream outsourcing for the following reasons:

- There is an erosion of wages and conditions associated with these operations.
- This involves the loss of offline activities which have traditionally been allocated to older or restricted employees.[9] Ironically, a system of labour utilisation and employee control sold as quintessentially modern turns out to be quintessentially macho and ageist!
- The company belief is that all restricted or elderly employees will want to leave the company through a separation or early retirement agreement. This is not true in many cases, and will ultimately mean that employees who have today been accommodated on lighter work will be forced to carry out functions beyond their age or medical capabilities.
- This leads to a lack of future investment in people: reduced or no apprenticeships and personnel development, especially where training and development are limited by an instrumentalist attitude to workers and their progress.
- It also leads to the break-up of the industrial social structure of a particular area. For example it particularly affects long-service employees who have worked on a particular area and have valuable industrial skills which will be lost to the business. The impact of this on workers, their families and locale needs to be assessed.

Worker and Trade Union Responses to Lean Initiatives and the Importance of the Quality of Working Life

There is a fundamental need to build a consensus amongst the trade union membership of total opposition to the arguments advanced by lean production. This is a basic requirement in the fight against lean. The ideology and the consequences of lean are powerful, and profoundly affect the working lives of millions of workers, not only in the automotive industry. Thus, it is crucial that workers on the shopfloor are involved at every possible level, and from the beginning. This involves basic education about the politics of lean.

As we saw in the example of Vauxhall-GM, constant engagement with production politics in a way that drew in many workers not normally involved with workplace politics was crucial in the early stages of pushing back the threat of lean to jobs and union organisation.

Labor Notes, the Canadian Auto Workers' Union and Transnational Information Network (TIE) were all involved at an early stage in developing a critical consciousness about lean production. Today, it is important that young workers are drawn directly into debates about the lean politics of production. This raises confidence and prepares for a new generation of shopfloor activists. Young workers of all national origins must be engaged in this battle, and this is especially the case today since so many in the auto sector in the United Kingdom are agency workers who have recently migrated from mainland Europe.

In this respect, a major threat to unions and their capacity to resist is the presence of agency firms whose role is effectively to 'outsource' workers by reducing the core establishment. This cheapens labour while deepening insecurity, and consequently the ability to resist further attacks on labour standards. Maintaining the pay and conditions of agency workers in UK plants could be extended to those working for the same companies in countries with lower rates of pay. In addition to debates at European Works Council (EWC) level, this issue could be included in debate with a wide range of members at plant level, which could have the important affect of extending the ongoing and plant-wide critique of lean production.

These concerns in turn raise broader issues of inter-plant coalitions which need to be strengthened. One of the potent factors in the employers' agenda has been the ability to fight back where they can use whipsawing (inter-plant competition on concession bargaining) to undermine union and worker solidarity. This has proved to be an especially noxious weapon in the employer's class struggle from above. In the case of GM and the round of bidding for the new Astra which occurred in 2006, whipsawing certainly allowed the company to push back a range of worker benefits and labour standards. Nonetheless, while GM eventually moved to end Astra production at its Antwerp plant, the capacity of the unions to protect recent agreements remains strong, if continually under assault. (See too the wildcat strike at Ellesmere Port in 2008. In May 2007 the union at Antwerp ended a two-week strike called after the failure to land the new Astra, but the union won concessions – until 2009 – from GM on relocation and a production commitment for the Chevrolet.)

The point to this was that unions at plant level, and not only via the EWC – although this was vital – developed an important dialogue on GM's strategy. This requires sustained development, and could include many younger workers brought into the debate about sectoral politics. Their participation would help to democratise the union by drawing in new blood to shop stewards' committees, while spreading outwards the critique of lean as part of the employers' latest offensive, which likes to present the problems of closure and redundancy as a logical response to the ebb and flow of the market rather than anything to do with lean. The company via its employer-driven belief in company–worker coalition (which is stronger in the United States) wants to argue that because of global developments it can do little to save everyone's job, but that without lean production things would be worse – although if they are about to close your plant it is difficult to see what this 'worse' might consist of.

This productivity coalition is really a pact that destroys workers' and their unions' capacity to resist attacks on jobs and job standards. A different type of pact is one formed with workers, not just at sectoral level but in supplier companies too, an international solidarity pact (Babson 1995) which allows workers from different plants and countries to meet regularly and prepare an agenda to challenge employers right across the product sector. This would aim in the first instance to take workers' employment (and in consequence living) standards out of the competition equation. Steve Babson's argument from the mid-1990s about the necessity for the regulation of workplace standards and a rejection of the employers' competition agenda is still crucial today.

A significant way to enforce this is to institute worker-centred, trade-union led controls linking workplace change to a quality of working life index. This was advocated by the Canadian Auto Workers in the 1990s but has not come to very much in the wider scheme of things. Where lean practitioners advocate and utilise benchmarking for a range of production criteria, unions need to begin to push for a quality of working life benchmark which would begin to flush out and describe the deleterious impact of lean production on workers' quality of life at work and at home in the community. In consequence, community involvement in this process is very important. The 'better' companies would be those in which there is trade union leadership of the health and safety agenda. Finally, union controls on work determination might also include the ability to regulate the form and conditions of outsourced labour, including the wages and conditions of workers in other countries.

Worker-centred benchmarking would also seek to assess the impact of lean on workers' health outside the plants, including its effects on workers over the recent and longer period of their working lives, by researching issues around absence, early retirement or other reasons for early exits from relatively well-paid employment (see Stewart and Murphy 2009). Why does lean have a detrimental affect on workers and their families while both employers and governments continue to extol its questionable social and other virtues? This apparently unyielding ideology needs to be addressed by shopfloor and community action which is underpinned by continually updated research.

Developing this approach will make it more likely that the following agenda can be developed and sustained:

- The necessity for industrial action, up to and including strike action when required. Maintain a language and practice of opposition even when industrial action is not considered because it educates members for the context in which conflict will occur.
- Fight to secure agreements, both locally and nationally. It is vital that independent framework agreements sustain autonomy and the integrity of workers and their unions.
- Appeal to the local and national community when strike action or other forms of industrial conflict are used.
- Involvement of local and national media is crucial.
- Consumer awareness with radical green activists in the context of the next point.
- Build coalitions with labour organisations and other social movements. Especially when jobs and plant are threatened, the involvement of MPs and local councillors is important, but must be constrained by the agendas and decisions of workers in the assembly plants.

APPENDIX 1

SURVEY OF CAR WORKERS BY THE TGWU AND CARDIFF UNIVERSITY TRADE UNION RESEARCH UNIT (QUESTIONNAIRE 1996)

Transport & General Workers Union

and

Cardiff University Trade Union Research Unit

SURVEY OF CAR WORKERS

Dear Brothers and Sisters
The T&GWU is working with a research team from Cardiff University to monitor the experience
and attitude of the work force to new management techniques€(NMTs), particularly with respect
to job control, health and safety and union organisation. We need your help and ask you to take
the time to fill in this questionnaire. All responses will be treated in the strictest confidence.

Instructions
This questionnaire will take about 15 minutes to complete. the questions are divided into 5
sections convering different aspects of your work in relation to NMTs. Each question requires
you to tick in the box beside the appropriate answer. We welcome further comments and leave
space at the end of the questionnaire. Please return your completed questionnaire to your union
representative.

Section 1 About you

1.1 Are you a
⌐ union officer   ⌐ union member

1.2 To which union do you belong?
⌐ T&GWU   ⌐ AEEU   ⌐ MSF

1.3 Are you   ⌐ male   ⌐ female

1.4 In which part of the plant do you work?
⌐ Body welding
⌐ Paint
⌐ Trim
⌐ Engine & exhausts
⌐ Final assembly
⌐ Other

1.4 How long have you worked in this
plant? _____ years

1.5 How old are you? _____ years

1.6 What is your job?
⌐ welding, metal finishing
☐ rectification, spotting
⌐ paint-colour1,colour2,wax
⌐ trim-glass,carpets seats,
☐ engine
⌐ final finish
? inspection
? other

Section 2 Impact of New Management Techniques (NMTs)

2.1 To what extent have NMTs affected
your work in the plant?
⌐ a great deal
⌐ a fair amount
⌐ a small amount

2.2 Which view most appropriately
describes your attitude towards NMTs?
⌐ strongly positive
⌐ mostly positive
⌐ neutral
⌐ mostly negative
⌐ strongly negative

2.3 What effect have these changes had
on your job?

⌐ more ⌐ same ⌐ less   **skilled**
⌐ more ⌐ same ⌐ less   **technical**
⌐ more ⌐ same ⌐ less   **physical**
⌐ more ⌐ same ⌐ less   **mental**
⌐ more ⌐ same ⌐ less   **interesting**

2.4 How much do you move around the
plant in terms of the jobs that you do?
⌐ a great deal
⌐ a fair amount
⌐ a small amount

2.5 How does this level of mobility
compare with 5 years ago?
⌐ more ⌐ same   ⌐ less

2.6 How would you describe your current
physical work load (moving and lifting
objects, loading and unloading machines,
air tool torque etc.)?
⌐ much too heavy
⌐ too heavy
⌐ not a problem

2.7 Do you work harder, in terms of
physical work load, compared to 5 years
ago?   ⌐ yes   ⌐ no

2.8 How would you describe your current
work speed or work pace?
⌐ much too fast
⌐ too fast
⌐ about right
⌐ too slow
⌐ much too slow

2.9 Do you work faster, in term of work
pace, compared to 5 years ago?
⌐ yes   ⌐ no

2.10 In general , how much are skilled
staff doing the jobs previously done by
production-line staff?
⌐ a lot   ⌐ a little   ⌐ not at all

2.11 Is this plant-wide or just in certain
sections?
⌐ throughout the plant
⌐ only in certain sections

2.12 In general, how much are production-line staff doing the jobs previously done by skilled staff?

¬ a lot   ¬ a little   ¬ not at all

2.13 Is this plant-wide or just in certain section?

¬ throughout the plant

¬ only in certain sections

2.14 Which view most appropriately describes your attitude towards this reduction in job demarcation?

¬ strongly positive

¬ mostly positive

¬ neutral

¬ mostly negative

¬ strongly negative

2.15 Have you received training in the use of NMTs?   ¬ yes   ¬ no

2.16 How do you rate this training?

¬ good

¬ adequate

¬ inadequate

¬ poor

2.17 How satisfied do you feel that you have received adequate financial reward for participating in NMTs?

¬ very satisfied

¬ satisfied

¬ neutral

¬ dissatisfied

¬ very dissatisfied

2.18 In your view, are NMTs necessary for the survival of the company?

¬ yes   ¬ no

2.19 In your view, how important were the following in the company's decision to use NMT? (rank the following from 1 to 5)
__ increase flexibility
__ increase quality of product
__ make better use of technology
__ reduce staff levels
__ reduce costs

3.1 How easy is it for you to change the things that you do not like about your job?

¬ very easy

¬ easy

¬ neither easy or difficult

¬ difficult

¬ very difficult

¬ impossible

3.2 How has this been affected by NMTs?

¬ for the better

¬ unchanged

¬ for the worse

3.3 How closely is your work performance monitored by management?

¬ very closely

¬ closely

¬ not closely

¬ not at all

3.4 How has this been affected by NMTs?

¬ for the better

¬ unchanged

¬ for the worse

3.5 How often can you talk with other workers at work outside of breaks?

¬ rarely, if ever

¬ rarely

¬ sometimes

¬ often

¬ quite often

3.6 How has this been affected by NMTs?

¬ for the better

¬ unchanged

¬ for the worse

3.7 Would it be easy for you to get time off for personal reasons such as illness in the family or a medical appointments?

¬ very easy

¬ easy

¬ difficult

¬ very difficult

¬ impossible

Section 3 Job Control/Autonomy

3.8 How has this been affected by NMTs?
- ¬ for the better
- ¬ unchanged
- ¬ for the worse

Section 4   Health and Safety

4.1 In the last month how many days have you worked with physical pain or discomfort which was caused by your job?
- ¬ every day
- ¬ most days
- ¬ half the time
- ¬ a few days

4.2 On average what part of each day is spent in physically awkward positions?
- ¬ all the time
- ¬ three quarters
- ¬ half
- ¬ one quarter
- ¬ none

4.3 In the last month how tense and wound up have you been at work?
- ¬ very tense
- ¬ moderately tense
- ¬ a little tense
- ¬ not tense at all

4.4 Compared with 5 years ago, does your job make you
- ¬ more tense
- ¬ same tension
- ¬ less tense

4.5 Could you work at the pace of your current job until you retire?
- ¬ yes   ¬ no

4.6 In the last month, how often have you felt exhausted after 8 hours of work?
- ¬ every day
- ¬ most days
- ¬ half the time
- ¬ a few days
- ¬ never

4.7 How does this compare with 5 years ago?
- ¬ more tired
- ¬ same amount of tiredness
- ¬ less tired

4.8 In the last month, how often has tiredness due to work restricted your participation in family and social activities'
- ¬ every day
- ¬ most days
- ¬ half the time
- ¬ a few days
- ¬ never

Section 5   Union Involvement

5.1 What do you consider to be the level of union influence over the implementation of NMTs?
- ¬ very influential
- ¬ quite influential
- ¬ marginal influence
- ¬ no influence

5.2 On a scale of 1 to 5, how would you rate the level of negotiation involved in the implementation of NMTs? 1 represents a negotiated agreement and 5 represents imposed conditions (please circle)

1   2   3   4   5

5.3 How has the influence of the union been affected by NMTs?
- ¬ greatly increased
- ¬ increased
- ¬ unchanged
- ¬ decreased
- ¬ greatly decreased

5.4 In general how would you describe the industrial relations climate in the plant at present?
- ¬ very positive
- ¬ positive
- ¬ neutral
- ¬ negative
- ¬ very negative

5.5 How does this compare with 5 years ago?

⌐ more positive

⌐ unchanged

⌐ more negative

5.6 Is the recruitment of new members changing?

⌐ much more difficult

⌐ more difficult

⌐ unchanged

⌐ easier

⌐ much easier

Thank you for taking the time to complete this questionnaire

Please use the space below to add any comments

APPENDIX 2

WORKFORCE SURVEY ON WORKPLACE ISSUES

WORKFORCE SURVEY ON WORKPLACE ISSUES

Instructions: It is important that you answer all the questions. Please answer each question by filling in the space that best fits your job situation. Sometimes none of the answers fit exactly. Please choose the answer that comes closest. **All responses will be treated strictly confidentially. Please make sure to read and complete all pages of the survey.**

A. DESCRIBING YOURSELF

1. **Sex:** Male ☐   Female ☐   **2. Age:**

3. **How long have you worked for your current employer:** _____ years.

4. **To which union do you belong?** ☐ T&GWU   ☐ AEEU   ☐ MSF ☐

5. **In what part of the plant are you currently working?**   (Mark X where appropriate)
   Stamping ____   Body Shop ____   Paint ____   Engine Line _____
   Trim _____   Off Line/Sub-assembly_____ Other Assembly

6. **Are you currently employed as:**
   ____ **Direct** production worker (Machine or Press Operator, Assembler, Painter, etc.)
   ____ **Indirect** production worker (Inspector, Material Handler, Forklift Driver, Relief, Sweeper, etc.)
   ____ **Skilled Trades** worker (Electrician, Machine Repairer, Spot Welder, etc.)

7. **Are you an active Union member** yes ☐ no ☐

8. **How many hours in total did you work in the last 2 weeks?** _____ hours

9. **Have you changed jobs within the plant in the last six months?** Yes ☐   no ☐

10. **Do you work rotating shifts? (example one week days, one week nights)** yes ☐ no ☐

11. **Which shift do you work?** Day ? yes ☐ no ☐   Night?   yes ☐ no ☐

12. **Have any of your relatives worked in this plant?** yes ☐ no ☐

B. DESCRIBING YOUR HEALTH

1. **How much do you know about new management practices and work reorganization?**
   a great deal ☐   a fair amount ☐   some ☐   very little ☐   nothing at all ☐

2. **Can you name at least 3 new management practices used in your plant? (eg team work, etc)**
   i) _____ ii) _____ iii) _____

3. **How involved has the union been in telling you about new management practices and work reorganization?**
   very involved ☐   involved ☐   not very involved ☐   not involved at all ☐

4. **How involved has management been in telling you about new management practices and work reorganization?**
   very involved ☐   involved ☐   not very involved ☐   not involved at all ☐

5. **How involved has the union been in trying to improve health and safety conditions?**

very involved ☐   involved ☐   not very involved ☐   not involved at all ☐

6. **How involved has the union been in getting management to modify work practices?**

very involved ☐   involved ☐   not very involved ☐   not involved at all ☐

7. **In the last month at work, how often have you worked with physical pain or discomfort?**

every day ☐   most days ☐   half the time ☐   a few days ☐   never ☐

8. **In the last month at work, how often have you been concerned about exposure to chemicals?**

every day ☐   most days ☐   half the time ☐   a few days ☐   never ☐

9. **In the last month at work, how tense and wound up were you?**

very tense ☐   somewhat tense ☐   not very tense ☐   not tense at all ☐

10. **What part of each day do you work in physically awkward positions?**

all the time ☐   three quarters ☐   half ☐   one quarter ☐   not at all ☐

11. **What part of each day would you describe your work as boring or monotonous?**

all the time ☐   three quarters ☐   half ☐   one quarter ☐   not at all ☐

12. **Do you ever feel that things are getting on top of you during your shift?**

a great deal ☐   a fair amount ☐   some ☐   very little ☐   none at all ☐

13. **How much control do you have sorting out problems that prevent you from doing your job?**

a great deal ☐   a fair amount ☐   some ☐   very little ☐   none at all ☐

14. **What is the risk of your becoming ill or being injured from doing your job in the next twelve months?**

zero ☐   low ☐   moderate ☐   high ☐   very high ☐

15 a). **Do you ever feel bullied at work?**

a great deal ☐   a fair amount ☐   some ☐   very little ☐   never at all ☐

b). **By Fellow worker?** a great deal ☐   a fair amount ☐   some ☐   very little ☐   never at all ☐

Team Leader? a great deal ☐   a fair amount ☐   some ☐   very little ☐   never at all ☐

Other Manager? a great deal ☐   a fair amount ☐   some ☐   very little ☐   never at all ☐

16. **Do you worry about work outside working hours?**

a great deal ☐   a fair amount ☐   some ☐   very little ☐   never at all ☐

17. a) **Do you ever worry about the amount of alcohol you consume?**

a great deal ☐   a fair amount ☐   some ☐   very little ☐   never at all ☐

b) **Has this increased much over the last 3-5 years?** a great deal ☐   a fair amount ☐

some ☐   very little ☐   not at all ☐

C. DESCRIBING YOUR JOB

1. **Over the course of a working day, how much can you vary your pace of work (for example, work harder for part of the day so you can work less hard at other times)?**

a great deal ☐   a lot ☐   some ☐   a little ☐   not at all ☐

2. **Outside of breaks, how often can you talk with other workers while working?**

rarely if ever ☐   rarely ☐   sometimes ☐   often ☐   quite often ☐

3. **Do you have arrangements with the people you work with which allow you to rotate jobs?**

yes ☐   no ☐

4. **To what extent are these job rotation arrangements management policy?**

completely ☐   a lot ☐   some ☐   a little ☐   not at all ☐

5. **In the last month, how often has tiredness due to work restricted your participation in family and social activities?**

every day ☐   most days ☐   half the time ☐   a few days ☐   never ☐

6. **How concerned are you about losing your job in the next three years?**

very concerned ☐   concerned ☐   not concerned ☐

7. Do you consider the workers in your area work in a team? yes☐   no☐
8. To what extent have these teams been formed as part of a management policy?

    completely ☐   a lot☐   some☐   a little☐   not at all☐

9. To what extent does management raise issues such as lay-offs, outsourcing or even plant closure when discussing the need for change at this workplace?

    all the time ☐   a lot☐   some☐   a little☐   not at all☐

10. To what extent does management talk about co-operation when discussing the need for change at this workplace?

    all the time ☐   a lot☐   some☐   a little☐   not at all☐

D. ON WORKLOAD

1. Are there enough people in your area to do the work assigned?

    far too many ☐   too many☐   about right☐   too few☐   far too few☐

2. In the last month, how often have you felt exhausted after your shift?

    every day☐   most days☐   half the time☐   a few days☐   never☐

3. Is your current manual work load (for example, positioning and fastening pieces, moving and lifting sub-assemblies, air tool torque):

    much too heavy☐   too heavy☐   about right☐   too light☐   much too light☐

4. Is there adequate relief staff in your work area so that you can easily leave your job to attend to personal matters (for example, going to the toilet, etc.)?

    far too many ☐   too many☐   about right☐   too few☐   far too few☐

E. ON WORK PACE AND INTENSITY

1. How much time do you have to do the work currently assigned to you?

    far too much ☐   too much☐   about right☐   too little☐   far too little☐

2. Could you work at the pace of your current job until age 60?

    yes☐   likely☐   not likely☐   no☐

3. When you reach 60, do you expect there will be an easier job available for you at this workplace?

    yes☐   likely☐   not likely☐   no☐

4. For what part of each day do you work as fast as you can so you don't fall behind?

    all day☐   75% of the time☐   50% of the time☐   25% of the time☐   never☐

5. Is your current work speed or work pace:

    much too fast☐   too fast☐   about right☐   too slow☐   much too slow☐

6. How easy is it to get light duty work without overloading other workers?

    very easy☐   easy☐   neither☐   difficult☐   very difficult☐

F: ON TRAINING, CONTROL AND CHANGES IN YOUR JOB

1. How long would it take to train someone to do your job?

    over 1 month ☐   2-4 weeks☐   1 week☐   a few days☐   1 day☐   a few hours☐

2. How easy is it for you to change the things you do not like about your job?

    very easy☐   easy☐   neither☐   difficult☐   very difficult☐

3. Since the last reorganization of your workplace :
    a) How tired are you lately after finishing your shift?

    more tired☐   the same☐   less tired☐

    b) Is the work speed or work pace on your current job?

    faster☐   the same☐   slower☐

    c) How much time do you have to do the work assigned in your current job?

    more time☐   the same☐   less time☐

d) Is the manual work load on your current job?(positioning & fastening pieces, moving & lifting sub-assemblies, rolls or bundles, air tool torque)

heavier ☐   the same ☐   lighter ☐

4. How much influence do you have on the way you do your job?

a great deal ☐   a lot ☐   some ☐   a little ☐   not at all ☐

G: LABOUR RELATIONS

1. Over the last two years, was it easy for you to get time off to attend to personal needs such as a doctor's appointment, an ill child or a wedding?

very easy ☐   easy ☐   difficult ☐   very difficult ☐

2. How closely is your work performance monitored by management?

very closely ☐   closely ☐   some ☐   not closely ☐   not closely at all ☐

3. Are management policies reasonable and fair at this workplace?

very fair ☐   fair ☐   neither ☐   unfair ☐   very unfair ☐

4. How interested is management in your welfare?

very interested ☐   interested ☐   neutral ☐   not interested ☐   not interested at all ☐

5. How satisfied are you with your immediate supervisor at this workplace?

very satisfied ☐   satisfied ☐   neutral ☐   dissatisfied ☐   very dissatisfied ☐

6. To what extent do you feel consulted over company policy?

a great deal ☐   a lot ☐   some ☐   a little ☐   not at all ☐

THANK YOU FOR COMPLETING THE SURVEY

Additional Comments

If you would like to make any additional comments concerning conditions at your workplace, or comments about the survey, please do so in the space provided below:

APPENDIX 3

WORKING ON THE LINE 'AFTER FORDISM': A DIARY

Jim McSheffrey agreed to keep a diary of his first few weeks on the assembly line at a General Motors plant in the United Kingdom. While he did not remain long in the plant, and his diary was incomplete (and has been tightly edited down here), nevertheless we feel it offers a glimpse into a new worker's first impression of his experience of working the assembly line in a world of work supposedly beyond the hard toil of Fordism. It is particularly interesting that a number of the issues we grapple with throughout the book come quickly to the surface in Jim's brief account of his initial experiences, and in his record of conversations with other workers, some of whom have worked for GM for many decades.

My first day, Monday. I didn't realise it would be so tough, mentally as much as anything else.

To make sure we started for the 7.00 am shift and since we had to pick up Johnnie's son Patrick we had to get up at 5.30. We were only around 30 minutes from the plant. Johnnie had been to Dublin for a lads' weekend and also to get a chance to see Dublin in the Gaelic footie – they'd got to the quarter final of the all-Ireland, so he had today out for a bit of recovery.

I'm staying with Eddie for a few weeks until I get something a bit more long term so that's been really good.

Get locker set up and then Eddie takes me down to the body shop to meet the foreman – he's OK. A friend I know in the union [T&G] had told me there were some jobs going so I'd applied and when I got the job after tests – mostly basics but also about my attitude as much as anything – I was looking forward to it as it's pretty good money for manufacturing but mostly for this part of the world.

We start 7.00 am on 'the bell'. I'm put immediately on my jobs, which are hood, fender, hinges (for the hood) and tailgate (four varieties). I feel I'll never work out the sequence and jig placement. Seems to take me ages to get it right without a problem somewhere along the line. Before I do that, though, Jean shows me how to place and take the hood from the stack. It is more awkward than it seems and requires more balance than I thought – you're always on the move which would be fine if you were in training for a sport but the floor is hard and your legs and feet really feel like they're on fire or swollen up. Anyway, I drop the hood onto the jig as you're supposed to do, making sure it's in position correctly, then lever the clamps to ensure it's properly locked in position – then draw the jig along the line by two straps. The jig is then placed on the front of the door frame and fixed into position making sure the hinges are not caught up and then with my air gun I fix it with two torque bolts. Then I unclamp the jig, pull it back the same way I brought it to the car and do that again. For two hours. Then the fender. The same kind of thing of placing everything carefully in line and fixing it to the jig and so on. But I said, then the fender. Bastard job! Bolts on right-hand side. I keep forgetting either front two or one by body door pillar. Or sometimes the wheel arch. Jean says not to worry because they can pick it up later in inspection although she tells me they'll track it back to me from the place and time of the work but that since I'm new they'll assume it's what she calls 'beginner's nerves'. Or so she hopes. She also tells me that someone in Italy, Hungary, or Germany or even the UK is driving one of 'my' pieces of handiwork. Thanks Jean!

The next two hours I work on the other side of the Astra. OK, so I seem to be getting the hang of it but now the damn jig isn't working properly – all we need. Maintenance sorts it out, but apparently it's a constant problem so he stays by the tool and just reads a paper till it jams up again, then sets off to sort it out. By now, like everyone else I'm able to work up the line by several cars but the guys and later the foreman tells me that it's slow at the moment anyway because the model is coming to the end of its life span and we're only on around 41 per hour (instead of about 45–8 per hour). But the other thing is that I'm on fenders not the hood, which I'd found tough. And that's something I didn't realise, that even though pretty much all the jobs I do are tool and power assisted some are just that bit harder than others, so the fender is both lighter anyway but also requires less work on it. Even though I thought I was getting fast my mate on the other side of the line could read snatches of his paper waiting for me. Maybe in time I'll catch the hang not just of the job

– what goes where etc. – but also the knack of doing it the fastest way for me. As Gary says, 'Find your own knack and keep it to yourself.' He certainly has it but I can't see for the life of me how he does it that much more quickly and efficiently than me, but somehow he does. It's only a matter of seconds but I guess it adds up to a few minutes in the day, which is what you need to read the paper and a take a few slugs of liquid.

At 2.00 pm the line stops for everyone to do their Five Ss [Toyota-speak for quality assurance and management of worker behaviour].

Last two hours I do the tailgate – decide this is another bastard job. Four variations of it plus changes to the jig itself (hatchback/ SRI, estate/standard). It takes all my time to work it out then I put the damn door on but forget one hinge bolt. But as usual the guys are really helpful and look after me well – but still find it funny. Glenn is the only one to take the piss. Afternoon break I'm 30 or so seconds late and he jokes, 'If you're fuckin' doin' this, do it properly!' Then he laughs, and so do I.

Everyone is chatting away when they can, and then someone asks about Tom, who has been off for a few weeks with back pain from an injury he got when lifting a hood onto a jig when the automatic feeder broke down. It's like lifting the lid on a pressure cooker. Some can't stop talking about their various physical injuries. Things they 'just have to carry on with'. But it's not only the physical pain, which someone points out to me later most people have to put up with 'as long as you can cope', but also the mental stress of not making mistakes, and it's worse too with the mental isolation.

Tuesday – still in the body shop but due to staff shortage put in 'cell from hell' with Gerry. He's got restricted movement in both wrists after a traffic accident some years previously and the only job he can do is in the 'cell from hell'. This is where the various components of the hood are assembled prior to being placed on the jig and assembled on the job I was doing yesterday. Three functions. Put hood in jig 'box', place small mental addition, then press button, door slides down – bang! Same with other components to complete operation in two separate booths.

Gerry tells me that that the job is very isolating. At lunch break he comes over to where I'm eating and tells me about his feelings about the job. He feels that 'they like it like this and if they could get everyone to work that way they'd be happy – stops us all nattering amongst ourselves about issues'. 'They don't like you talking and mouthing off about the set-up and if it wasn't for the unions keeping them in check fuck knows what it would be like'. 'They measure everything you do.' 'Up in there see [the foreman's office above and to the side of the line] the SS *Titanic* it is.' They measure the robot's movement and so when the box is open it reads as down time. So the longer you take to load, the longer you're not working, and really it's only seconds but it adds up. It's open in fact for two or three minutes in every cycle – that's an hour, so that's 16–24 minutes every day. 'So according to them I'm not working 24 minutes, which is crap because as you've just done it, you're constantly moving, aren't you, and you have to wait for the box to close.'

Every small chance you might get to take a blow [breather], they want to cut it out [rest time], and the blows you have are pretty far between. In May Gerry says they claimed he was two hours down in one day, so he went and got Ronnie [foreman] and showed him it was bollocks. But it's the pressure all the time. Gerry says they want you isolated in the cells so as they can monitor you. He says he goes out of his mind here sometimes. He says nights though are the worst. He says you can't switch off so easily from the stuff that really gets you down. He says, 'Isn't that when you're supposed to dream about other stuff?'

I wondered later about Gerry's situation, and thought it was weird, and decided that it was a crazy life. That his view of the job already seemed reasonable to me, and that the problem wasn't his, or at least it wasn't him who alone had a problem. It was the job that was the problem, and he was being bashed over the head in a way into accepting that that's how it was, and that he should just accept it and get on with it. He was the problem if he couldn't cope. Madness.

Been told I'm in on Saturday and due to staff shortages I'll be on door trim line.

I'm on door trim today – taken along by Johnnie where I'm introduced to the team leader who seems unsure where to start me off – a bit humourless. I'm shown the ropes by Big Ears, Doc Halliday and Peter Rabbit! Great teachers and good guys to boot. Although they can't get me to put the wing mirrors on properly, or not all the time at any rate. They show all the little knacks for doing the job properly and try to teach me all of them, but it's not their fault I keep mixing up the right and left mirrors! They are perfectionists even if I am not – or find it difficult to learn what it takes to be one. At lunch when I mention the fact that I saw a number of people with bandages on their arms, just as on Monday, a number of people talk about the pressure of the job, of how they are forced to work harder and harder. Tim, an amateur boxer, also has physical problems – RSI in his lower arm – which he is concerned about.

Thursday: Still on wing mirrors – they've decided – someone obviously hasn't seen the mess I make. On this line, though, the odd thing is the banter, and catcalls are all directed at the different managers who from time to time come along the track. I talk to people at lunch about how things have changed over the years. A reasonable mix of ages so some idea of the changes over time. Pretty much universal recognition of the fact that especially since the late 1980s the 'push nature' of the job has become more obvious. People felt that managements and team leaders who replaced the old charge hand have made things worse in terms of the ability to cope with the job. The union was seen as helping a lot, particularly when it came to holding management back, and also in terms of fighting for compensation and support for those injured on the job. It is a hard job that was matched by a gallows humour.

Terry [a T&G steward] who was working with me on door trim has booked two weeks off next week but it was going to be tough to stay away – 'The thing is I'm really worried about the next couple of weeks of not getting in here! You know it's like 3.30 and I'm really upset, I just don't want to leave. You know Sammy, the worst is every week come Friday. I think, God, what am I going to do till Monday!' Then his mate added, 'It's depressing, Terry isn't it? You're right mate, vacation is the worst time of all. I have to get tablets – it's like a bereavement.' Someone else then added, 'Have you heard Vauxhalls have a new scheme for you when you pop off? Like they're making coffins Astra shaped, but it depends how long you worked here, you know. Some have been here so long they're going down below in a Vauxhall Viva shape [an early model assembled at Ellesmere Port in the 1970s]. From the cradle to the grave. It's like the fuckin' Co-op.'

During this exchange the line has been moving and I've been unable to keep up, so Terry grabs my torque gun and 'catches' up for me. But it seems characteristic of the work overall. People begin the jobs, it's mind-numbing and then someone breaks the tedium with a joke or some casual good-humoured banter, then everyone focuses on the job in front of them.

Saturday week two: Lunchtime no one speaks – everyone is simply exhausted. It's the same most days from what I can see. I've been moved again this time, to final trim as cover. Final trim and I cannot speak either when working, or not as much as in the body shop. It's tiring. Much more than any of the other lines I've been on. Young or old – although there are many fewer older people on this line, which is hardly surprising as it requires more speed and agility, with all the work of jumping in and out of the moving car, fixing the wire harnessing [electrical wiring units] and crash pads [dashboards]. Ian tells me this is definitely the hardest part of the car to work on, that this is the one they can't yet automate so they've more labour in the shop. He said that other shops have their boredom factor and others have a fair bit of heavy lifting despite the robots, so you might get hurt in other ways or just due to RSI or whatever. But here you've got the speed factor, plus it's awkward positions you're working in, plus then you get bored and that's a recipe for injury. When you just lose a bit of concentration, then you pull something or just overstretch that little bit, and the back goes or something.

Ian told me that at nights when he's on days he sometimes gets cold sweats just thinking about it all. He then goes on about the continuous improvement programmes and the threat these pose to people's jobs: that people just don't see it sometimes that the improvement set-ups where you do away with someone else's job is a big problem. He reckons some people just don't see the bigger picture. They think that's great we've improved this or that so it's quicker, but then what happens in the next round of negotiations? [Ian had been a T&G steward.] The company say that such and such a line did the job faster than the agreement in a CI meeting and why can't we agree on that? Then what happens? 'Two less jobs.' He said that people don't seem to see the bigger picture sometimes.

NOTES

Chapter 1, Understanding the Lean Automobile Industry

1   Letter to all Ellesmere Port employees, May 2006, on the occasion of the crisis over the plant's future funding for the new Astra. By the end of June around 1,000 workers had been forced to take a voluntary severance package.

2   There have been a number of exemplary accounts and critiques of lean production, including some from trade union and research members of the Auto Workers' Research Network. One particular view we reject is that of Paul Adler, a critical researcher in the United States, whose analysis of lean production gained an important prominence. Notably we do not accept his argument that lean production offers the possibility for what he terms 'democratic Taylorism'. See Paul Adler and Paul Landsbergis' debate on lean production and workers' health, available from kennym@talk talk.net and paul.stewart.100@strath.ac.uk.

3   The IVMP was coordinated by the Massachusetts Institute of Technology.

4   Gerpisa is the French-based network, Permanent Group for the Study of the Automobile Industry and its Employees.

5   The keenest of these voices can be found in the collection edited by Kochan, Lansbury and MacDuffie (1997), which includes contributions by MacDuffie, a lean protagonist, and the Canadians Kumar and Holmes, and the Europeans Jurgens and Roth, all significant critics of the IMVP agenda.

6   According to the Department for Business Enterprise and Regulatory Reform (BERR) (2009), the United Kingdom is Europe's third-largest automotive market. More than 2.4 million new cars were sold in 2007, 'equivalent to 17% of European vehicle registrations'. The BERR sees the United Kingdom as Europe's 'most diverse and productive vehicle manufacturing location and as a global centre of excellence for engine development and production'. This is a sector in which over 40 firms are active in production of vehicles for all niches, and 1.5 million autos were produced in Britain in 2007. According to BERR, 'the UK accounts for some 2.4% of worldwide vehicle output and 8.7% of European assembly, ranking it fourth in Europe and twelfth globally' (BERR 2009).

7   Only Ellesmere Port, the GM-Vauxhall plant in the north-west of England, survives although the V6 engine plant has long gone. While the Oxford Cowley plant remains, it was effectively transformed into a

greenfield facility by BMW in 2000 (Mini production was launched in April 2001, sales commenced in July 2001) and little remains of the previous era when it was British-owned. See Chapter 6.

8   Lewchuk, Stewart and Yates (2001), Lewchuk and Robertson (1996, 1997), Stewart et al. (2004).

9   This is part of the implicit bargain on offer. Workers play the game and 'make it work' because it is easier, as many report, to simply get on with the teamworking exercises, and especially because in many instances these take people way from boring work routines. We write 'lock workers into production' because often they report feelings of compulsion and restraint in an insecure inducing environment in which there is perceived to be an absence of choice. The objective is to tap into the 'gold' of workers' knowledge, as managers have often referred to it, including their ideas for improving production.

10   As we write the UK Civil Service has received a copy of its commissioned report on the 'benefits' of lean production.

11   See Hyman (1991) and Pollert (1991) on flexibility.

12   Between January 1992 and March 1997, the TGWU organised a series of major European seminars on lean production. The objective was to educate shopfloor leaders on the nature of lean production, with a very strong emphasis on the scope for minimising its worst elements. In attendance were shopfloor representatives from up to five other EU countries, plus union activists from Canada and the United States. See Chapter 4 and Stewart and Martinez Lucio (2008).

13   'The whole point of "lean" production is to produce more with less: that is, to increase economic output per unit of labor power purchased. [It is important] to eliminate the "pores" in the working day. In traditional Fordist automobile plants workers actively labored forty-five seconds each minute. In the typical lean production auto plant, in stark contrast, workers are engaged in productive activity around fifty-seven seconds a minute. If we assume a ten second per minute differential applied to a plant of 2,000 workers, then 2,667 extra work hours are performed over the course of an eight-hour shift as a result of this speed-up. Some 13,335 extra work hours are added over a five-day week. This is equivalent to hiring an extra 333 workers to work a forty hour week. Or, to put it another way, this is equivalent to each worker performing the equivalent of more than an extra day's pay every five day week.'

(Smith 2000: 60)

14   Let us choose just one example from the many that we could pick from virtually any sector. As of late summer 2006, Renault planned to roll out 26 new models by the end of the decade under the auspices of the Commitment 2009 agenda to push up sales. Speaking of 'waste' in this context is especially salutary when we consider the impact this agenda is having on the technical staff at Renault's state-of-the-art R&D centre at Guyancourt, as revealed in the quote in Chapter 1. The whole thrust

of the political economy of lean production is to produce more with less. But the question of what there is increasing production of, and at what cost to the environment, including both raw materials and human resources, is never even considered to be an issue for the gurus of a waste-free world. Then, as with all lean rhetoric, they assume that lean is for their clients, and their competitors can figure out the problems of flabbiness alone. Some waste in global terms – what irony!

15 See *The Japanisation of British Industry*, by two early exponents of the manufacturing benefits of lean production, Oliver and Wilkinson (1988, 1992). By the early 1990s, the political-cum-technical problems associated with using the term Japanisation led to its being replaced by the more culturally acceptable 'lean production'. This also marked a shift from an explicitly academic attempt to interpret 'lean', where it became increasingly associated with the promotion of managerial and sectoral interests under the auspices of company consultancy. See, *inter alia*, Oliver et al. (1993, 1994) and Andersen Consulting (1993). There were a number of early critics of the Japanisation approach. Among the most prominent (not all of whom had a specifically labour movement focus) were Nohara (1993), Nomura (1993); Coriat (1993), da Costa and Garanto (1993), Grant (1994, 1996), Humphrey (1995), Watanabe (1993) and Totsuka (1996).

Chapter 2, The Prehistory of Lean Production

1 Taken from an interview with Peter Titherington in 1992 when he was TGWU convener at Vauxhall-Ellesmere Port, in which he was making a broader point about the impact of managerial payment strategies from the postwar period across the sector, rather than just at Vauxhall, where Measured Day Work was introduced in 1956. Peter Titherington was one of the leading stewards in the company who campaigned to 'control lean', as he put it. (See Chapter 3.)

2 With annualised hours the notion of a regular five-day week is replaced by an annual total of hours worked. This is supposed to allow for variations in output to match demand. It involves a payback measure: if there are downtime and layoffs, the company continues to pay workers at the normal rate. Then when more production is required, they must 'pay back' the hours paid but not worked in the form of overtime working until the hours worked and paid are in alignment.

3 See especially the research of the International Auto Workers' Research Network in Canada, Britain, Italy and Brazil. Texts in particular include Lewchuk, Stewart and Yates (2001)and Stewart et al. (2004).

4 At time of writing Vauxhall unions continue to be engaged in a series of disputes over salaries, labour utilisation – see above – and the future viability of the plant. For historical contextualisation see Lewchuk and colleagues (2001) and Ackroyd and Thompson (1999).

5 The so-called 'British system' was at its height during the postwar

period. As a system of production it was admirably suited to the UK context. The companies picked up very specific elements of Fordism, including 'greater mechanisation and use of engineering studies in internal component manufacturing. Fixed-capital and plant-integration levels remained low compared with recovering European manufacturers' (Whisler 1999: 182). The common view of many critics was that products (and components) were much too diverse, and that while this might have suited a quality product market, given the scale of the UK-owned sector, it simply did not deliver sufficiently high output. Moreover, in contrast to Ford, which relied on extensive mechanisation to boost output, the British firms typically invested a larger percentage of revenue in variable capital through extended job hire programmes.

6 As Whisler argues, 'Management believed that it controlled the strategic aspects of production, but the goals of economies of scale and capacity expansion without high capital levels revealed that executives pursued Fordist objectives without Fordist methods. On the shop floor piecework and mutuality empowered labour' (1999: 184–5).

7 Whisler cites the establishment view that 'labour at Ford and Vauxhall had long accepted MDW, industrial engineering, capital-intensive production methods and centralised bargaining'. However, not only was bargaining always plant-centred at Vauxhall, but the idea that the 'American' (Fordist) approach inhibited conflict is really quite an unsubstantiated, eccentric view. It was, on the contrary the so-called Fordist methods that led to the quite bitter conflicts of 1979 – the 'We Will Manage' dispute.

8 It is worth noting that a strong element of the local remains today, even after the traumas to the sector and unions caused by the more or less effective levelling of the employment relationship caused by lean production. For example, the famous 1992 *Rover Tomorrow* agreement heralding the introduction of lean production at what was then Rover, dominated by Honda, nevertheless had four separate plant agreements, which even by this stage covered issues of labour mobility and the sickness and absence regime. More significantly lean production agreements between Vauxhall and the trade unions – Ellesmere Port, 1989 and Luton, 1992 – continued the tradition of local bargaining that began with ordinances introduced in 1942. According to Turner, Clack and Roberts, 'Vauxhall signed a district negotiating agreement with the AEU and NUVB ... at the same time formalising its existing joint consultative arrangements as an elected Management Advisory Committee and announcing a managerial "open door" to workers and union representatives' (1967: 194).

9 Notably, the government was not convinced that formalisation of industrial relations as recommended by Donovan was enough. While Barbara Castle, secretary of state at the Department of Employment and Productivity (after April 1968), was concerned about the increase in unofficial strikes, she was not convinced that to proceduralise industrial relations at

company and plant level would resolve the problem. The Ford Motor Company, for instance, had procedural agreements in place and eschewed piecework but was still far from strike-free (Croucher 2000: 38).

10   Until the late 1960s, trade union representation in the sector comprised the following main unions: AEW (Amalgamated Engineering Workers' Union), NUVB (National Union of Vehicle Builders), TGWU (Transport and General Workers' Union), NUGMW (National Union of General and Municipal Workers), DATA (Draftsmen's and Allied Technicians' Association) and UCATT (Union of Construction, Allied Trades and Technicians). These were the main organisations although a number of others existed. They eventually amalgamated or consolidated into what became AEEU (Amalagamated Engineering and Electrical Union) and MSF (Manufacturing, Science, Finance) (which in turn both merged in 2002 to form Amicus) and the TGWU. The TGWU and Amicus merged in 2009 to form UNITE, which now represents in excess of 90 per cent of union membership across the sector.

11   By differentials is meant the wage drift that developed after the war, rising to prominence as a major source of discontent in the sector from the 1950s through to the 1970s. Turner and colleagues discuss the period from the mid-1950s until the mid-1960s. With regard to the significance of pay differentials they conclude that these developed as a result of 'the force of "compulsive comparison" ... the effect of information about earnings at other firms and plants [was] transmitted through the unions and joint shop stewards' organisations' (Turner et al. 1967: 142).

12   See Whisler (1999) and IWCMG (1978) for different perspectives on the way in which late-1970s management used MDW from the standpoint of control.

13   According to Willman and Winch, MDW received a mixed response, with some 'commentators' feeling that 'the scheme created considerable problems, and contributed to the reduction of productivity observed throughout the industry in the early 1970s' (1985: 66).

Chapter 3, From 'Embrace and Change' to 'Engage and Change'

1   This chapter was originally published in *New Technology, Work and Employment* 13(2), September 1998. It is republished here with permission from Blackwell.

2   Streeck (1986) made an important intervention which emphasises the positive role played by unions in the negotiation of (especially) technological innovation. However, he went on to suggest, in similar vein to Marsden and colleagues, that the leverage of the unions was dependent on the market circumstances of British Leyland, on whose fate his analysis largely depended.

3   In particular, this applies to their diagnosis and remedy for what they termed the 'British disease' of 'low productivity, poor quality, inadequate control of labour costs, and weak management' (Willman and Winch 1985: 174).

4   Specifically, the fragmentation of union strategies in the face of competitive pressures from Europe and Japan, including new management strategies, rationalisation, the demise of corporatism and the inappropriateness of traditional union structure in the face of these concerted 'histories' (Marsden et al. 1985: 157–73, 187–92).

5   Positive > neutral > negative, but the differences between each category are not necessarily equal.

6   Employees' attitude towards NMTs, A*, depends on their characteristics and their perceptions of the implementation and impact of NMTs, such that $A^* = \beta'X + \varepsilon$ (where ε is the error term and is distributed with a mean of zero and a variance of 1). A* is not observed but is measured by A, an ordinal variable which takes on the values positive, neutral or negative as follows:

A is negative if $A^* \leq 0$
A is neutral if $0 \leq A^* < \mu_1$
A is positive if $\mu_1 \leq A^* < \mu_2$

The ordered probit technique estimates the βs and μs to maximise $\sum \ln(Pj)$ where Pj is the estimated probability of observing each of j responses (positive, neutral, negative). Thus the probability of observing

A = negative if $1 - \phi(\beta'X)$
A = neutral if $\phi(\mu - \beta'X) - \phi(-\beta'X)$
A = positive if $1 - \phi(\mu - \beta'X)$

7   The implications of joint ownership, or jointness, as the UAW in the United States defines it, were not lost on the stewards.

8   Out of a total of 22,000 hourly paid employees, the majority in favour of *Rover Tomorrow* was 168 at the final (second) count. This reflected the divisions within the company and the trade unions themselves, but left many with the impression that the agreement had been imposed.

9   At Rover, by contrast, the number was less than ten (interview with education officer, Region 1).

10 While there are differences between these, for present purposes they will for the most part be considered together.

11 These findings are reported in detail in Stewart and Garrahan (1995).

12 The data used in this analysis are weighted so that each company is represented equally and so that the proportion of employees in each group (body shop, assembly line, shop stewards and ordinary members), are represented according to their prevalence in the population of the company.

Chapter 4, Striking Smarter and Harder

1   This chapter was originally published in *Capital and Class*, 1997. It includes additional interviews and an addendum drawn from statistical data comparing Vauxhall and Rover plants. The interviews and

questionnaire were collected between early 1995 and the end of February 1996 and were not used in Stewart (1997).

2   See Tables 4.1 and 4.2 on the deteriorating industrial relations climate (Stewart and Wass 1997).

3   See Vauxhall (1992). For a general defence of lean production see, inter alia, Womack, Jones and Roos (1990), Oliver (1991) and Oliver and colleagues (1994).

4   The breakdown by union was:

   TGWU 83.1% in favour of strike action, 16.9%against
   AEEU 72.6% in favour, 27.4% against.

5   See *Samizdat* 1–4 on stewards' shopfloor responses at a number of critical moments throughout the 1990s.

6   After a difficult six months for both workers and unions, there was still a majority, though small, in favour of continuing with the action. The vote in mid-February 1996 on Vauxhall's final offer was 1,820 in favour, 1,850 against. According to Tony Woodley, the TGWU national secretary of the Automotive Group, and chief union negotiator, '[This] ballot has taken place against a background of threats and sustained pressure from Vauxhall management on our members to secure a vote for acceptance of the deal. Despite that, and also despite the fact that members of the AEEU had last week voted by nearly four to one to accept the management offer, our members rejected it.'

7   For a management-sponsored interpretation of the changes at Luton see Hamblin (1994: 6), who records marginal managerial benefits at the level of employee acceptance of the demands behind teamworking under lean production.

Chapter 5, Round Table Discussion

1   Transnational Information Exchange-Ellesmere Port TGWU conference, Liverpool, January 1992.

2   Parker and Slaughter (1988) and Parker (1985).

3   Bought by GM in 1989.

4   See Chapter 7 and Project Olympia. In January 2001, GM announced the closure of the Vauxhall-Luton assembly plant.

5   This was borne out in May 2006 when Vauxhall-GM called for 1,000 redundancies. The target was met within a few weeks.

6   Team leaders were selected by the company. At first it was the old group leader who evolved into the team leader, but as time went on team leaders came to be appointed by management.

Chapter 6, Rover-BMW

1   For a detailed account of the significance of the plant and community-based movement against the closure, see Hayter and Harvey (1993).

2   This refers to management-initiated task-based involvement schemes such as quality circles and teamworking.

3   Someone unfortunately seemed to have forgotten that deals not involving wages had been negotiated outside a wage review for some time.

Chapter 7, From 'Engage and Change' to Endless Change

1   Robert H. Guest's intriguing site data from an exploratory visit to Luton and Ellesmere Port in the spring of 1974 (in the Robert Guest Archive, Modern Record Office, University of Warwick) provide riveting testimony to the strength of shopfloor organisation and its origins in traditional and aggressive management and combative labour traditions founded on what one of his interviewees described as a legacy of 'bitter class struggle'.

2   On Monday 5 February 2001 Vauxhall announced that Ellesmere Port was to become a 'flexi-plant' producing both the Astra and Vectra models.

3   Competition and worker insecurity at GM-Vauxhall is intensified by use of the 'EP Performance vs Rest of Europe' monthly data sheet comparing a range of indices relating to production at Antwerp, Bochum, Ellesmere Port and Gliwicw. Whipsawing is the dark presence lurking behind this. And of course, all the other GM-Europe plants have similar internal 'information' sheets.

4   Screwdriver plants is the colloquial term for a facility where a large majority of components have been manufactured elsewhere, including much of the metal bashing (and sometimes stamping), and transported to the final assembly plant where they are assembled into the shape of the final product 'on the line'.

5   Guest reports Ellesmere Port's 11,000 employees working on three variations of the Viva from '14 large presses, 42 medium and 48 small'. Engine assembly and seat production were also critical to the plant's activities at that time.

6   Indeed in the case of Ellesmere Port the union has been able to improve conditions of workers in outsourced companies: see the round table discussion, Chapter 5, and interviews 2004.

7   Certainly in 2006, as we wrote this, the threat to Ellesmere Port had become evident. See the Conclusion.

8   This could never guarantee security in the medium, let alone long term. By 2007, after more bitter whipsawing games between the Astra plants, Ellesmere Port, Bochum and Antwerp, GME chose the last of these for closure.

9   'The financial problems caused by the over capacity across Europe, the under-utilisation of plant and equipment within GM Europe, combined with the currently strong pound and our higher freight costs leave the UK plants vulnerable at a time when critical decisions are about to be made' (Vauxhall *Update* no 2, 30 March 1998).

10   Agreement Plant Oxford (APO), May 2001 was to apply retrospectively from 1 November 2000 and run until 31 October 2002. APO instituted a

range of 'modern' management performance measurement practices that included payment by 'Results, Cooperation in the Group, Initiative, Willingness to change, Business Awareness' (p. 13). One of the key and most modern of all the innovations in the control of workers' time was the end to the outdated time-wasting practice of 'togging time' which was paid for by the company. The 'togging allowance' allowed workers miniscule time to kit up ready for work in the company's time. 'Payment for togging can no longer be justified in today's manufacturing environment. It is a basic requirement that Associates should be properly equipped and available at their place of work at the designated shift start time' (p. 14). (Just imagine the money being squandered!) Then again, it is extraordinary that labour had retained this 'privilege' until the twenty-first century.

11 Compare the Vauxhall agreements with Agreement Plant Oxford of May 2001.

12 The Management Performance scale is a summative scale based on the last three questions in Table 7.3. Responses were coded from 4 to 0 with a great deal/very fair/very interested coded as 4. This group of questions had an internal consistency reliability (Cronbach's Alpha) of 0.732.

13 Responses to each were coded from 3 (very involved) to 0 (not involved at all). This group of questions had an internal consistency reliability (Cronbach's Alpha) of 0.8632. Mean scores are presented in Table 7.5.

14 We undertook a bivariate correlation analysis (using Spearman's rho correlation tests).

15 Compare with the Blue Diary available from Stewart and Murphy.

16 A summative scale of employee autonomy was based on these four questions. Responses to each were coded from 4 (a great deal/very easy) to 0 (none at all/very difficult). This group of questions had an internal consistency reliability (Cronbach's alpha) of 0.6542.

17 See the Blue Diary, available from authors Stewart and Murphy.

18 A summative scale of workplace stress was based on four questions. 'In the last month how often have you worked with physical pain or discomfort?' and 'How often have you felt exhausted after your shift?' both had scales of every day/most days/half the time/a few days/never and were coded from 4 to 0. 'Do you ever feel that things are getting on top of you during your shift?' had a scale of a great deal/a fair amount/some/very little/none at all, and was coded from 4 to 0, and 'How tense and wound up were you at work?' had a scale of very tense/somewhat tense/not very tense/not tense at all, and was coded from 3 to 0. This group of questions had an internal consistency reliability (Cronbach's alpha) of 0.8262.

19 A bivariate correlation analysis (using Spearman's rho correlation tests) was used.

20 The dependent variable and two independent variables (autonomy and management performance) were all treated as interval level variables since they were regarded as sufficiently analogous to a genuine interval variable (see, for example, Harley 1999). The remaining variables were recoded dummies.

Conclusion

1   *Hazards* magazine has highlighted the fact that suicides in Britain related to stress, bullying and work overload are not included in figures for those killed at their workplace, although it estimates these to be in the order of 250 per annum, which is more than the total number of fatalities attributed to accidents at work (*Hazards* 102, April–June 2008).

2   Miliband considered the role of the state and its various agencies, and he also saw the media and education processes as playing their part in helping capital wage its asymmetrical war to control and subjugate labour. While the postwar settlement saw the rise of workplace regimes based upon social compromise, which included the growth in the social wage, in the 1970s class struggle from above in the form of neoliberalism witnessed an assault on these social gains. This class struggle from above has made it increasingly difficult to maintain, let alone extend, progressive health and safety agendas based on worker-defined norms. They are not impossible to achieve but are everywhere limited and threatened by the judiciary and the recalcitrance of the executive, notably against the backdrop of the demise of social democracy, as the reduction in the power and scope of the Health and Safety Executive (HSE) makes clear. This is unambiguous: the assault upon workplace protections for labour is the vital agenda pursued by capital in its desire to push back labour gains. This is for the very reason that it is these that moderate or shackle the drive by capital to accumulate, whatever the cost. The fact that it cannot always or even straightforwardly do just at it pleases, and that consensus is the preferred route, when labour organisation has been cowed, does not detract from this observation.

3   In so far as management think of the social character of lean production, they view it as an inherently progressive system of work organisation. Miliband reminds us that his notion of class struggle from above bears a resemblance to Michael Burawoy's concept of 'despotic regime' (1986).

4   The example of Renault from our introduction serves to remind us again of the wider canvas upon which these tragedies are taking place. The workers who took their own lives at the company's Technocenter at Guyancourt in 2007 were the cream of Renault's technical and design staff, their quintessential high fliers. Yet while Renault disputed culpability in the matter, CEO Carlos Ghosn rushed to shore up his staff, flagging in physical and emotional energy, with the announcement of more staff to keep the ship afloat. The state too did its best. It claimed that at least one of the deaths should be considered a 'workplace accident'. If what constitutes a workplace accident might seem obvious, it is perhaps easy to understand why many other such deaths are filed as unrelated to work. After all, the first death was caused when the worker, a computer technician, leaped from the fifth storey of his work building onto the glass roof of the canteen below, and the second worker drowned himself in an onsite pond. If the state found no connection to work in these tragic

cases of workers' suicides, 500 of their colleagues thought differently, when they staged a silent demonstration putting the blame squarely on Renault's plan for market dominance. (It calls for 26 models by the end of 2010. One key element of Contract 2009 is the perfection of the new Laguna, and another is Renault's plan to average eight vehicle launches per year instead of the traditional four as it expands into new segments.)

It was only after the third death that the state did indeed seek to go beyond the usual institutional *cordon sanitaire* of confining deaths to breaches of health and safety regulations, when a decision was taken to open a criminal investigation 'in view of the word that he left and to make this affair totally transparent'. The worker had left a note blaming work conditions on his state of mind. The state decided to consider the extent to which laws were violated, and their investigation would also consider the claims of employee harassment by supervisors. A CGT official called for an independent investigation 'to bring to light all the causes of the anguish at the Technocenter that have pushed several employees to [take their own lives]'. It is the unions who are making the running in arguing that the deaths are not just linked to breaches in health and safety regulations, but that the personal responses to the pressure of working conditions have been driving people not simply to high achievement but also to low self-esteem when failure, inevitable for many, kicks in. The CFDT was quoted as saying, 'For the last two years, the pressure on employees is much too much. The reorganization (of work) has disturbed a certain number of employees for whom the situation is often difficult to detect' (union spokesperson quoted in *WardsAuto*, 21/2/2007). The CGT was cited in *Libération*, 25 July 2007, as arguing that work, among a number of other factors, was responsible for the suicides. The unions got it exactly right. It was a 'crime' for sure, but it was a 'collective crime' insofar as it represented the tip of the iceberg of the quotidian assault by capital on labour inside and outside the factory.

5   The type of views we include are not those aimed at increasing production but rather those that balance production with worker interests, including those concerned with enhancing the quality of working life.

6   Contact Ken Murphy for details.

7   See note 4 on Renault's push for 26 new models before 2010.

8   This could be deeply ironic were we to consider that in many respects what lean, as central to the lean society, achieves is the absurdity of production of new (superficially or otherwise) commodities for its own sake. Production for production's sake, and let the worker take the strain. And if they cannot take it, there should be plenty of others ready and willing. What wasted lives, as Bauman might put it.

9   'Restricted employees' is a term used to refer to those with temporary or long-term disabilities unable to carry out regular job responsibilities.

BIBLIOGRAPHY

Ackroyd, S., Burrell, G., Hughes, H. and Whitaker, A. (1988) 'The Japanisation of British industry?' *Industrial Relations Journal* 19(1) (September), 11–23.

Ackroyd, S. and Thompson, P. (1999) *Organisational Misbehaviour*, London: Sage.

Adler, P. and Landsbergis, P. (nd) 'Debate on lean production.' Mimeo available from Paul.stewart.100@strath.ac.uk or Kennym@talktalk.net

Andersen Consulting (1993) *The Lean Enterprise*, Benchmarking Project Report.

Appelbaum, E. and Batt, R. (1994) *The New American Workplace: Transforming work systems in the United States*, Ithaca, NY: Cornell University/ILR Press.

Arrowsmith, J. (2002) 'Pacts for employment and competitiveness: case studies. GM Vauxhall Motors.' Dublin: European Foundation for the Improvement of Living and Working Conditions.

Ashton, D. and Sung, J. (2002) *Supporting Workplace Learning for High Performance Working*, Geneva: ILO.

Babson, S. (ed.) (1995) *Lean Work Empowerment and Exploitation in the Global Auto Industry*, Detroit, Mich.: Wayne State University Press.

Barratt Brown, M. and Coates, K. (1996) *The Blair Revelation: Deliverance for whom?* Nottingham: Spokesman.

Bauman, Z. (2004) *Wasted Lives: Modernity and its outcasts*, Cambridge: Polity.

Beaumont, P. (1985) 'New plant working practices', *Personnel Review* 14(5), 15–19.

Berggren, C. (1988) '"New production concepts" in final assembly – the Swedish experience', in Dankbaar, B., Jurgens, U. and Malsch, T. (eds), *Die Zukunft der Arbeit in der Automobilindustrie*, Berlin: WZB.

Berggren, C. (1993) 'The end of history?' *Work Employment and Society* 7(2) (June), 163–88.

Berggren, C. (1995) 'Japan as number two: competitive problems and the future of alliance capitalism after the burst of the bubble economy', *Work, Employment and Society* 9(1) (March), 53–95.

BERR (2009) 'BEER's automotive page', Department for Business Enterprise and Regulatory Reform [online] www.berr.gov.uk/whatwedo/sectors/automotive/index (accessed 28 May 2008).

Beynon, H. (1984) *Working for Ford*, 2nd edn, Harmondsworth: Pelican.

BLMC (1975) 'Obsession with Measured Day Work', British Leyland Motor Corporation Combine Committee Executive, MSS 309/t/1/1/4, 30 January.

BMW (2001) *Agreement Plant Oxford*. Oxford: BMW.

Bowden, S., Foreman-Peck, J. and Richardson, T. (2001) 'The post-war productivity failure: insights from Oxford (Cowley)', *Business History* 43(3), 64.

Boyer, R. and Freyssenet, M. (1996) 'Des models industriels aux strategies d'internationalisation', in *L'Industrie Automobile Mondiale: Entre homogénéisation et hiérarchisation*, Paris: Gerpisa, June.

Brenner, M., Fairris, D. and Ruser, J. (2004) '"Flexible" work practices and occupational safety and health: exploring the relationship between cumulative trauma disorders and workplace transformation', *Industrial Relations* 43, 242–66.

Bunting, M. (2004) *Willing Slaves: How the overwork culture is ruling our lives*, London: Harper Perennial.

Burawoy, M. (1986) *The Politics of Production; Factory regimes under capitalism and socialism*, London: Verso.

CAW (1993) 'Workplace issues, work reorganisation: responding to lean production.' Willowfield, Ontario: CAW Research and Communications Departments.

Church, R. (1994) *The Rise and Decline of the British Motor Industry*, London: Macmillan.

Clark, A, (2006) 'Half of Ford's workforce take redundancy', *Guardian*, 30 November.

Coffey, D. (2006) *The Myth of Japanese Efficiency: The world car industry in a globalizing age*, Cheltenham: Edward Elgar.

Cohen, S. (1998) *What's Happening?* London: Trade Union News Discussion Forum.

Cooper, C., Dewe, P. and O'Driscoll, M. (2001) *Organizational Stress: A review and critique of theory, research and applications*, London: Sage.

Coriat, B. (1993) 'Incentives, bargaining and trust: alternative scenarios for the future of work', paper for DGB (German TUC) Conference on Japanese Lean Production, Hattingen, November.

Coupar, W. and Stevens, B. (1998) 'Towards a new model of partnership: beyond the "HRM versus industrial relations" argument', in Sparrow, P. and Marchington, M. (eds), *Human Resource Management: The new agenda*, London: FT Pitman.

Croucher, R. (2000) 'The Coventry Toolroom Agreement, 1941–1972, Part 2: abolition', *Historical Studies in Industrial Relations* 9 (Spring), 37–71.

Da Costa, I. and Garanto, A. (1993) 'Entreprises japonaises et syndicalisme en Europe', *Le Mouvement Social* (Jan–Mar), 95–128.

Danford, A. (1999) *Japanese Management Techniques and British Workers*, London: Routledge.

Danford, A. (2005) 'New union strategies and forms of work organisation in UK manufacturing', in Harley, B., Hyman, J. and Thompson, P. (eds),

Participation and Democracy at Work: Essays in honour of Harvie Ramsay, Basingstoke: Palgrave Macmillan.

Danford, A., Richardson, M., Stewart, P., Tailby, S. and Upchurch, M. (2005) *Partnership and the High Performance Workplace: Work and employment relations in the aerospace industry*, Basingstoke: Palgrave Macmillan.

Dankbaar, B., Jurgens, U. and Malsch, T. (eds) (1988) *Die Zukunft der Arbeit in der Automobilindustrie*, Berlin: WZB.

Delbridge, R. (1995) 'Surviving JIT: control and resistance in a Japanese transplant', *Journal of Management Studies* 32(6) (November), 803–17.

Donnelly, T. and Thoms, D. (1989) 'Trade unions, management and the search for production in the Coventry motor car industry, 1939–75', *Business History* 31(2), 98–113.

Donovan, Rt Hon. Lord (1968) *Report of the Royal Commission on Trade Unions and Employers' Associations 1965–1968*, Cmnd 3623, London: HMSO.

Durand, J. P. (2007) *The Invisible Chain: Constraints and opportunities in the new world of employment*, Basingstoke: Palgrave Macmillan.

Edwardes, M. (1983) *Back from the Brink: An apocalyptic experience*, London: Collins.

Electoral Reform Ballot Services (1995) *Trade Dispute with Vauxhall Motor Company Including All Matters Arising out of and in Consequence of the Dispute, Report of Voting of TGWU and AEEU Members*, London.

Elger, T. and Smith, C. (1994) *Global Japanization: The transformation of the labour process*, London: Routledge.

Elger, T. and Smith, C. (2005) *Assembling Work: Remaking factory regimes in Japanese multinationals in Britain*, Oxford: Oxford University Press.

Ellegard, E. (1993) *The Creation of a New Production System at the Volvo Automobile Assembly Plant in Uddevalla, Sweden*, Paris: Gerpisa.

Ellegard, K., Engstrom, T. and Nilsson, L. (1992) *Reforming Industrial Work: Principles and realities in the planning of Volvo's assembly plant in Uddevalla*, Stockholm: Arbetsmiljofonden.

Fairbrother, P. (1996) 'Workplace trade unionism in the state sector', in Ackers, P., Smith C. and Smith, P. (eds), *The New Workplace and Trade Union: Critical perspectives on work and organization*, London: Routledge.

Fairbrother, P. and Waddington, J. (1990) 'The politics of trade unionism: evidence, policy and theory', *Capital and Class* 41, 15–56.

Fisher, J. (1995) 'The trade union response to HRM in the UK: the case of the TGWU', *Human Resource Management* 5(3), pp 7–23.

Fosh, P. (1993) 'Membership participation in workplace unionism: the possibility of union renewal', *British Journal of Industrial Relations* 31(4), 577–92.

Friedman, A. (1977) *Industry and Labour: Class struggle at work and monopoly capitalism*, London: Macmillan.

Fucini, J. and Fucini, S. (1990) *Working for the Japanese: Inside Mazda's American auto plant*, New York: Free Press.

Fujita, E. (1997) 'Changes in employment practices, personnel management and the wage system at Toyota in an era of globalisation and an ageing society', *Journal of Humanities and Social Sciences* 3 (November), 287–95.

Gallie, D., Felstead, A. and Green, F. (2001) 'Employer policies and organizational commitment in Britain 1992–1997', *Journal of Management Studies* 38(8), 1081–1101.

Garrahan, P. and Stewart, P. (1992) *The Nissan Enigma: Flexibility at work in a local economy*, London: Cassell.

General Motors Europe (1997, 1998) GME Works Council Papers (1997–1998).

Gerpisa (1993) 'Trajectories of automobile firms', *Proceedings of the Group for the Study of the Auto Industry and its Employees*, Paris: Université d'Evry-Val d'Essone.

Gerpisa (1996) *The Global Automotive Industry: Between homogenization and hierarchy*, Paris: Université d'Evry-Val d'Essonne.

Gordon, A. (1998) *The Wages of Affluence: Labor and management in postwar Japan*, Boston, Mass.: Harvard University Press.

Graham, L. (1995) *On the Line at Subaru-Isuzu: The Japanese model and the American worker*. Ithaca, NY: ILR Press.

Grant, D. (1994) 'New style agreements at Japanese transplants in the UK: the implications for trade union decline', *Employee Relations* 16(2), 65–83.

Grant, D. (1996) 'Japanisation and the new industrial relations', in Beardwell, I. J. (ed.), *Contemporary Industrial Relations: A critical analysis*, Oxford: Oxford University Press.

Hamblin, D. (1994) *Vauxhall Luton Plant Team Work Report*, University of Luton.

Hamper, B. (1992) *Rivethead: Tales from the assembly line*, London: Fourth Estate.

Harley, B. (1999) 'The myth of empowerment: work organization, hierarchy and employee autonomy in contemporary Australian workplaces', *Work, Employment and Society* 13(1), 41–66.

Hayter, T. and Harvey, D. (eds) (1993) *The Factory and the City: The story of automobile workers in Oxford*, London: Mansell.

Hazami, H. (1997) *The History of Labour Management in Japan*, Basingstoke: Macmillan.

Hazards (2006) 'Employer to blame for suicide', *Hazards*, April–June, 8.

Hazards (2008a) *Hazards* 101 (Jan–March).

Hazards (2008b) *Hazards* 102 (April–June).

Heery, E. (2002) 'Partnership versus organising: alternative futures for British trade unionism', *Industrial Relations Journal* 33(1), 20–35.

Heery, E. and Kelly, J. (1995) 'Conservative radicalism and nostalgia: a reply to Paul Smith and Peter Ackers', *Work, Employment and Society* 9(1), 155–64.

Higgs, P. (1969) 'The convenor', in R. Fraser (ed.), *Work: Twenty personal accounts*, London; Penguin.

Hirst, P. and Zeitlin, J. (1991) 'Flexible specialisation versus post-Fordism: theory, evidence and policy implications', *Economy and Society* 20(1), 1–56.

Hodson, R. (2001) *Dignity at Work,* Cambridge: Cambridge University Press.

Holloway, J. (1995) 'Capital moves', *Capital and Class* 57 (Autumn), 137–44.

Humphrey, J. (1995) 'The adoption of Japanese management techniques in Brazilian industry', *Journal of Management Studies* 32(6) (November), 767–87.

Huxley, C., Rinehart, J. and Robertson, D. (1991) 'Team concept: a case study of Japanese production concepts in a unionised Canadian auto plant', paper for Labour Process Conference, Manchester, April.

Hyman, R. (1991) 'Plus ça change? The theory of production and the production of theory,' in Pollert, A. (ed.), *Farewell to Flexibility?* Oxford: Blackwell.

Hyman, R. and Elger, T. (1981) 'Job controls, the employers' offensive and alternative strategies', *Capital and Class* 15 (Autumn).

Institute of Workers Control Motors Group (IWCMG) (1978) *A Workers' Enquiry into the Motor Industry*, London: CSE.

International Labour Organization (ILO) (1998) 'When working becomes hazardous', *World of Work* 26 (September/October).

ILO (2000) *The Social and Labour Impact of Globalisation in the Manufacturing of Transport and Equipment,* report by P. Bailey, Geneva: ILO.

Japan Automobile Workers' Unions Confederation (JAW) (1992) *Towards Coexistence with the World, Consumers and Employees*, February.

Jones, D. (1992) 'Lean production breaking the Japanese worker: a response to the report by the JAW', *Engineering News*.

Jones, D. (1992) 'Lean production (an update)', paper for 'Lean Production and European Trade Union Co-operation', TGWU Centre, 6–11 December 1992, Eastbourne, England.

Jurgens, U., Malsch, M. and Dohse, K. (1993) *Breaking From Taylorism: Changing forms of work in the automobile industry*, Cambridge: Cambridge University Press.

Kawanishi, H. (1992) *Enterprise Unionism in Japan*, London: Kegan Paul International.

Kelly, J. (1996) 'Union militancy and social partnerships', in Ackers, P., Smith, C. and Smith, P. (eds), *The New Workplace and Trade Unions: Critical perspectives on work and organization*. London: Routledge.

Kenney, M. and Florida, R. (1991) 'Transplanted organisations: the transfer of Japanese industrial organization to the US', *American Sociological Review* 56 (June), 381–98.

Kenney, M. and Florida, R. (1993) *Beyond Mass Production: The Japanese system and its transfer to the US*, Oxford: Oxford University Press.

Kochan, T. A., Lansbury, R. D. and MacDuffie, J.-P. (eds) (1997) *After Lean Production: Evolving employment practices in the world auto industry*, Ithaca, NY: ILR Cornell.

Kumazawa, M. (1996) *Portraits of the Japanese Workplace: Labor movements, workers and managers*, New York: Westview Press.

Laurent, L. (2007) 'Peugeot and Renault's suicide woes', *Forbes*, 18 July [online] http://www.forbes.com/2007/07/18/peugeot-citroen-renault-markets-equity-cx_ll_0718markets15.html (accessed 6 May 2009).

Leary, E. and Menaker, M. (nd) *Jointness at GM: Company unionism in the 21st century*, Woonsocket, R.I.: New Directions.

Lewchuk, W. and Robertson, D. (1996) 'Working conditions under lean production: a worker-based benchmarking study', *Asia Pacific Business Review* (Summer), 60–81.

Lewchuk, W. and Robertson, D. (1997) 'Production without empowerment: work re-organisation from the perspective of motor vehicle workers', *Capital and Class* 63, 37–65.

Libération (2007a) *Libération*, 25 July.

Libération (2007b) 'Safety at work', *Libération*, 29 November.

Linger, D. T. (2001) *No One Home: Brazilian selves remade in Japan*, Stanford, Calif.: Stanford University Press.

Linhart, R. (1981) *The Assembly Line*, London: John Calder.

Lowe, J., Delbridge, R. and Oliver, N. (1996) 'Performance and practice of autocomponents plants in the world motor industry', paper for 'The Globalization of Production and the Regulation of Labour' Conference, University of Warwick.

Lyddon, D. (1996) 'The car industry, 1945–79: shop stewards and workplace unionism', in C. Wrigley (ed.), *A History of British Industrial Relations 1939–1979: Industrial relations in a declining economy*, Cheltenham: Edward Elgar.

Macdonald, W. (2003) 'Work demands and stress in repetitive blue-collar work', in Peterson, C. (ed.), *Work Stress: Studies of the context, content and outcomes of stress*, New York: Baywood.

MacDuffie, J. P. and Pil, F. K. (1999) 'What makes transplants thrive: managing the transplant of "best practice" at Japanese auto plants in North America', *Journal of World Business* 4, 372–92.

MacDuffie, J. P. (1995) 'Human resource bundles and manufacturing performance: organizational logic and flexible production systems in the world auto industry', *Industrial and Labor Relations Review* 48(2), 199–221.

MacEwan, A. (1994) 'Globalisation and stagnation', *Socialist Register*, London: Merlin.

McKinlay, A. and Melling, J. (1999). 'The shop floor politics of productivity: work, power and authority relations in British engineering, c. 1945–57', in Campbell, A., Fishman, N. and McIlroy J. (eds), *British Trade Unions and Industrial Politics, Volume One: The Post-War Compromise, 1945–64*, Aldershot: Ashgate.

Marsden, D., Morris, T., Willman, P. and Wood, S. (1985) *The Car Industry: Labour relations and industrial adjustment*, London: Tavistock.

Martinez Lucio, M. and Stewart, P. (1997) 'The paradox of contemporary labour process theory: the rediscovery of labour and the disappearance of collectivism', *Capital and Class* 62 (Summer), 49–77.

Martinez-Lucio, M. and Weston, S. (1992) 'Human resource management and trade union responses: bringing the politics of the workplace back into the debate', in Blyton, P. and Turnbull, P. (eds), *Reassessing Human Resource Management*, London: Sage.

Masami, N. (1993) 'Farewell to "Toyotism"? Recent trends of a Japanese automobile company', Gerpisa, February.

Mayhew, C. (2003) 'Exploration of the links between workplace stress and precarious employment', in Peterson, C. (ed.), *Work Stress: Studies of the context, content and outcomes of stress*, New York: Baywood.

McCormack, G. (2002) 'Breaking the iron triangle', *New Left Review* 13 (Jan–Feb), 5–23.

McIlroy, J. (1999) 'Notes on the Communist Party and industrial politics', p. 240 in J. McIlroy, N. Fishman and A. Campbell (eds), *British Trade Unions and Industrial Politics: Volume Two,The High Tide of Trade Unionism, 1964–79*, Aldershot: Ashgate.

Miliband, R. (1989) *Divided Societies: Class struggle in contemporary capitalism*, Oxford: Oxford University Press.

Milkman, R. (1991) *Japan's Californian Factories: Labour relations and economic globalisation*, Los Angeles, Calif.: Institute of Industrial Relations, University of California.

Le Monde (2006) 'Redundancies at Volkswagen,' *Le Monde*, 5 December.

Moody, K. (1997) *Workers in a Lean World: Unions in the international economy*, London: Verso.

Moore, J. (ed.) (1997) *The Other Japan: Conflict, compromise, and resistance since 1945*, Armonk, N.Y.: M.E. Sharpe.

Morris, J. and Wilkinson, B. (1995) 'The transfer of Japanese management to alien institutional environments', *Journal of Management Studies* 32(6) (November), 719–30.

Morris, J., Munday, M. and Wilkinson, B. (1992) *Japanese Investment in Wales: Social and economic consequences*, Cardiff Business School, mimeo.

Murden, J. (2005) 'Demands for fair wages and pay parity in the British motor industry in the 1960s and 1970s', *Historical Studies in Industrial Relations* 20, 1–27.

Murphy, K. (2008) 'Making more cars than ever', in Cohen, S. (ed.), *What's Happening: The truth about 'work life balance*, London: TU Publications.

Newsquest (2004) 'Astra production halted by walkout', Newsquest Media Group Newspapers, 27 November.

Nichols, T. (1997) *The Sociology of Industrial Injury*, London: Mansell.

Nichols, T. and Beynon, H. (1977) *Living with Capitalism: Class relations and the modern factory*, London: Routledge and Kegan Paul.

Nohara, H. (1993) 'The average worker of a large Japanese company', Japan: University of Hiroshima.

Nomura, M. (1993) '"The end of Toyotism": recent trends in a Japanese automobile company', paper for 'Lean Workplace Conference', Wayne State University, Detroit, 3 October.

Oliver, N. (1991) 'The dynamics of just-in-time', *New Technology, Work and Employment* 6(1), 19–27.

Oliver, N., Delbridge, R., Jones, D. and Lowe, J. (1993) 'World class manufacturing: further evidence in the lean production debate', paper for British Academy of Management Conference, Milton Keynes, September (mimeo, Cardiff Business School).

Oliver, N., Jones, D., Delbridge, R, and Lowe, J. (1994) *Worldwide Manufacturing Competitiveness Study: Second Lean Enterprise Report*, Andersen Consulting.

Oliver, N. and Wilkinson, B. (1988) *The Japanisation of British Industry*, Oxford; Blackwell.

Oliver, N. and Wilkinson, B. (1992) *The Japanisation of British Industry*, Oxford; Blackwell.

Panich, L. (1994) 'Globalisation and the state', *Socialist Register,* London: Merlin.

Parker, M. (1985) *Inside the Circle: A union guide to QWL.* Boston, Mass.: South End Press.

Parker, M. and Slaughter, J. (1988) *Choosing Sides: Unions and the team concept*, Boston, Mass.: South End Press.

Parker, M. and Slaughter, J. (1994) *Working Smart: A union guide to participation programs and reengineering*, Detroit, Mich.: Labor Notes.

Pilkington, A (1996) *Transforming Rover: Renewal against the odds, 1981–94*, Bristol: Bristol Academic Pres.

Pollert, A. (1991) 'The Orthodoxy of flexibility' in Pollert, A. (ed.), *Farewell to Flexibility?* Oxford: Blackwell.

Price, R. (1986) *Labour in British Society*, London: Croom Helm.

Quality Network Production System (QNPS) (1988) Vauxhall/General Motors.

Ramsay. H. (1977) Cycles of control: workers' participation in sociological and historical perspective', *Sociology*11: 481–506.

Rinehart, J., Huxley, C. and Robertson, D. (1997) *Just Another Car Factory? Lean production and its discontents*, Ithaca, NY and London: ILR Press.

Rinehart, J., Robertson, D., Huxley, C. and Wareham, J. (1994) 'Reunifying conception and execution of work under Japanese production management? A Canadian case study', in Elger, T. and Smith, C. (eds), *Global Japanization? The transnational transformation of the labour process*, London: Routledge.

Roberts, I. (1993) *Craft, Class and Control: The sociology of a shipbuilding community*, Edinburgh: Edinburgh University Press.

Robertson, D. (1992a) 'Canadian trade union experiences of the new management techniques and the development of counter strategies', paper for TIE/Vauxhall Shop Stewards' Committee Conference on 'New Management Techniques', Liverpool, January/February.

Robertson, D. (1992b) 'The Canadian experience', paper for 'Lean Production and European Trade Union Co-operation' seminar, TGWU Centre, 6–11 December. Eastbourne, England.

Rover (1992) *Rover Tomorrow,* Rover Group.

Rudder, B. (1983) 'The inside story at Toyota and BL', book review, *Labour Review* 1(7) (August).

Smith, P. (1995) 'Change in British trade unions since 1945', *Work, Employment and Society* 9(1), 137–46.

Smith, T. (2000) *Technology and Capital in the Age of Lean Production: A Marxian critique of the 'new economy',* New York: SUNY Press.

Stephenson, C. (1995) 'The different experience of trade unionism in two Japanese transplants', in Acker, P., Smith, C. and Smith, P. (eds), *The New Workplace and Trade Unionism,* London: Routledge.

Stewart, P. (1994) 'A new politics for production? Trade union networks in the European automotive industry, the case of GM', in Totsuka, H., Ehrke, M., Kamii, Y. and Demes, H. (eds), *International Trade Unionism at the Current Stage of Economic Globalization and Regionalization,* Tokyo: Friedrich Ebert.

Stewart, P (1996) 'Introduction' in P. Stewart (ed.), *Beyond Japanese Management: The end of modern times,* London: Frank Cass.

Stewart, P. (1997) 'Striking smarter and harder: the new industrial relations of lean production', *Capital and Class* 61, 3–11.

Stewart, P. (2006) 'Marginal movements and minority struggles? The case of the Japanese minority social and labour movements', *Sociological Review* 54(4) (November), 753–73.

Stewart, P. and Garrahan, P. (1995) 'Employee responses to new management techniques in the auto industry', *Work Employment and Society* 9(3) (September), 517–36.

Stewart, P., Lewchuk, W., Pulignano, V., Ramalho, J., Santana, M., Yates, C., Saruta, M. and Danford, A. (2003) 'Patterns of labour control and the erosion of labour standards in regimes of hegemonic despotism: towards an international study of the quality of working life in the automobile industry (Brazil, Canada, Italy, Japan and the UK)', Paper for 27th encontro anual da 2003, Brazil.

Stewart, P., Lewchuk, W., Yates, C., Saruta, M. and Danford, A. (2004) 'Patterns of labour control and the erosion of labour standards: towards an international study of the quality of working life in the automobile industry (Canada, Japan and the UK)', in Charron, E. and Stewart, P. (eds), *Work and Employment Relations in the Automobile Industry,* Basingstoke: Palgrave Macmillan.

Stewart, P. and Martinez Lucio, M. (1996) 'New models, hybrids or societal effects? The development of the employment relationship in General Motors Europe' in *L'Industrie Automobile Mondiale: entre homogénéisation et hiérarchisation*, Paris: Gerpisa, June.

Stewart, P. and Martinez Lucio, M. (1998) 'Renewal and tradition in the npew politics of production', in Thompson , P. and Warhurst, C. (eds) , *Workplaces of the Future*, Basingstoke: Macmillan.

Stewart, P. and Martinez Lucio, M. (2008) 'New management practices: the never ending story of the never ending case study', Paper for Annual International Labour Process Conference, UCD, April.

Stewart, P. and Murphy, K. (2009) 'Surviving lean injury: redundancy and retirement in the lean society', paper presented to the International Labour Process Conference, Edinburgh, April.

Stewart, P., Richardson, M., Danford, A. and Pulignano, V .(2006) 'The employment relationship -European aerospace and automotive industry', *Document for Work Package* 4, Deliverable D5 ESEMK (The European Socio-Economic Models of a Knowledge-Based Society). Priority 7: Citizens and governance in a knowledge-based society.

Stewart, P. and Wass, V. (1995) 'Working harder and suffering longer: interim report prepared for the TGWU on the occupational health and safety consequences of lean Production at Rover and Vauxhall Motors', paper for TGWU National Industrial Policy Conference, Birmingham, July.

Stewart, P and Wass, V. (1997) *Final Survey Report, for Rover and Vauxhall stewards*, unpublished, available from Paul.Stewart.100@strath.ac.uk.

Stewart, P. and Wass, V. (1998) 'From "Embrace and Change" to "Engage and Change": trade union renewal and new management strategies in the UK automotive industry', *New Technology, Work and Employmkent* 13(2) (September), 77–93.

Streeck, W. (1986) *Industrial Relations and Industrial Change in the Motor Industry: An international view*, Warwick: University of Warwick Industrial Relations Research Unit.

Tabata, H. (1989) 'Changes in plant-level trade union organisations: a case study of the automobile industry', Institute of Social Science, University of Tokyo Occasional Paper.

Thornett, A. (1987) *From Militancy to Marxism: A personal and political account of organising car workers*, Oxford: Left View Books.

Thornett, A. (1998) *Inside Cowley: Trade union struggle in the 1970s: who really opened the door to the Tory onslaught?* London: Porcupine Press.

Titherington, P. (1991) 'Teamworking: rethinking our strategies', *Trade Union News* (May).

Todd, S. (2007) 'Practices at Renault Technocentre in Paris under official judicial investigation after three staff suicides', *Personnel Today*, 28 February.

Tolliday, S. (1988) 'Competition and the workplace in the British automobile industry: 1945–1988', *Business and Economic History* 17, 62–77.

Tolliday, S. and Zeitlin, J. (1992) 'Shop floor bargaining, contract unionism and job control: an Anglo-American Comparison', in Tolliday, S. and Zeitlin J. (eds), *Between Fordism and Flexibility: The automobile industry and its workers*, New York: St. Martin's Press.

Totsuka, H. (1996) 'Transformation of Japanese industrial relations: a case study of the automobile industry', *Bulletin of the Centre for Transnational Labour Studies* 1 (March), 9–23.

Transport and General Workers Union (TGWU) (1995) *Change at Work*, London: TGWU.

Turnbull P. and Wass, V. (1997) 'Dockers and deregulation in the international port transport industry', in McConville, J. (ed.), *Transport Deregulation Matters*, London: Pinter.

Turner, H. A., Clack, G. and Roberts, G. (1967) *Labour Relations in the Motor Industry: A Study of industrial unrest and an international comparison*, London: Allen and Unwin.

Vauxhall Motors (1989) 'V6' Agreement, Ellesmere Port plant agreement.

Vauxhall Motors (1992) *Working Together to Win*, Luton plant agreement.

Vauxhall Motors (1995–96) *Negotiations Update*, Issues 1–10 (Aug. 1995–Feb. 1996).

Vauxhall Stewards (1998) *Joint Trade Union Document – GM Ellesmere Port and Luton Trade Unions*, Ellesmere Port and Luton.

Jarry, E. (2007) 'France studies work stress after car plant suicides', *Wards Auto*, 9 July.

Warman, B. (1992) Address to the 'Lean Production and European Trade Union Co-operation' Conference, TGWU Centre, Eastbourne.

Watanabe, B. (1993) 'The Japanese auto industry: is lean production on the way out?', paper for 'Lean Workplace Conference', Wayne State University, Detroit, 3 October.

Whisler, T. R. (1999) *The British Motor Industry, 1945–94: A case study in industrial decline*, Oxford: Oxford University Press.

White, M., Hill, S., Mills, C. and Smeaton, D. (2004) *Managing to Change: British workplaces and the future of work*, Basingstoke: Palgrave Macmillan.

Williams, K., Cutler, T., Williams, J. and Haslam, C. (1987) 'The end of mass production', *Economy and Society* 16(3), 404–38.

Williams, K., Haslam, C., Adcroft, A. and Johal, S. (1993) 'The myth of the line: Ford's production of the Model T at Highland Park, 1909–16', *Business History* 35(3) (July), 66–87.

Williams, K., Haslam, C. and Williams, J. (1992a) 'Ford – v – "Fordism": the beginning of mass production?' *Work Employment and Society* 6(4) (December), 517–55.

Williams, K., Haslam, C., Adcroft, A. and Johal, S. (1992b) 'Against lean production', *Economy and Society* (August), 321–54.

Williams, K., Haslam C., Adcroft, A. and Johal, S. (1992c) 'Factories or warehouses', mimeo.

Williams, K., Haslam, C., Williams, J. and Johal, S. (1994) *Cars: Analysis, history, cases*, Oxford: Berghahn.

Williamson, H. (1989) *Back in the Melting Pot? Rethinking trade union perspectives on Japanese motor industry investment in Britain and 'Japanese-style' industrial relations*, London: CAITS.

Willman, P. (1988) 'The future of the assembly line in the UK car industry', in Dankbaar, B., Jurgens, U. and Malsch, T. (eds), *Die Zukunft der Arbeit in der Automobilindustrie*, Berlin: WZB.

Willman, P. and Winch, G. (1985) *Innovation and Management Control: Labour relations at BL Cars*, Cambridge: Cambridge University Press.

Wilson, P. (2008) 'Britain going global hits our rights', in S. Cohen (ed.), *What's Happening: The truth about work and the myth of work–life balance*, London: TU Publications.

Womack, J. P., Jones, D. T. and Roos, D. (1990) *The Machine that Changed the World: The triumph of lean production*, New York: Rawson Macmillan.

Wood, S. (1988) 'Some observations on industrial relations in the British car industry 1985–87', in Dankbaar, B., Jurgens, U. and Malsch, T. (eds), *Die Zukunft der Arbeit in der Automobilindustrie*, Berlin: WZB.

Woodley, A. (1992) 'End of conference statement' for 'Lean Production and European Trade Union Co-operation' Conference, TGWU Centre, Eastbourne.

Yamamoto, K. (1990) 'The "Japanese style industrial relations" and an "informal" employee organisation: a case study of the Ohgi-Kai at T-Electric', Institute of Social Science, University of Tokyo Occasional Paper.

Yamamoto, K. (1992) 'Labour relations in big Japanese corporations: the formal framework and the informal in-house organisations', Institute of Social Science, University of Tokyo Occasional Paper.

Yates, C., Lewchuk, W. and Stewart, P. (2001) 'Quality of working life in the automobile industry: a Canada-UK comparative study', *New Technology, Work and Employment* 16(2) (July), 72–87.

INDEX